Parables of Jesus
INTRODUCTION AND EXPOSITION

SPCK Large Paperbacks

Parables of Jesus

INTRODUCTION AND EXPOSITION

Eta Linnemann

LONDON

S·P·C·K

First published in 1966
Second impression 1971
First published in paperback 1975
S.P.C.K.
Holy Trinity Church
Marylebone Road
London NW1 4DU

Made and printed in Great Britain by
Hollen Street Press Ltd., Slough

Translation © S.P.C.K. 1966

Translated by John Sturdy from the third edition (1964) of *Gleichnisse Jesu, Einfuhrung und Auslegung*, first published 1961 by Vandenhoeck and Ruprecht, Göttingen

SBN 281 02891 5

TO MY PARENTS

Publisher's Note

Thanks are due to the following for permission to quote in this translation from copyright material:

Basil Blackwell and Mott, Ltd: *The History of the Synoptic Tradition*, by R. Bultmann.

William Collins, Sons and Co., Ltd: *The Gospel of Thomas*, translated by A. Guillaumont and others.

Hodder and Stoughton, Ltd, and Harper and Row, Inc.: *Jesus of Nazareth*, by G. Bornkamm.

James Nisbet and Co.: *The Parables of the Kingdom*, by C. H. Dodd.

S.C.M. Press, Ltd: *Studies of the Historical Jesus*, by E. Fuchs, and *Promise and Fulfilment*, by W. Kümmel.

S.C.M. Press, Ltd, and Charles Scribner's Sons: *The Parables of Jesus*, by J. Jeremias.

Contents

PART ONE
THE BASIC PRINCIPLES OF PARABLE INTERPRETATION

PART TWO
EXPOSITIONS

ix

148

Introduction

When Miss Eta Linnemann was asked to write this book, the commission given her was that it should help the teacher of Religious Knowledge.

Every lesson becomes a good one as soon as the pupil joins in the work. Miss Linnemann, with this in mind, simply leads teacher and pupil together in their work on the text, by showing them step by step how one deals with the text methodically as an expositor. The text is the parables of Jesus. Not all of them—that would take too long, and is also quite unnecessary—but a selection. The selection is so made that at the same time the question of authenticity must be considered. In every case, even in a case of unauthenticity, i.e. when we cannot ascribe the text to Jesus, it is Jesus himself who gains by this.

An extremely exciting introduction into the particular nature of parables and the technique of expounding them is therefore followed by a group of individual expositions. The whole is written in a completely intelligible manner. The present position of scholarship is set out in the section of notes at the end of the book. This part carries further the discussion among the scholars in a way that is not only learned but also intelligible and relevant; it shows the reader that no one needs to be discouraged here, when once he has realized how others have done it.

Every genuine parable is spoken from a community and for a community. From this its setting in life can be determined. Miss Linnemann teaches us that we can often take hold of this setting in life quite assuredly if we pay attention to the "interlocking", to the concessions to a common experience, which a parable prefers to make use of. This is her own discovery, and it is one of far-reaching significance. The parable speaks to the man who answers up to it, as we might put it, modifying a well-known phrase of a philosopher.

Good instruction presupposes nothing, but it awakes in us pleasure, pleasure in the actual lesson too. This exceptionally good book does this, I believe. It is written so readably because it is the result of years of work—and this is a good omen for all who are minded similarly to work away at their teaching. Discipline in method leads to disciplined instruction; and what results from this is a free and enjoyable manner, in fact a partnership of learning, both in the lecture hall and in the most modest class room. Later on we shall also be discussing the book with its author in a lively way. But this is just what we want, so that the Spirit can blow mightily.

Marburg   ERNST FUCHS
April 1961

Foreword

This book owes its origin to a commission from the Catechetical Office of the Hanover Landeskirche. For this I must warmly thank its director, Professor Karl Witt, as well as the Office of the Landeskirche (it need hardly be said that responsibility for the contents of the book rests solely with the author, and that neither the Catechetical Office nor the Landeskirche Office are identified with its conclusions).

The manuscript was accepted by the Kirchliche Hochschule of Berlin as a dissertation under the title of "Die Gleichnisse Jesu" (The Parables of Jesus)— Rector, Professor Karl Kupisch; Supervisor, Professor Ernst Fuchs; Joint-Supervisor, Professor Martin Fischer.

I have received much generous assistance in my work. I owe warm thanks above all to Professor Rudolf Bultmann, Professor Joachim Jeremias, Frau Ellen Loch, Frau Professor Helene Ramsauer, Professor Martin Stallmann, and Professor Hans Stock.

I must further thank my colleagues in the Catechetical Office, Herr Ahlers, Pastor Baldermann, and Dozent Heinz Kittel, as well as Herr Bloem, Herr Emmerich, Frau Hilde Fischer, Frau Isenbeck, and Frau Weeber.

My warmest thanks are due to my honoured teacher, Professor Ernst Fuchs, and include not only all that he has done for this book, but all that I owe to him.

Berlin 1961   ETA LINNEMANN

Foreword to the Third Edition

The third edition examines the literature that has appeared meanwhile. (Some French articles, and the books of Buzy and Hermaniuk on the parables, were unfortunately inaccessible to me.) The introduction and the expositions have for the most part been left unaltered; but the notes have been expanded. This slight change of balance in the book was, however, inevitable if I was to remain faithful to the principle of giving information conscientiously about other interpretations. In some cases, however, I have not dealt with opposed interpretations, where the differences of approach in method were so great that the discussion would have gone beyond the limits of this book.

Berlin 1964   ETA LINNEMANN

PART ONE

The Basic Principles of Parable Interpretation

1

Similitudes, Parables, Illustrations, Allegories

The parable is a universally used figure of speech. Jesus was by no means the first teller of parables. He did not invent this stylistic form, but took it over; though it must be said that he handled it with extreme skill.

The parable includes several types of "figurative" speech, each of which has its own characteristics, a knowledge of which is indispensable for the interpretation of the parables.[1] These types are: 1. The similitude. 2. The parable proper. 3. The illustration. 4. The allegory.

Similitude and Parable

The parable in the wider sense includes the similitude, but in a narrower sense is contrasted with it. The *similitude* tells of "a typical situation or a typical or regular event", the *parable* "some interesting particular case".[2]

"The image in the *similitude* is taken from real life as everyone knows it, and refers to things that happen every day, to circumstances that even the most ill-willed must admit exist": this is how it always happens when leaven is added to meal (Matt. 13.33), when someone sows mustard-seed (Matt. 13.31f), when grain ripens to harvest (Mark 4.26–9). This is how every master behaves to his servant (Luke 17.7–10), how every father gives his son good gifts (Luke 11.11–13). This is how everyone rejoices at finding a lost sheep or a lost coin again (Luke 15.4–10). And would not everyone do all he could to secure for himself a treasure trove (Matt. 13.44–6)? For that reason many similitudes begin with the words "Which of you . . . ?" (Luke 11.5; 11.11; 14.28; 15.4; 17.7; etc.).

In the *parables proper* on the other hand we are told freely composed stories. "We are not shown what everyone does, what simply cannot be different, but what someone did once, whether or not other people would do it the same way."[3] "There was a rich man who had a steward . . ." (Luke 16.1). "There was a man who had two sons . . ." (Matt. 21.28). "There was a man who gave a great banquet . . ." (Luke 14.16). "In a certain city there was a judge . . ." (Luke 18.2). These are typical beginnings of parables.

"The *similitude* appeals to what is universally valid, the *parable proper* to what has happened only once. . . . The similitude guards against any opposition, since it only speaks of established facts; the parable hopes to avoid all opposition, by telling its story so attractively, so warmly and freshly that the listener simply does not think of objections. It makes it all seem so probable to him that he does not ask if it is true. What the similitude gains from the authority of what is generally known and recognized, the parable replaces by its *perspicuity*. The parable is even a higher form, because it is more subtle, and its bias less obvious. The similitude uses words like 'no one', 'no . . .', 'everyone', 'whenever', 'as often as', etc.; it tries as it were to overwhelm the listener by the weight of its generalizations, of its 'semper, ubique et ab omnibus'. The parable gently gives up this use of force, it says: 'Listener, let me tell you just one story; if it doesn't win you over I'll be silent. . . .' The individual instance comes before the eyes of the listener with total objectivity, the story-teller never allows himself, and what he thinks and feels, to look through the meshes of his net. But the parable has, like the Sibyl, become richer by renunciation; a well-composed story creates the impression of a law to which one must submit, even more strongly than if it is proclaimed in advance that by the laws of human behaviour everyone must act in such a way under such and such circumstances."[4]

The Illustration

Illustrations must be distinguished from similitudes and parables. Among them are to be found in the Gospels the story of the good Samaritan (Luke 10.29–37), of the rich fool (Luke 12.16–21), of the rich man and Lazarus (Luke 16.19–31), and of the Pharisee and the tax-collector (Luke 18.9–14).

Illustrations have this in common with parables proper, that they are invented stories and are subject to the same laws of story-telling.[a] They too are meant to be a form of argument.[b] But the way they work is different: the parable adduces a correspondence (analogia) but the illustration produces an example (exemplum). The parable gets its power of argument from the fact that what is admitted in one case can hardly be contested in another exactly corresponding case. The illustration works by reality itself, on the evidence of the example, appearing to prove the narrator right.[c]

The difference between illustration and parable or similitude can be further elucidated by some examples:

Both in the similitudes of the lost sheep and coin (Luke 15.1–10) and in the illustration of the Pharisee and the tax-collector the subject is the relationship of Jesus to tax-collectors and sinners, and the standing of sinners before God. In the similitudes a correspondence (analogy) to the case is set out; the meaning of loss and rediscovery is portrayed by the lost sheep and the lost coin, so that what is obvious to the listeners in reference to a sheep or a coin can win agreement in reference to tax-collectors and sinners. The illustration on the other hand mentions tax-collectors and Pharisees directly. It presents a (particular) Pharisee and a (particular) tax-collector in a situation which shows by its example what is at issue.

A comparison of the parable of the unjust steward (Luke 16.1–8) with the illustration of the rich fool (Luke 12.16–21) also shows this difference. Both try to urge upon the listener wise, prudent conduct (on this point they agree; otherwise their meaning is different). The parable demonstrates the conduct which the situation requires by corresponding (analogous) conduct from economic life. The illustration produces an example of the question at issue. In the parable the evaluation that the narrative compels one to make has to be carried over to another level (from "picture" to "reality"). In the illustration it refers directly to the reality and only needs to be generalized.[5]

Allegory

The allegory, like the parable proper, is a coherent, freely composed narrative, and, just like the parable, it is not told for the sake of conversation, but to bring the listeners to understand something. But this is as far as the similarity between them goes.

[a] Cf. below, pp. 10ff.
[b] Cf. below, pp. 23f.
[c] In fact the narrator has stamped his example with the meaning that the reality has for him, and in so far as the example appears to be clearly a piece of real life and the narrator retreats behind the narrative, it is a masterpiece of the stage-production of the narrator—though this is not necessarily conscious on his part.

"Allegory tries to portray for us a . . . truth in an expressive form by painting it in a series of pictures, which hint at the reality that is meant and yet veil it." [6] It gets its name from saying something other than what it means.

> The allegory in Matt. 22.1–14 for example speaks of servants and *means* prophets and apostles; it speaks of a king and *means* God; it speaks of recalcitrant guests, who maltreat and kill the messengers who summon them to the feast, and *means* the people of Israel, which "kills the prophets and stones those who are sent to it" (Matt. 23.37); it speaks of the punitive expedition of the king against the unwilling guests, which destroys their city, and *means* the destruction of Jerusalem, and so on. The allegory in Ezek. 17.1–10 speaks of an eagle and means the King of Babylon; it speaks of a twig from the top of a cedar, and means the king and princes of Judah; it speaks of a seed of the land, and means one of the seed royal, and so on.
> The parable by contrast means what it says.
> In Luke 14.15–24, for example, the host is a man who invites people to a banquet. The messenger is just any slave, the guests are acquaintances and friends of the host. Everything that the parable mentions is meant *in its proper sense*.

The allegory does not, however, mention just anything in the place of what is meant, but something that is similar to it.

This similarity does not in fact need to be obvious; and it may be merely asserted. We can use the example of terms of abuse to clarify the connection between what is mentioned and what is meant. "If terms of abuse mention an animal, they do not really mean what they mention, but the man for whom the insult is designed. They want as it were to deprive the man who is so insulted of his own proper name." [7] They give him a new name, and so assert (for the name is the expression of the essential nature) that he is what he is being called.

So an evaluation is being made when one thing is mentioned and another meant. "The new name should . . . remind men of the attitude that is to be taken to what is really meant." [8] This brings us to the decisive function of allegory: it passes on an evaluation of the reality, so that it can be shared by the listeners or readers. It does this by placing a "picture" in front of the "reality", behind which this (apparently) disappears. Strictly speaking what happens is as if two tracings were laid one over the other, of which the lower one contains the outlines, the upper one the colours: the allegory in its entirety allows the reality with which the author is concerned in the allegorical narrative to show through it. It takes its outlines from it: the narrative is modelled on the reality, but gives it its colouring: it gives an evaluation to the situation.

One can see very clearly in the allegory Matt. 22.1–14 how the narrative is modelled on the reality: although in v. 4 the banquet is already prepared, the new guests are only invited after the punitive expedition. This makes for an unnatural feature in the flow of the narrative.

This point can be seen still more clearly in the allegory in Ezek. 17. There v. 7 says: "the vine bends its roots towards the eagle"! This feature can only be understood from the reality referred to.

How the narrative makes an evaluation of the reality is shown in Ezek. 17, especially in v. 5; the vine was set "beside abundant waters" as a riverside plant: that is, the vine was placed in the best conditions possible; this makes its later fate all the more regrettable. The picture here expresses something which cannot be evident in the historical situation (note that this feature has no corresponding one in the interpretation of the allegory, 17.11ff).

In Matt. 22 the evaluation results from making the murder or manslaughter of the servants of the king the answer to the very friendly invitation to the wedding.

An allegory cannot therefore be understood unless one knows not only the allegorical narrative but also the state of affairs to which it refers. Anyone who does not have this key can read the words, but the deeper meaning is hidden from him. Allegories therefore may serve to transmit encoded information, which is only intelligible to the initiated. In every case an understanding must exist between the author and those addressed. Without this understanding the allegory cannot become effective: those addressed will not understand it or will not concede its validity. Here there is an important difference between allegory and parable. The parable speaks (for preference) to opponents, the allegory to the initiated. The parable is used to reconcile opposition, the allegory presupposes an understanding.

For the uninitiated the allegory is a riddle, which needs to be interpreted. Since the allegorical narrative in its entirety allows the reality to which it refers to show through it, every feature of the allegory must have its interpretation. In a parable on the other hand a transference of the individual features would be completely misplaced: here what matters is a single point of comparison.[d]

An ideal example of how an allegory is to be interpreted is found in Ezek. 17. Every feature of the allegorical narrative that is mentioned in vv. 3–10 corresponds to a feature of the reality that is meant in vv. 12–21.

[d] See below, p. 23f.

There are very few allegories in the Gospels. The only passage that we can regard with certainty as an allegory is the pericope of the royal wedding (Matt. 22.1–14). This is, however, a later reshaping of the parable of the great supper (Luke 14.15–24). An application has certainly been appended to the parables of the sower (Mark 4.3–9), of the net (Matt. 13.47f) and of the tares among the wheat (Matt. 13.24–9), in which they are interpreted feature by feature in the style of an allegory; but it can be said with considerable certainty that these interpretations are not original. If, however, the interpretations are disregarded, at least the parables of the sower and of the net do not give the impression of allegories. Two further parables which have been suspected (in my opinion wrongly) of being allegories are the parables of the wicked husbandmen (Mark 12.1–12) and of the wise and foolish virgins (Matt. 25.1–13).

Nevertheless for centuries all the parables of Jesus have been understood and interpreted as allegories. Traces of this view of them can already be found in the Gospels. It was Jülicher in his comprehensive work on the parables who was the first to prove irrefutably that the parables of Jesus are not allegories. This realization is to-day shared by all commentators, at least for the great bulk of the parables. The only matter for argument now is whether Jesus also composed one or two allegories *alongside* the similitudes and parables.

2

The Narrative Laws of Similitudes and Parables

Similitudes and parables do not exist for their own sakes like fairy-tales, sagas, riddles, or songs, but serve a particular purpose. They are subject to particular laws to suit what they are trying to do: they are formulated to fit their purpose.

1. The *similitude* takes up a regular or typical occurrence: i.e. it borrows its material from reality. Reality is always manifold and complex. To present clearly the occurrence that is to serve as a similitude, the narra-

tor has to take it on its own and ignore everything else that is connected with it in real life.

In the similitude of the mustard-seed (Mark 4.30–2) what matters for the narrator is that the grain of seed which is proverbially the smallest produces a shrub as big as a tree. This certainly means that it produces a very large yield as well; but that does not matter to the narrator, who ignores it, while emphasizing the difference in size between seed and plant.

In the similitude of the sower (Mark 4.3–9) on the other hand the narrator completely ignores the difference in size between the seed and the ear, and stresses instead the yield: thirtyfold, sixtyfold, a hundredfold.

In the similitude of the seed growing secretly (Mark 4.26–9) the narrator ignores the yield and the difference in size between seed and plant, and stresses instead that the seed, when once it has been sown, ripens to harvest without any help from the farmer.

From one field of reality the most varied features can be drawn on for a similitude—as this comparison of Jesus' harvest similitudes shows. But each time only one is important; the others are ignored. The parable-teller makes use of the most varied narrative devices to stress the point that matters to him at the expense of the others:

He divides up the decisive saying, and so gives it greater fullness: "The earth produces of itself, first the blade, then the ear, then the full grain in the ear." He may connect this division with a gradation: "Thirtyfold, sixtyfold, a hundredfold." He may use antithesis: "The smallest of all seeds—the greatest of all shrubs"; "He leaves the ninety-nine on the hills and goes in search of the one; and if he finds it . . . , he rejoices over it more than over the ninety-nine."

These are only a few examples from a host of possibilities that are open to an experienced narrator.

The narrator gives the material of the similitude the form that most clearly shows what is common to the event that the similitude describes and the reality for which it is designed. It must be made quite clear in what respect the two are comparable. The point of comparison, the "tertium comparationis", must be clearly brought out. Usually the narrator arranges it so that it comes at the end of the similitude, and the climax and the conclusion of the similitude coincide. This makes it particularly easy to remember.

Only what bears immediately on this point of comparison is said. A similitude is formulated as briefly as possible. Embellishments are always open to suspicion as later additions. The narrator avoids them, because they distract the listener's attention from the point of comparison.

2. While the similitude draws on a typical occurrence of real life, the *parable* in the narrower sense offers a freely composed story. But since it is composed with a specific aim, this story, like the similitude, is formulated to fit its purpose.

All the freedom that the author of a freely composed story has, is in the parable put at the service of the impression which it is to make on the listener. Like a good stage-producer, the narrator is careful to find the arrangement of characters, sets, and properties that best suits his purpose:

The "wicked servant" (Matt. 18.23–35) runs into his fellow-servant who owes him a debt just at the moment when he comes out from the king, who has let him off his great debt: it is just this temporal coincidence, a stage-artifice, that makes the verdict of the king in v. 33, "You too should have had mercy", seem compelling to the listener. The parable would have been ineffective if it had said: "Some years later the servant met one of his fellow-servants."

The father sees his "prodigal son" (Luke 15.11–32) already at a distance: by means of this trait the narrator makes room for the gesture of the father hurrying to meet his son.

The elder son does not come from the field until the feast is already in progress (Luke 15.25): this improbable feature also helps the movement of the narrative: it allows the protest of the elder son against the feast to come to light in his refusal to go in, and the generosity of the father to his sons is seen when he repeats the gesture of going out.

The steward of the vineyard is ordered by its owner (Matt. 20.1–16) to begin with the last in paying the wages: by this device the first comers are made to witness the generous payment of the last, which is necessary for the development of the story.

The owner of the vineyard is present at the payment of wages, although this is not usual if it is done by the steward. By this means the production ensures the smooth development of the story: this is the only way the dialogue between the grumbling day-labourer and the owner can be made to follow immediately on the payment of wages.[a]

The listener to a parable is quite content with such "stage-production" as long as it passes only the bounds of probability and not of possibility. If the story as a whole seems credible, he will not be worried by small divergences from what is customary in real life.

[a] Cf. now also Eichholz, "Das Gleichnis als Speil", p. 318: "So . . . we can say . . . that to fit what has to be said often enough a story is told, which is far from being everyday. . . . Individual scenes and the sequence of scenes, monologue and dialogue, leading parts and minor parts, are *staged*, as they are required to fit what has to be said."

Like the similitude, the parable is so arranged that the point of comparison comes out clearly. The narrative of a parable has a strong direct flow, which is determined by the point of comparison. Without halts and detours the narrative runs on to the point of comparison. All the individual features of the narrative join in this dramatic movement, and have a function in the development of the narrative. Only when the flow of the narrative has reached its goal is the listener released from suspense.

It can be seen from the following double example how the individual features of the parable are included in the flow of the narrative.

One of the most noticeable features of the parable of the great supper (Luke 14.16–24) is the *twofold* invitation of the substitute guests. It proves, however, to be necessary to the flow of the parable: the point of comparison is the proclamation of the host that none of the guests that are late shall taste of the meal. This proclamation follows on from the measures that the master of the house has taken to exclude the original guests. They lead up to the point that the house must be full, so that there is no room left for them. To bring out the point of comparison the narrator must describe as effectively as possible the intention of the host to fill the house right to the last place. The order for the (first) invitation of the substitute guests in v. 21 does not allow this, since the anger of the host must first be described. The narrator therefore uses the second exchange between servant and master (vv. 22f) to bring in this motif. He picks it up not only in the servant's inquiry ("still there is room"), but also in the master's answer ("that my house may be filled"), and uses this repetition to ensure that it cannot be overlooked.

The variant of the parable of the great supper, the "royal wedding" (Matt. 22.2–5, 8, 9)[b] has a different point of comparison. In consequence the motif that the house must be filled is lacking, and with it the double invitation of substitute guests. The point of comparison here is: "those invited were not worthy" (v. 8). In a comparison of this variant with the passage in Luke one notices that the host is here a king, and also in what detail the second invitation at the hour of the meal is given. In this case, however, the unworthiness of the guests depends on the worthiness of the host. There must be no doubt of this. The mention of the king derives therefore from the development of the narrative, even though here the standard image of King for God is picked up. The detailed form of the invitation underlines its value. The listeners will then agree all the more readily with the verdict of v. 8. It is therefore not a superfluous decoration, but assists the development of the narrative to the point of comparison.

[b] I distinguish between the *allegory* of Matt. 22.2–14 and the *parables* underlying this allegory, Matt. 22.2–5, 8, 9, and Matt. 22.11–13. In the *parable* of the royal wedding we see a later variant of the parable of the great supper.

The point of comparison forms the end of the parable. The upshot of the stories is not told: the listener does not learn whether the grumbling labourer in the end admits the owner is right (Matt. 20.1-16), whether the elder son allows himself to be persuaded to share in the joy of the father (Luke 15.11-32), whether the steward by his deceit achieves his aim (Luke 16.1-8). His attention would otherwise be left on the characters of the narrative and not turn as the narrator wishes to the reality for which the parable is coined.

3. In general the parables are subject to the laws of popular narrative. We are grateful to be allowed to quote the classification of these stylistic laws which Bultmann gives in his *History of the Synoptic Tradition*:

"The *conciseness* of the narrative is characteristic. Only the necessary *persons* appear. Thus in the story of the Prodigal Son there is no mother, or in the parable of the Importunate Friend no wife of the disturbed sleeper. There are never more than three chief characters, and for the most part only two: slave and master (Luke 17.7ff), the widow and the judge (Luke 18.1ff), the importunate man and his friend (Luke 11.5ff) . . . the Pharisee and the publican (Luke 18.9ff), etc.

"But often there are three: the creditor and his two debtors (Luke 7.41f), the king and the two debtors (Matt. 18.23ff), the father and the two sons (Matt. 21.28ff), etc. If there are not two (or three) persons, there are two (or three) parties or groups; the wicked husbandmen and the master (Mark 12.1ff), the host and the guests (Luke 14.16ff), the master of the vineyard and the labourers (Matt. 20.1ff), the master and his servants (Matt. 25.14ff), etc. *Groups* of people are treated as a single person (the wicked husbandmen, Mark 12.1ff, the fellow servants, Matt. 18.31; 24.49; etc.) and only differentiated so far as it is necessary (the guests who make excuses, Luke 14.18ff, the labourers hired at different times, Matt. 20.1ff, the debtors, Luke 16.5ff, the priest and the levite, Luke 10.29ff, etc.). The law of *stage duality* is operative, i.e. only two persons speaking or acting come on at a time. If others are present, they remain in the background. If more than two have to speak or act, they have to do it in separate successive scenes. The steward deals with his master's debtors one by one (Luke 16.5-7); the father asks his sons one at a time to go into his vineyard (Matt. 21.28-30); the servants come with their talents one after another to their master, and he does not receive a report from all three before he distributes rewards and punishments, but everyone receives his reward immediately he has given an account of himself (Matt. 25.19ff).

"There is also the *law of the single perspective*, i.e. one is not asked to watch two different series of events happening at the same time. In the parable of the prodigal son the whole story is told from the point of view of the prodigal. How the father took his son's departure, and what he thought while he was absent, is never stated. The parable of the unmerciful servant is similarly told. Admittedly the King and the servant come in turns to the forefront, but even so the scenes are so arranged that they never overlap. What the visitor thought or did in Luke 11.5-8 while his friend went to his neighbour is also unrecorded. The only time when it is otherwise is in Luke's version of the parable of the talents, but that is due to secondary editing. In Matthew the story flows from a single perspective, and where the master was between his first and second appearances we are not told.

"Only seldom are the *characters* portrayed by some attribute, like the judge who 'feared not God and regarded not man' (Luke 18.2) or the ten virgins of whom five were wise and five foolish (Matt. 25.2). For the most part people are characterized by what they say or do, or how they behave, like the prodigal son and his loving father, or the magnanimous king and his unmerciful debtor, or the two so different sons, etc. Or it may be that in the story itself some characterizing judgement is made of one of the actors: the king upbraids the unmerciful servant as 'you wicked servant'; the first two servants who bring their talents back with interest are praised as 'good and faithful servant', while the third is rebuked as 'you wicked and slothful servant'; and God calls the rich farmer who is concerned only about his worldly prosperity a 'fool'.

"*Feelings and motives* are mentioned only when they are essential for the action or the point. Thus in the parable of the unmerciful servant, as the servant fell down before the king and entreated him we read: 'And out of pity for him the lord . . . released him'; when the servant then mercilessly threw his fellow-servant into prison: 'When his fellow-servants saw . . . they were greatly distressed'; and finally when the king heard what had happened: 'In anger . . . he delivered him . . .'. It is said of the Good Samaritan, 'He had compassion', as it is of the father when he sees his lost son returning home; and the shepherd who finds his sheep puts it on his shoulder 'rejoicing'. But for the most part feelings are only portrayed indirectly or left to the hearer's own imagination. The feelings of the prodigal are indicated at best simply by 'when he came to himself', and for the rest are conveyed by the account of what he said and did. In the same way the feelings of the Pharisee and the publican are presented only in their prayers and gestures. And there is e.g. no description of feelings at all in the parables of the importunate friend, the wicked judge, or the ten virgins.

"*Subsidiary characters* are described only in so far as it is necessary. In Luke 10.30–5 there is no description of either the man who went down to Jericho or the innkeeper. The widow who importuned the judge is not characterized except by her persistency (Luke 18.1ff); nothing in fact turns on her motives and the justification for them. In the differentiation of subsidiary characters the parables are governed by the judicious economy of popular story-telling: two debtors suffice in the parable of the unjust steward, and their debts and his fraudulent manipulation of them are presented in identical form, with slight variation in details. Three types of guests are brought into the parable of the supper. . . . In the parable of the labourers in the vineyard there are five groups of labourers; it is only the first and last groups that matter for the story, but the sharp contrast of the extremes has to be mitigated by some sort of intermediaries; otherwise the story would sound grossly improbable.

"*Motivation* in particular is absent from the presentation, because it is irrelevant to the point being made. Thus the request of the younger son for his share of the inheritance (Luke 15.12f) and his journey into a far country are quite unmotivated. Similarly we are not told why the employer in Matt. 20.1ff needed so many labourers for his vineyard as to go out every three hours to take on more hands. From what motive the various travellers in Luke 10.29ff made their journey is not disclosed. Likewise the reason for the different answers and the different behaviour of the two sons in Matt. 21.28ff remains outside the story. . . .

"There is a similar economy governing the *description of events and actions*. Anything unnecessary is omitted; e.g. we are not told how the steward dissipated his master's wealth. There is no description of how the widow importuned the judge, but just a very brief indication that she did, etc. In distinct contrast to this whatever is reported is described in very concrete terms. The debts of the two debtors in Luke 7.41f amount to 500 and 50 denarii, in Matt. 18.23ff to 10,000 talents and 100 denarii; Luke 16.5ff gives 100 measures of oil and 100 measures of wheat. The prodigal son becomes a swineherd; when he comes home the father clothes him with the best robe, adorns him with a ring, and kills the fatted calf for him. The luxury of the rich man and the lamentable state of Lazarus are vividly portrayed. The wage of the workers in the vineyard is concretely stated as one denarius. The owner of the unfruitful fig-tree has come already for three years to find no fruit, etc. All this conforms to the art of popular story-telling.

"So does the rich *use of direct speech and soliloquy*. For the first we need only to think of the similitudes of the Lost Sheep and the Lost Coin [Luke 15.4–10], . . . of the Master and the Servant [Luke 17.7–10], . . . or of the parables of the Barren Fig Tree [Luke 13.6–9] (for this reason the vinedresser has to appear beside the owner), of the Labourers in the Vineyard [Matt. 20.1–16] (for the same reason there has to be a steward), of the Sowing of the Tares [Matt. 13.24–30], of the Great Supper [Luke 14.15–24], etc. . . . Soliloquies can be found in the parables of the Prodigal Son, the Unjust Steward [Luke 16.1–8], the Unjust Judge (Luke 18.1–8), the Rich Fool (Luke 12.16–21), the Unfaithful Servant (Luke 12.45), the Wicked Husbandmen (Luke 20.13 expanded). Under this category we must include the prayers of the Pharisee and the publican. . . .

"We can find other elements of style typical of popular story telling, like the *law of repetition*: the phrase 'Have patience with me and I will pay you all' appears twice in the parable of the Unmerciful Servant. The confession of the prodigal son comes twice. The servants in Matt. 25.20ff present their accounts and receive their reward in words that are repeated; similarly, with variations, are recorded the excuses of the invited guests Luke 14.18ff, and the dealings of the steward with the debtors Luke 16.5ff. A *threefold repetition* can be found in the parable of the Great Supper: three types of guests make their excuses; also Matt. 25.14ff: three sorts of servants who are entrusted with money; Luke 10.29ff: Priest, Levite and Samaritan go down the Jericho road. . . . There is also the law of *End-stress*, i.e. the most important thing is described last. The clearest example is Mark 4.3ff: the fruitful seed is mentioned last of all . . . ; Luke 18.9ff: the publican is introduced after the Pharisee; Matt. 25.14ff: the servant who has not used the money entrusted to him is presented last, so as to accord with the hortatory nature of the story. . . .

"Finally it is important to notice how and why the *hearer's judgement* is precipitated. The *moral* quality of the man who found the treasure [Matt. 13.44] or of the pearl-merchant [Matt. 13.45f] is not the subject of judgement; naturally, too, there is no verdict intended on the institution of slavery (Luke 17.7ff) or upon imprisonment for debt (Matt. 18.23ff). It is plain that the steward is fraudulent and the judge unscrupulous, but not in order that they should be judged on those grounds, but that we should realize that it is possible to learn something even from such rascals as these. In other instances we are required to pass a *moral* verdict on some action, . . . in the parable . . . of the talents, of the unmerciful servant, of the two sons, where the point of the parable is directed to just this verdict. Naturally *some* judgement is in general required by all parables, and their argumentative character is often expressed in their form. . . . Such a purpose is also often served by the *antithesis of two types*: the two debtors (Luke 7.41f), the two sons [Matt. 21.28–30], the wise and foolish virgins [Matt. 25.1–13], the faithful and unfaithful servants (Luke 12.42ff), the rich man and the poor man, the Pharisee and the publican, the Priest and Levite and the Samaritan." [9]

3

Introductory Formulas and Applications

Many of the parables begin just like an ordinary story:

"A man planted a vineyard" (Mark 12.1), "There was a rich man" (Luke 12.16), "There was a man who had two sons" (Luke 15.11), "Two men went up into the temple" (Luke 18.10), "A nobleman went into a far country" (Luke 19.12).

Other parables, however, are introduced by a formal phrase:

It is fullest in the parable of the mustard-seed in Mark's version: "With what can we compare the kingdom of God, and what parable shall we use for it? It is like . . ." (Mark 4.30f). In Luke the introduction to this parable runs differently: "What is the kingdom of God like? And to what shall I compare it?" (Luke 13.18f, cf. Luke 7.31f). Luke has a considerably shorter introduction for the parable of the leaven: "To what shall I compare the kingdom of God? It is like . . ." (Luke 13.20f, cf. Matt. 11.16). But very often this formula is so abbreviated that only the "like" or "just as" is left. So we find in the parable of the Talents: "As when a man going on a journey" (Matt. 25.14, cf. Mark 13.34), in the parable of the Great Supper: "The kingdom of heaven is like a king . . ." (Matt. 22.1, cf. Matt. 18.23, Matt. 13.24). "Then shall the kingdom of Heaven be like ten virgins . . .", we read in Matt. 25.1 (cf. Matt. 13.44,45).

In no case are we to take these introductory formulas literally. They are not intended for this. The kingdom of God in Mark 4.31 is not "like" a grain of mustard seed but "it is the case with the kingdom of God as with a grain of mustard seed". "In Matt. 13.47 the kingdom of Heaven is not compared to a seine-net, but the situation at its coming is compared to the sorting out of the fish caught in the seine-net." [10] It can also be seen how such introductions are not meant literally from the imprecise way that Matt. 13.44 says, "The kingdom of Heaven is like a treasure" while Matt. 13.45 says, "The kingdom of Heaven is like a merchant", although the two parables otherwise correspond completely.

The introduction, "The kingdom of Heaven is like . . ." is found in Matthew very much more frequently than in Luke. "Thus we have to do with an introductory formula which Matthew . . . prefers, and we must admit the possibility that it has been inserted in various cases, e.g. Matt. 22.2 (otherwise in Luke 14.16 . . .)." [11]

Numerous parables begin the narrative at once without an introductory formula, and many of them end the narrative without a word said beyond it. This is quite in order, because the original hearers could understand immediately from the situation what was meant by the parable, so that they needed no further help.

In other parables we find an *application*, that is a saying which gives an indication what the reality is to which the parable should be applied. Frequently this application is attached to the parable by "so" or "therefore".

"So also my heavenly father will do", it says in the parable of the unmerciful servant (Matt. 18.35), "So you also . . ." in the similitude of the servant's reward (Luke 17.10). "Even so there will be joy in heaven", is the conclusion derived from the similitude of the lost sheep (Luke 15.7).

In others the application takes the form of an imperative, for instance in the parable of the ten virgins, "Watch therefore . . ." (Matt. 25.13).

Some of the applications belonged from the beginning to their parables. But in many cases they are a help to understanding for a later reader, not for the original listener. This can easily be seen in those places where the application is a saying of Jesus transmitted by the other Evangelists in another position.

> So we find the application of the parable of the labourers in the vineyard, the saying about the last who shall be first (Matt. 20.16, cf. 19.30) used again in Luke 13.30 in another context. The saying with which Luke ends the parable of the Pharisee and the tax-collector (Luke 18.14b) he has already used at Luke 14.11.

Sometimes the lack of correspondence between application and parable reveals that the application has been added later.

> This is true e.g. of the parable of the Pharisee and the tax-collector; for when the actual circumstances are examined, it is not true either that the tax-collector has "humbled himself" or that the Pharisee has "exalted himself". The saying about the first and the last in Matt. 20.16 also does not fit the parable, because it only relates to a subsidiary feature of it.

Occasionally a second application has been appended to the first in the course of transmission:

> The final verse of the parable of the royal wedding, that "many are called but few are chosen" (Matt. 22.14), is also given by some manuscripts after the parable of the labourers in the vineyard (Matt. 20.16). The parable of the unjust steward (Luke 16.1–8) is followed by no less than six different applications—all of them attempts to overcome by interpretation the difficulties this parable gave rise to when its original meaning was no longer understood. If Mark 12.10f is compared with Matt. 21.43 and Luke 20.18, it can be established that each of the Evangelists has expanded the application in Mark's text in his own way.

4

The Parable as a Form of Communication

The parable (using the word in the wider sense[a]) is a form of speech. Its original situation is communication, dialogue.

[a] Where it is not otherwise specified, the word is always used in its wider sense in this and the following chapters, except when a specific parable is mentioned.

A parable is an urgent endeavour on the part of the speaker towards the listener. The man who tells a parable wants to do more than utter something or make a communication. He wants to affect the other, to win his agreement, to influence his judgement in a particular direction, to force him to a decision, to convince him or prevail upon him. Even when it is only the narrator who speaks, a conversation is really taking place. He has already anticipated the possible objections of the hearers, because it is to overcome such resistance that he has chosen the parable as his form of speech.

It is of the essence of a parable that there is achieved in it a *dialegesthai*, a con-versation, a dialogue *between* the narrator and the listener.[12] The type of conversational situation which a parable arises from can, however, be very varied.

A parable can be used for *instruction*. It overcomes the difficulties of comprehension by explaining what is unknown or hard to grasp through what is familiar and easy to grasp.

Thus the Palestinian scribes frequently used parables in their lectures. "The Rabbis said, 'Let not the parable be a small thing in your eyes, for through a parable a man can attain to understanding of the Torah [the Divine Law]. Like a king, who has lost a gold coin in his house or a precious pearl, can he not yet find it again by a wick of the value of an as [a small copper coin]? So too let not a parable be a small thing in your eyes, for through a parable a man can attain to understanding of the Torah.'"[13]

The parable is also used for *exhortation*. Its power of persuasion is used to overcome the resistance that stands in the way of doing good.

Thus the Rabbis used the following parable to give point to an exhortation to repent while it is still to-day, because every day can be the last and no one knows the moment of his death: "Like a king, who invited his servants to a banquet without giving them a fixed time. The wise among them made themselves smart and sat down at the entrance to the palace. They said: 'Is anything likely to be lacking in the house of the king?' (In his household everything is always on hand, so the meal could start at any moment.) The foolish among them went off to their work. They said: 'Is there ever a banquet without laborious preparation?' Suddenly the king called for his servants. The wise among them appeared before him, just as they were, smart and ready; the foolish among them appeared before him, just as they were, dirty. The king was pleased with the wise and was angry with the foolish. He said: 'These, who have made ready for the meal, are to sit and eat and drink; but those, who have not made themselves ready for the meal, are to stand and look on.'"[14]

The parable is also used readily when a man has to hold another responsible for his deeds and omissions. By setting the action of the other man in the light of the parable he compels him to pass his own verdict on himself, and in this way can convict him.

The classical example of this is Nathan's parable, 2 Sam. 12.1–12.

The parable was also used by the Rabbis, the Jewish scribes, in *scholarly arguments*.

So in the discussion of the school of Shammai with the school of Hillel whether the earth or heaven was made first, each school taught a parable to support its view:
The school of Shammai, which took the view that heaven was made before the earth, said: "The matter is like a king who has made himself a throne, and after he has made it he makes his footstool."
The school of Hillel, which took the view that the earth was made first, said against this: "The matter is like a king who built himself a palace. After he had built the ground floor, he built the first floor." [15]

The parable was furthermore a favourite weapon of the Rabbis in *controversy dialogues*. There was no better means to reduce the view of an opponent *ad absurdum*, because with a parable he could be convicted through his own verdict. However, these were more or less superficial victories. The underlying cause of the controversy was seldom reached. Often all that mattered was to make a fool of one's opponent.

Gamaliel answered a philosopher who asked why God was not wroth with the idols but with the idolators: "With what can this be compared? With a king of flesh and blood, who had a son; and this son had brought up a dog to which he gave his father's name (i.e. he called it 'Abba', my father). Thereafter whenever he took an oath he said, 'By the life of the dog Abba!' When the king heard of it with whom would he be angry? Would he be angry with the son or would he be angry with the dog? Of course he would be angry with the son!" [16]

The parable plays its most significant rôle in another situation, of which we will first give an example before we try to characterize it:

We are familiar from Roman history at school with the saga of Menenius Agrippa, which we are given in Livy 2.32:
The unity of Rome was threatening to break up, and the continued existence of the city was in danger. The plebeians, compelled year by year to bear arms instead of cultivating their fields, had been reduced to poverty and

given over to serfdom. Consoled again and again by empty promises, they were finally not ready to bear their misery any longer. Returning from a campaign and still under arms, they demanded the fulfilment of the promises. The danger of an insurrection threatened. To find some temporary solution the consuls sent the plebeian legions, which were still bound to them by oath, out of the city. But they entrenched themselves over against Rome, on the Mons Sacer, and the position was more dangerous than ever. If any of the many enemies of Rome were to make use of it and an external war break out, the fate of the city might well be sealed. The unity of the citizens must at all costs be restored. The patricians therefore sent Menenius Agrippa as a mediator to the plebeian legions. "When he was admitted to the camp, he is supposed . . . to have simply told the following story: 'At the time when not everything yet agreed in harmony within Man as it does now, but each single limb had its own will and its own power of speech, the other limbs were angry because their care, labour and service provided everything for the stomach; the stomach, at ease in their midst, did nothing more than make itself comfortable with the delights offered. They took an oath that the hands would bring no more food to the mouth, the mouth would not accept anything offered, the teeth would not grind anything. While they tried in their anger to break the stomach through hunger, at the same time the limbs themselves and the whole body were completely wasted away. By this it was shown that the stomach was not idle but gave its service and nourished as well as was nourished, because it shared round equally into the veins and gave back to all parts of the body the blood that gives life and strength, fortified by digestion of the food.' Because he thus showed by a comparison how similar the internal mutiny of the body was to the animosity of the plebeians against the patricians, he altered the feelings of the crowd." [17]

Three things can be learnt from this example:

1. The parable is used to induce the listeners to make a decision after the mind of the narrator in a concrete historical situation.

2. The situation is characterized by the greatest conceivable opposition which exists between the assessment of the situation by the narrator and by the listeners.

3. The narrator, who has at his disposal nothing other than the power of language, is able to prevail upon his listeners, because through the parable he offers them a new understanding of the situation.

While the plebeians understood their situation as infamous exploitation by the patricians and so were ready for revolt, Menenius Agrippa gives them the chance of understanding it from the natural differences within the body of the State, and the needs resulting from this.

The parable is acted out in between the differing verdicts of the speaker and of his listeners, but upon the same set of facts, and means to induce them to agree with him, even if it cannot compel them to do so. The narrator with his parable throws a bridge over the chasm of opposition. Whether the listener steps on to this bridge and finds his way over to him is, however, not under his control. He must be content to have made it possible. He can compel his listener to a decision; but what the decision is rests with the listener.

It is the firmly established result of the latest era of parable interpretation, characterized by the names of Cadoux, Dodd, and Jeremias, that the parables of Jesus (like the parable of Menenius Agrippa) refer to an historical situation. Jesus' parables are not for instruction, still less for learned argument; only in rare and exceptional cases do they give an exhortation,[b] or make it their object to convict the listener of something.[c] Though almost all uttered to opponents, they do not intend to reduce the opponent *ad absurdum*, but make it their aim to win his agreement. The opponent is not dismissed with superficial arguments, but the depths of the conflict are reached.[d] By this means he is given the chance of a genuine decision, which in controversy dialogues is normally lacking.

Although a parable always has its origin in a dialogue situation, it is only in this last case that the original situation is essential for the understanding of the parable. It is not just an accidental occasion to which the parable owes its origin, and from which it can be loosed without loss as a general utterance. A parable of this sort becomes a factor in the historical situation in which it originates, and can be understood only in the context of the other factors which are at work in it. The expositor who is inquiring into the meaning of such a parable must therefore examine specifically its original situation. It is not enough to consider what ideas the narrator has connected with the parable; it must also be observed what ideas, images, and evaluations were at work in the hearers of the parable, in what the opposition between the narrator and his listeners consisted, and how accordingly his words must have

---

[b] E.g., the illustration of the rich fool, Luke 12.16–21, though it is questionable whether this goes back to Jesus.

[c] Mark 12.1–12 is probably the only example of this.

[d] The evidence for this must be given in the interpretation of the parables.

acted on them. In other words, what the narrator was saying by such a parable can be grasped only when we know what the parable conveyed to its original listeners in that concrete situation.

5

The Structure of the Parable

The parable is a form of argument. Although we are used to talking of pictures and parables in the same breath, parables are something different from pictures. They are neither illustrations nor communications in pictorial language. This is true of the parables of Jesus too. We must not be led astray by the fact that many of his parables are introduced by the words: "The kingdom of Heaven is like . . .".[a] These parables do not at all communicate revelations in picture language of what the kingdom of Heaven is like, but intend to move the hearer to assess correctly what is needed now, at this moment.

> Thus the parable of the ten virgins (Matt. 25.1–13) is intended to help one to the recognition that those who neglect to prepare themselves for a lengthy time of waiting until the coming of the Son of Man are in danger of losing their share in the kingdom of God. The parable of the "royal wedding" (Matt. 22.2–5,8f) does not mean to give information on what it is like at the banquet in the kingdom of God; it is intended to compel the listener to the verdict: "Those who do not comply with God's invitation show by this that they do not deserve it. It is their fault, not God's!"

Parables are meant to be forms of argument. It is for this reason that they have only one point of comparison. One can hardly argue several things at once. For this reason we must carefully distinguish between what a parable is arguing and what it assumes. As soon as we draw from a parable a number of different significant ideas, we can be sure that we are missing the meaning that the parable had for its first narrator. This is also true when we do establish the point of comparison, but then set alongside it other important ideas which the parable seems to

[a] Cf. pp. 16f.

give us. We do not then do justice to the parable, because it makes its effect only through this concentration on one point.

This point of comparison, the *tertium comparationis*, is the cardinal point, which binds together the picture and the reality for which it is coined: or, as it is usually put, the "picture part" and the "reality part".

The terms "picture part" and "reality part", or "picture and reality", make the distinction between what the narrative portrays and what it means, what the parable is intended to say. This distinction should prevent us from mixing the two together from the start, and make us consider the relationship which picture and reality have to one another.

> In the parable of the school of Shammai quoted above (p. 20), the "picture" or "picture part" is what is said about the king, the throne, and the footstool. The "reality" or "reality part" is the view that God made heaven first, and then the earth. The point of comparison is the factually determined sequence of events; as one does not make a footstool until the throne is ready, so the earth was only after the heavens.
>
> In the parable of Menenius Agrippa (see pp. 20f) the "picture" or "picture part" is the story of the stomach and the limbs, the "reality" or "reality part" the position of the patricians and plebeians in the State. The point of comparison is the thought: "As the limbs which refused to serve the stomach did themselves harm, so too the rebellion of the plebeians against the patricians must cause harm to themselves."

The use of the terms "picture part" or "reality part" can easily mislead if its context is not considered. The description of the narrative as "picture *part*" does not mean that this is incomplete when taken on its own and needs amplification through an interpretation. The parable narrative is *all* the narrator says to his original listeners.[b] They do not need an interpretation; they can understand the parable immediately from the situation. It is only for the later commentators and readers who do not know the situation or at least are not in it that the meaning of the parables is added as a second part to the narrative—since they must find it out more or less laboriously. The concepts "picture *part*" and "reality *part*" are therefore shaped to fit the point of view of the commentator and are only meaningful in this context.

Picture and reality have only a single *tertium comparationis*; this can be definitely established. But beside this it should be noticed that numerous

---

[b] The question of the applications can in this connection be disregarded.

further connections can exist between the parable and the reality to which it alludes.

The choice of material for the parable by the narrator already implies the assertion that a correspondence exists between the parable and the reality to which it alludes. Sometimes this correspondence is obvious:

E.g. in the parable of the son's request (Matt. 7.9–11): as a son makes petitions to his father, so man stands before God as a petitioner.

Sometimes it is provided by a tradition:

The school of Shammai refers to Isa. 66.1 for the parable quoted above (p. 20): "Thus says the Holy One (blessed be he): 'Heaven is my throne and the earth is my footstool'." [18]

The parable of the wise and foolish virgins (Matt. 25.1–13) is able to assume that the wedding is a current image for the time of the end.

But in other cases the correspondence between the material of the parable and the reality is not predetermined at all. The narrator in his choice of parable material is then carrying out the function of "claiming one thing as another". Objects and situations do not have an unequivocal meaning simply as they exist: they only acquire their meaning from the way they are understood. It depends on our own understanding what a reality means for us. Understanding is, however, guided by the way this reality "enters into language". [19] The narrator brings the reality "into language" by his assertion of the correspondence between the material of the parable and the reality, and so opens up the possibility of understanding it (anew). This function is exercised by the narrator primarily in cases where the assessment of the situation is in dispute between him and his listeners, and he wants to present the listeners with his understanding of the situation through the parable, so that they share it. Here are some examples of this:

In the parable of Menenius Agrippa the point of comparison is that the limbs in refusing to serve the stomach do themselves harm. This only acquires validity for the situation described, however, because the parable *claims* that the position of the plebeians in the Roman State is like the place a limb has in a body.

The point of comparison of the parable of the great supper (Luke 14.15–24) lies in the fact that the guests who are late miss sharing in the meal. When Jesus tells this parable to Pharisees who call blessed whoever partakes of the meal of the kingdom of God, he is claiming that their conduct is like the behaviour of guests who still do not want to appear although the meal has already begun.

The point of comparison of the similitudes of the lost sheep and coin (Luke 15.1–10) is the joy of rediscovery. When Jesus tells these parables to those who protest because he spends his time with the lost, he is claiming the situation as the moment of rediscovery in which one must rejoice.

Such is the way in which the line of argument of the parables, which comes to a climax in the point of comparison, works in with their function of "claiming one thing as another".

But to claim one thing as another is only possible if one is successful in making a correspondence clear. It must become clear to the listener that the parable is alluding to the opposition between him and the narrator, and in such a way that he cannot deny a "moment of truth" to this allusion. We find therefore in the parables numerous correspondences between picture and reality:

> Just as the stomach appears to be an inactive parasite in comparison with the limbs (see pp. 26f), the plebeians regard the patricians as people who enrich themselves at their expense.
>
> The prodigal son (Luke 15.11–32) leads a life which is in opposition to the commandments of God, like the sinners; he even takes himself off, like the tax-collectors, to serve the gentiles. But the elder brother has never yet transgressed a command of his father: which corresponds to the Pharisees' faithfulness to the law.
>
> The attitude of those who worked for the whole day (Matt. 20.1–16), who have "borne the burden and heat of the day", towards those who worked for the last hour, who went idle the whole day, corresponds to the attitude of the Pharisees who have toiled all their life long with patience and zeal to fulfil the law towards the tax-collectors and sinners.

Such correspondences do not detract from the independence of the parable narrative. The parable always "means" what it says. Picture and reality do not coincide, as in an allegory; it is only parallels that exist between the two.

To put it more exactly, the parallels consist in the fact that the relevant feature in the parable evokes the same or at least a similar attitude as the listeners have taken to the reality in question.

> In the parable of Menenius Agrippa the feature that the stomach (apparently) lives as an inactive parasite at the expense of the limbs evokes the same attitude as the listeners take to the position of the patricians.
>
> In the parable of the prodigal son it is not that the younger son "is" or "signifies" the publicans, but the attitude that the listeners must take after

the first verses to the younger son corresponds to that which they take to the tax-collectors and sinners, while their attitude to the elder son at first corresponds to their estimation of their own obedience to the law.

In the parable of the labourers in the vineyard the comparison of the labourers for the whole day with the labourers for the last hour, between the busy and the idle labourers, evokes an attitude similar to that which the (pharisaic) audience feel when they compare themselves with the tax-collectors.

The correspondences between picture and reality depend therefore on the narrator allowing room in the parable for the evaluation of his listeners. They signify a concession to the listeners; the narrator *concedes them something*. Through what he concedes them he can get them to listen to his parable at first simply as being something said about this reality, in order to establish the connection between the parable and the point in dispute. The more unusual his demands on his listeners are when he claims by the parable that his own view of the situation is correct, the more careful he must be to concede his listeners something. Otherwise he would be talking at cross-purposes, and his parable would be a waste of effort.

This "claiming one thing as another" together with the "concession" produces the phenomenon of *interlocking*. In the parable the verdict of the narrator on the situation in question "interlocks" with that of the listener. Both evaluations of the situation go into the parable. The choice of material, the point of comparison, and with it the course of the narrative, are of course primarily determined by the verdict of the narrator. But the verdict of the listeners on the situation also leaves its deposit in the parable. The narrator takes it up by conceding something to the listeners, so that they must recognize the reference of the parable to the reality. The opposed judgements do not simply appear in the parable side by side, but they are interlocked with one another or interwoven in the concise single strand of the narrative. In this the narrator's verdict naturally remains predominant. The verdict of the listeners on the situation on the other hand, so far as it comes into the parable, undergoes a process similar to the refraction of a ray of light as it enters another medium:

The protest of the Pharisee against Jesus' table fellowship is not the *same* as the protest of the elder brother against the feast that is celebrated because of the younger son. Nor is it the *same* as the protest of the grumbling day-labourer who complains that someone else is being paid the same for much less work. But one cannot say either that the contrast as it is found in the parable has nothing to do with the historical situation.

The result of this interlocking is, first, that deductions can be made back from the parable to the historical situation that is claimed in a particular sense in it, but secondly that such inferences are subject to strong reservations. The original evaluation of the situation by the listener, the true causes of his disagreement, and with them a clear picture of the opposition between him and the parable-teller, cannot be deduced from the parable alone. If the picture that the parable gives is simply identified with the reality, we are not only on the wrong track in assessing the historical situation, but an essential feature of the parable itself escapes us: the parable in its function of claiming one thing as another. As long as we do not notice this interlocking in the parables of Jesus, we have no access to what Jesus was really saying.

Among the points of contact which picture and reality have outside the one point of comparison are also the *unusual features*.

Several parables contain features which conflict with daily experience. Such features, which do not result from a natural context in the representation in the parable narrative, take their origin from the reality of which the narrator wishes to speak.[20]

> It is unusual for *all* the guests to send excuses. This feature of the parable of the great supper (Luke 14.15-24) cannot therefore be occasioned by the material, but only by the situation which Jesus has in mind.
>
> It is unusual for a father to send his son in after his maltreated servants. The sequence "sending of the servants—sending of the son" in the parable of the wicked husbandman (Mark 12.1-12) must therefore have been composed for reasons derived from the reality.
>
> It is unusual for the father to behave as he does at the return of the prodigal son (Luke 15.11-32); here too we have to suppose an allusion to the reality.

It is usually said that these features from the reality part have invaded the picture part. But this way of putting it obscures more than it clarifies. It cannot have been intended that in such places the picture part and the reality part should fall together. For in that case the narrator would have given up the power of analogy, and deprived the parable itself of the effect intended. Only if the parable narrative remains independent can it become effective as an *argument* about the reality. So the direct connection which exists in the unusual features between picture and reality does not mean that the narrator in these places combines the two. Although the reason for the introduction of an unusual feature is the connection with the reality, such a feature is in no way supported by the reality. It is the parable narrative that supports the unusual features too. They do not destroy the narrative but are kept under control by devices of the narrator. Our understanding of them is blocked if we limit ourselves to comparing what the parable narrates with our experience of the reality, instead of asking how the feature which contradicts our experience of reality has been built into the narrative. We should not be asking: "Does what is narrated ever happen in reality?" We must ask: "Does this as it is told strike the listener to the parable as unreal?" And here we should note that many an obstacle which can make the reader of the passage stop to think does not strike a listener.

Though it is unusual for *all* the guests to refuse (Luke 14.18f), the listener who accepts the story as it comes, as the record of an event that happened only once, will not have trouble over this, particularly since the flow of the narrative, building up tension as it goes, sweeps him along with it and prevents him from fastening on to this point.

The same is true of the action of the vineyard-owner (Matt. 20.1-16) who goes out several times in the day, and even for the last time at the eleventh hour, to hire labourers.

It is improbable that a father should send his son in after his servants have been maltreated, as in the parable of the wicked husbandmen (Mark 12.1-12). A comparison of this feature of the parable with reality gives a negative result. But the trait is built into the narrative by a motivation with which the father justifies the sending of the son. This motivation seems credible; one usually respects the son to a far higher degree than a slave as the representative of a person. Whether this is also to be expected of rebellious vinedressers is not relevant. It is enough that the motivation has the appearance of credibility, so that no break arises in the story, and the listener follows the narrator without objections from the fate of the servants on to that of the son.

The murder of the son by the husbandmen is also built in to the flow of the narrative by a motivation. It is the same with the conduct of the guests in the parable of the great supper, of the father in the parable of the prodigal son, etc.

To summarize, parables have only *one* point of comparison, but the connections between "picture part" and "reality part" are not exhausted by this. Behind the course of argument of the parable, which is based on the point of comparison, stand its other functions, of which the listener hardly becomes aware—indeed he should not—but which are no less effective for that. Their immediate effectiveness is of course largely limited to the original listeners. It is only these who lose nothing if they pay attention only to the argument of the parable. The later expositor on the other hand would lose something essential if he confined himself only to this foreground and thought his exposition complete when he had formulated a main thought which depends on the point of comparison.

This must be true at least for the parables which are intended to bridge over an opposition between the narrator and the listeners. In them the speaker makes a free gift to his hearers, which can be recognized in all its force only if one pays attention to the way in which the parable opens up for the listeners the possibility of coming into agreement with the narrator.

The utterance of the parable, which comes out of the point of comparison, alters its character and no longer remains the same if it is detached from this urgent and active concern for the listener. The original listeners participated immediately in this free gift of the speaker. The later reader and commentator only gets access to it when he traces the means which the narrator puts at their service.

6

The Parables as "Language Event"

A successful parable is an event that decisively alters the situation. It creates a new possibility that did not exist before, the possibility that the man addressed can come to an understanding with the man addressing him across the opposition that exists between them. This possibility depends on the narrator bringing into language in a new way the matter which is in dispute between him and his listeners, and so opening up a new understanding.[a]

This new possibility which the parable creates in the situation is significant even if understanding is not achieved. Even if the man addressed persists in his previous position, it is not simply "all as

---

[a] See above, p. 25. Cf. Fuchs, *Hermeneutik*, particularly "Prolegomena" §5 (pp. 67–72) and "Hermeneutik" §6 (pp. 126–33).

before". Just because a genuine opportunity has been opened up for him of giving up his previous position, this has lost its inevitability. Even if he persists in it he is really making a decision. His persistence acquires a different character; it becomes explicit opposition.

So a successful parable is an event in a double sense; it creates a new possibility in the situation, and it compels the man addressed to a decision. That is to say (as should be clear after what has been said above), it compels the making of a decision; it cannot decide the outcome of it. Anyone who risks a parable in such a situation is risking everything; but this is the only way he can win everything.

The deeper the opposition between the speaker and the man addressed goes, the more significant is the decision which the parable compels to be made. There are oppositions which reach right into the depths of existence, right to the ground that sustains the life of a man and determines it. The parables of Jesus—or at least most of them—are addressed to such an opposition.[b]

If a parable reaches the listener this depends on the moment of truth which the narrator knows how to make so effective for his purposes that his listeners are perplexed by it. This perplexity does not remove the opposition between the speaker and the listener, but it does remove the possibility of ignoring the opposition. For the man so perplexed, truth is now set against truth. On the one hand there is the truth that he himself represents with his entire existence—in so far as this opposition, even if it has appeared at a superficial level, reaches down into the depths of existence; and on the other hand there is that which forces itself on him inescapably as being truth in the words of the speaker—as truth whose validity he has always known, or at least could have known. He must decide; in fact he has already done so at the moment of listening. This is true even if this decision has not been at all conscious for him, because he persists in his previous position. By this persistence he has placed himself in active opposition to that moment of truth which the parable holds out to him. But if the listener follows the call of the truth which confronts him in the parable, he sets himself in opposition to what has till now been the truth of his existence.

Jesus, by compelling his listeners to a decision through telling a parable, gives them the possibility of making a change of existence, of understanding themselves anew from the depths up, of achieving a "new life". Such a change of existence no one can undertake in his own strength and on his own authority, for that would be like wanting to jump over one's own shadow or to pull oneself up by one's own bootlaces. The possibility can only come to a man from outside, only through a saying that reaches into the depths of his existence. A parable is such a saying if it succeeds in bridging an opposition that touches the depths of existence. Such sayings the parables of Jesus are.

We called the parables of Jesus a "language event", for something decisive happens here through what is said. We have already said that one who risks a parable in such a situation is risking everything; we must now add more exactly, he risks all on the power of language. The man who risks such a parable wants his listeners to come into agreement with him across this deep opposition. The deeper the opposition the less there is as a matter of course that he and his listeners have in common, to which he could refer with his parable. If it is only a matter of opposition in doctrine, the disputants will still always have common basic presuppositions, which none of them questions; if it is a matter of moral exhortation, the speaker and the man addressed are still at one in the basic recognition of the good, and also agree extensively on what the good is, apart from the point at issue. If it is a question of imparting knowledge we cannot even talk of opposition, because here only the difficulties of comprehension need to be overcome. If, however, the opposition reaches right down to the depths of existence, the parable teller can only find a common point of reference in the basic features of language. He is thrown back on the power of language. Here what a philosopher has said is true: "Language speaks. Language? And not man? . . . Man speaks in so far as he conforms to language. The conforming is listening."[21] Only when man succeeds in following the basic features of language does his word have force.[c]

Language, however, is subject to historical change. There are words that "no longer say anything to us". Others have for us "acquired a different ring". Language is bound up with its context in cultural history and with historical events. Although the essential nature of human existence persists at all times and is the same in all cultural settings, it must at the same time not be overlooked that it "comes into language" in ever new forms, and must do so.

[c] See Heidegger, *Unterwegs zur Sprache*, p. 33: "Everything depends on learning to stay within the utterance of language. For this continuous testing is needed whether and to what extent we achieve the essentials of conforming to language. . . . For man only speaks, in so far as he conforms to language." Cf. on this Fuchs, *Hermeneutik*, pp. 62–72.

The parables of Jesus have been passed down to us, but the "language event" that they effected cannot be passed down. It is not effected for us just by our reading or listening to the parables; we do not stand in the same situation as the original listeners. The opposition—even if it is basically the same—breaks out for us at a different point. Our language has changed in the course of history. The allusions of the parables no longer reach us, or at least not immediately.

The "language event" of the parables of Jesus cannot be transmitted. But it can be made intelligible—this is the task of exposition; and it can be repeated—this happens in Christian preaching. Preaching repeats the *event* that happened to Jesus' listeners through the parables of Jesus. It is the word that comes from outside, the *verbum externum*, that alone makes this change of existence possible for man, that helps him from unbelief to faith. For "faith comes by preaching" (Rom. 10.17). Preaching, however, not only receives instruction from the parables of Jesus on how it is to be done rightly, but is grounded in what Jesus did when he risked his word.

7

The Parables as Sayings of Jesus

Jesus' parables are not exhausted by being uttered; they effected an event in which something decisive happened. Only if we grasp this event as well shall we have grasped the original meaning of the parables.

This event, however, is an historical event. It binds the parables of Jesus to a particular historical situation in the past. They cannot be loosed from this historical place of origin as an "eternal truth", for which it is of secondary importance at what historical moment it first appeared. What binds them to this point of origin is more than an accidental historical form, which can be stripped off so that the valid content appears all the more clearly. They need to be grasped in their connection with their original historical situation, for this is precisely how they reveal their meaning, though it reaches far beyond that situation.

Although it is not an historical interest that guides us, we must for this reason postpone the question of what the parables of Jesus say to *us*, and try to understand the parables as Jesus' listeners heard them. In doing this we do not give up the question which is near our hearts, but as a matter of method we postpone it, because this is the best way we can hope to get an answer to it. For every attempt to master the parables of Jesus directly, without this return to the historical situation, only yields a theological utterance or a moral demand. This is, however, not only very much less than, it is something quite different from, the original meaning of the parables of Jesus.

Perhaps it is disturbing to learn that the sayings of Jesus are to such an extent historically time-bound. But this is only to say of them what is true of the whole Bible: it is the word of God, not as a revelation that has fallen from heaven without a history, but as the word of man, uttered at a specific historical moment. The words of Jesus are no exception to this: they too are the words of man, if it is indeed true as we have learnt in the catechism that Jesus is "true man", and "true God" *as* true man, and not to the neglect of his humanity.

The historical question forces us, so it seems, to stand at a distance from the text. In reality, however, it forces us to stand at a distance from our own thoughts and ideas, values, and hopes, from our usual language. It prevents us from taking without examination what strikes us immediately on reading it as the meaning of the text, and makes us examine it in detail. In this way the historical problem helps us against the danger of mistaking ideas that are dear and familiar to us for the word of God. While it makes long-familiar stories seem strange to us, it gives us the chance of understanding them anew.

If we want to try, so far as this is possible for us, to hear the parables of Jesus as their hearers did, we must always bear in mind two insights of far-reaching significance.

1. The only thing that could give weight to the words of Jesus was the words themselves.
2. The words of Jesus had to bridge over a deep opposition which existed between him and his listeners.

Let us first of all unfold the meaning of the first proposition: Jesus was true man. His words were heard as a word of man, not as the words of an authorized revealer of God's secrets.

It is hard for us to grasp this, because we picture Jesus as the first

Christians saw and described him, with the eye of faith. They painted together the "true man" and "true God" in one single picture, in the picture of the God-man. They proceeded like the pious masters of the Middle Ages, who on a background of gold painted the holy story in such a way that in what they painted one could also recognize at once what it signified. To see the historical situation correctly we have to forget this picture of Jesus which has been impressed on us, the picture of the divine Lord and Saviour. This is not at all to say we must give it up or question its truth. It is only a question of a methodological step: we set aside the advantage we have over Jesus' audience, because otherwise we could not hear the words of Jesus as they did.

For the original listeners to the parables of Jesus we cannot presuppose the belief that he is the Christ. There can be found only a few, if any, parables, which Jesus directed explicitly to his disciples: most are spoken to his opponents, to men who took offence at his behaviour or were indignant at his sayings. Jesus stood before these listeners as a carpenter from Nazareth, as a wandering Rabbi, like many at that time who wandered up and down the land with their disciples, as a preacher of repentance, of whom some supposed that he was a prophet. No acknowledged proof of divine authority gave weight to what he said, so that men had to listen to it in advance as a word of revelation. For even his miracles were no sort of authorization. Jesus was not the only wonder-worker of his time (cf. Matt. 12.27) and miracles were not an unequivocal proof for his contemporaries that the power of God was at work in the wonder-worker. They could just as well reproach Jesus with being in league with the devil (cf. Mark 3.22).

Nor were Jesus' words supported by the authority that an office gives a man. Jesus was not an ordained theologian nor a qualified teacher by profession. And he did not himself appeal to the Scriptures, as does an expositor of them, nor like a prophet to a special revelation from God.

The only thing that could give weight to the words of Jesus was the words themselves, and who Jesus is for his listeners depends entirely on what he becomes for them through his words.

Our second proposition ran: the parables of Jesus had to bridge over a deep opposition which existed between him and his listeners. This is true even when his listeners were not in the strict sense his opponents. It is connected with Jesus' proclamation of the arrival of the kingdom of God, which forms the centre of his message.

To understand the meaning of this proclamation we must know what the "arrival of the kingdom of God" meant for Jesus' listeners.

The concept of the kingdom of God had from of old been bound up with the faith and hope of Israel. This faith said: "The Lord is King for ever and ever" (Ex. 15.18). "The Lord has established his throne in the heavens, and his kingdom rules over all" (Ps. 103.19). "The Lord will reign for ever, thy God, O Sion, to all generations" (Ps. 146.10). This faith in the reign of God over the whole world, over all peoples and over all hostile powers, found its expression in the feast of the Enthronement of the Lord, which was celebrated in ancient Israel every year: "God reigns over the nations, God sits on his holy throne." "Clap your hands, all peoples! shout to God with loud songs of joy! For the Lord, the most high, is terrible, a great king over all the earth. He subdued peoples under us, and nations under our feet. He chose our heritage for us, the pride of Jacob whom he loves. God has gone up with a shout, the Lord with the sound of the trumpet" (Ps. 47.8, 1–5). With such psalms was the kingship of God extolled on this feast day.[a]

But opposed to this faith in the kingship of God was the fact that Israel, the only people which confessed this God and kept his commandments, and which had taken upon itself the "yoke of the kingdom of God", was subject to the heathen peoples of the world; and also the fact that powers hostile to God—tribulation, sin, and death—asserted themselves in the world. The belief that God is King therefore had to be connected with the *hope* that the kingdom of God would become manifest. "The revelation of the kingdom of God is the very essence of the hope, which will find its fulfilment only at the end of time. It is still hidden, still held back, the powers of evil—tribulation, sin, and death—are still in control, but the hope of the appearing of God's kingdom holds firmly and unerringly to a belief in his victory and to the certainty of his promise."[22]

In late Judaism at the time of Jesus the belief in the kingdom of God had shifted very strongly to the side of hope. In wide circles this hope was bound up with wishes for the nation: it was expected that at the end of time God would renew the old kingdom of David and exalt it over all the kingdoms of the world. Alongside this nationalist expectation for the future was the apocalyptic one,[b] which hoped for a "new heaven and a new earth" and nourished this hope with richly coloured

[a] See also Pss. 93 and 96.
[b] The word comes from the Greek: *apokalypsis*=revelation, unveiling. The reference is to the "unveilings" that the writings of these circles give about the time of the end, and the events preceding them. Cf. the Revelation (Apocalypse) of John.

pictures of the time of the end, and kept it alive with speculations about the moment of its coming. But "whatever political dreams or indeed whatever fantastic expectations of the destruction or rebirth of the world were bound up with the hopes of the Jews, it is of the essence of those hopes that the spirit of resignation which banishes God to a nebulous other world of ideals and which accepts the idea that no change is possible in this world, is totally strange to them. Even in its most distorted form their hope cannot be written off merely as a sudden reversion of feeling due to disappointment in the present, nor as a picture of the future sketched in glowing colours to offset the distress and despair of the present. Nietzsche's *ressentiment* theory does not apply here, however characteristic of the hope of the Jews these traits may be. At the ground of this hope lives the certainty that God is the Lord of this puzzling world, and will not always remain afar off but will reveal himself and vindicate his word. It is this certainty which makes the present lack of fulfilment the real difficulty for Jewish faith, and invests the hope of the coming of God's kingdom with its extreme tension." [23]

This expectation led to the question, "When"? The answer to this question was sought in various ways. The nationalist fanatics, the Zealots, tried to force the arrival of the kingdom of God by their armed revolt against the heathen occupation powers. The Pharisees were concerned to keep open the way for it by their strict obedience to the law and their representative repentance undertaken in voluntary fastings. The Apocalyptists tried to answer the question when the kingdom of God was coming "by means of observation of cosmic and historical events, or by fantastic numerical speculations and arrangements of epochs". [24]

Another answer was given by John the Baptist. He proclaimed that this day, for which the whole Jewish people was waiting, stood at the door (Matt. 3.2), and he called men to repentance, since the coming of the kingdom would mean inexorable judgement for the impenitent, which would devour them as fire does the winnowed-out chaff (Matt. 3.8–10,12).

Like John the Baptist, Jesus also put in the place of apocalyptic calculation the announcement of the kingdom of God. His message too can be summed up in the time-announcement: "The kingdom of God is at hand" (Mark 1.15). Just like John the Baptist, Jesus means to convey by this time-announcement what it is time for: "Repent and believe in the Gospel!"

But Jesus' proclamation is something other than a simple and direct continuation of the proclamation of the Baptist. For all the points in common and the connections that existed between the Baptist and Jesus, there is a basic difference between the two of them and their messages. It can be characterized as the difference "between the eleventh and the twelfth hour" (Bornkamm). For Jesus cries out, "The change of the eras is here, the kingdom of God is already dawning. Now is the hour of which the prophets' promise told: 'The blind receive their sight and the lame walk, lepers are cleansed and the deaf hear, the dead are raised up and the poor have good news preached to them'" (Matt. 11.5; cf. Isa. 35.5, etc.). [25] "If it is by the finger of God that I cast out demons, then the kingdom of God has come upon you" (Luke 11.20).

This simple formula, "The Baptist says, 'The kingdom of God is near'; Jesus says, 'It is here'", is, however, not enough to let us grasp fully the difference between the two. Jesus proclaims the dawn of the kingdom of God, but in many of his sayings, in which there is no direct question of this proclamation, he assumes, just like his contemporaries, that God's judgement and God's salvation, which belong indissolubly to the kingdom of God, are something future: "You *shall* be satisfied . . .", "You *shall* laugh", he says in the Beatitudes (Luke 6.21f); "You *shall* hunger . . .", "You *shall* mourn and weep . . ." in the Woes (Luke 6.25f). The men of Nineveh, the Queen of the South *will* arise at the judgement with this generation and condemn it (Matt. 12.41). "Many *will* come from East and West and sit at table with Abraham, Isaac and Jacob in the kingdom of Heaven . . ." (Matt. 8.11). But "whoever does not receive the kingdom of God like a child *shall* not enter it" (Mark 10.15).

A tension exists between the two groups of sayings of Jesus. [26] But this tension does not signify a want of consistency, an accidental and regrettable unbalance. It has a positive meaning: the future and the present aspects of the kingdom of God are related to one another in a new way. We said above that the belief and hope of Israel were bound up with the concept of the kingdom of God. In late Judaism the hope became autonomous over against the belief, and was nearly separated from it. People thought they were living in a present that was empty of salvation, and hoped for a future filled and even overflowing with salvation. In the message of Jesus this hope is now overtaken by faith, and it is in such an overtaking and incorporation of hope by faith that faith first really becomes faith. [27]

The preaching of Jesus takes place as an announcement that the time is fulfilled (Luke 10.23f; 10.18); in fact it appeals specifically to the signs of the time (Luke 12.54–6). And yet it is something other than the statement that the world clock has just moved on to twelve o'clock. To put it pointedly, the time which the Baptist announces as imminent, and Jesus as arrived, is not the same. The two "twelve o'clocks" are not identical.

John the Baptist understood the coming of the kingdom of God—like the whole of Judaism of his period—as the frontier of time, the frontier between two epochs, two radically different ages, which split up time very clearly into a before and an after; the frontier between the time in which man can still act and that in which he can do nothing more, because henceforth God alone is acting. The kingdom of God is near: this means, "The time is pressing in". "Even now the axe is laid to the root of the trees!" (Matt. 3.10). Now is the moment for men to repent, *before* the kingdom of God arrives.

It is different with Jesus. The coming of the kingdom of God is not for him the frontier of time, which by its pressing nearness gives its stamp to the present, and qualifies it. The coming of the kingdom of God is itself "Time to . . .", just as there is a time to sleep, a time to eat, a time to work; the lost is found, therefore it is time to rejoice together (Luke 15.3–10). Goodness appears and seeks to be understood (Matt. 20.1–16). The invitation to the banquet is issued and must be obeyed (Luke 14.15–24). The unique opportunity is there and demands to be seized decisively (Matt. 13.44–6).[28]

When both Jesus and John the Baptist say, "Repent, God stands at the door", the same words have different meanings for them. For the Baptist it means, "Repent *before* the decisive turning point happens"; but for Jesus, "*Now* the decisive turning point is happening; *therefore* repent and believe in the joyful message."[29] And repentance, conversion, is for Jesus in the last resort no different from believing in the joyful message.[c]

Once Jesus' proclamation of the arrival of the kingdom of God has become meaningful to us, we can better recognize why Jesus inevitably forced open a deep opposition between himself and his listeners with this proclamation.

Jesus' listeners had their firm ideas of what would happen when the change of the ages came in. For them it was therefore an unheard-of

---

[c] On the question what repentance means for Jesus, cf. the exposition of Luke 15.1–10.

paradox when Jesus announced the arrival of the kingdom of God, for they were able to see little or nothing of all that by their ideas went along with the arrival of the kingdom of God. It was inevitable that they should oppose Jesus' time-announcement. This opposition was not a dispute about ideas, it was about the question whether the decisive change to salvation had already happened.

Jesus' listeners regarded it as obvious that this question would be answered by what they could see before their eyes, that it had an "objective" answer which one could as an observer read off from the "object". Jesus' paradoxical time-announcement meant just this, that the question had to be answered by the decision of faith or unbelief, by a "subjective" decision, a decision of the "subject" which itself was decisive for him. Jesus concludes the utterance in which he characterizes the present as the time of salvation by, "The blind receive their sight and the lame walk . . . and the poor have good news preached to them" (Matt. 11.5), with the words, "Blessed is he who takes no offence at me", or as it should be translated, following the original text more exactly, "Well it is for him who does not trip up over me" (Matt. 11.6). He warns men against refusing belief in regard to the proclaimer of the message.

This message is concerned with the whole of life, with the whole man, with his very existence. It is about the question, What does a man base his existence on—on what is "before his eyes", that is, on an understanding of the world orientated on what is visible, or on what he comes to hear, the word that demands belief and makes it possible? The opposition which existed between Jesus and his listeners reaches down to the ground of human existence. Anyone who came into agreement with Jesus accomplished by this a change of existence; his life was set on a new base. In opposition to what had previously been a matter of course to him, he now lived by the truth of the word of Jesus.

The opposition which inevitably opened up between Jesus and his listeners over the heart of Jesus' preaching, his message of the arrival of the kingdom of God, must always be kept in mind in the exposition of the parables, since the parables were spoken by Jesus to bridge over the opposition between him and his listeners. They are striving for the agreement of those who hear them.

A man who risks a parable to bridge over such opposition indeed takes a risk. By his words he compels his hearers to a decision, without having the outcome of this decision in his own hands. He will have to bear the consequences! A direct line leads from the parables of Jesus to his crucifixion.[30]

One can hardly assume that Jesus did not know what he was risking with his parables. May one not say then that by his parables he put his life at stake, that he risked his life for the word that could bring his listeners into agreement with him, that made possible for them this change of existence, this faith?

"Crucify him, this man is blaspheming God." This was one of the answers that could be given to the parables of Jesus. But it was not the only possible one. There was one other: "Truly this is the Son of God."[31] This was the answer of those who came into agreement with Jesus, who admitted his unheard-of claim to speak for God. Since this word became truth for them, because they recognized it as the truth which had always been true, and which they had only failed to find, Jesus became for them the one who spoke in the name of God.

The witness of faith died on the cross. The testimony of faith arose as faith in the resurrection. Since then the flame of faith has never been put out. Faith leads to preaching, and preaching brings men to faith. But everywhere that men believe, Jesus is recognized as the one who has authority to speak and act in the name of God.

8

The Parables as Passages of the Bible

We said that we must try to hear the parables of Jesus with the ears of their first listeners to grasp their original meaning. But the parables do not come to us as the spoken word of Jesus of Nazareth, they appear before us as written passages of the Bible. We read them in the New Testament; we find them within the context of the Gospels. That is to say, the parables of Jesus have been passed down to us through the tradition of the Church.[a]

---

[a] Certainly to say that the Bible is a book of the tradition does not exhaust all there is to say about it; but it can be said, and needs to be.

Tradition, however, wherever it is not purely mechanical, is always exposition. What is transmitted is what has previously been understood, and it is as thus understood that it is passed on. The parables of Jesus as we read them in the Gospels have all passed through the understanding of primitive Christianity. They have been transmitted to us with a particular interpretation.

This is true in several respects: first of all in a very general sense:

1. The insertion of the parables within the context of the Gospels and their admission into the New Testament signifies a process of exposition which determines the understanding of these passages in a decisive manner. Even if no syllable of the passage has been altered, the parables of Jesus have, just through this, undergone a profound alteration.

The New Testament speaks of Jesus as the Christ, as crucified and risen, as the exalted Lord. Anyone who reads the parables in the context of the New Testament cannot hear them as Jesus' listeners must have done: as the words of a carpenter and wandering Rabbi from Nazareth. The scandal, the stumbling-block that the parables of Jesus signified for their first hearers has been lost.[b] The outrageous fact that Jesus lays claim to God in them loses its offence if one is listening to them from the start as the words of the Son of God. Put more exactly, the claim laid to God by the man Jesus of Nazareth, which demands belief, is replaced by a revelatory utterance of the Christ about God and his kingdom, which already presupposes belief in the authority invested in him by God. While the parables as they were uttered by Jesus first created agreement with Jesus and the change in existence which was necessary for this agreement, in the tradition of the Church they become instructions or exhortations which rest from the start on this basic agreement.[c]

2. The early Church understood the words of its Lord as the word that is true for his Church. It has therefore presented many parables that were spoken to opponents or to the crowd as parables for the disciples.[d]

[b] This is not to say that the Gospels as a whole have not preserved the stumbling-block.

[c] The agreement here comes about through the missionary preaching of the Church. The parables of Jesus that have been passed down now have a use within the Church.

[d] It would be a misunderstanding to see this only as a mistaking of the historical situation, rather than a confession that this Jesus of Nazareth is the Lord and his

The parable of the lost sheep (Luke 15.4–7; Matt. 18.12–14), spoken according to the redactional but probably correct account of the situation in Luke
(15.1–3) to Pharisees´and scribes, becomes in Matt. (18.1) a parable for the
disciples. The parable of the labourers in the vineyard (Matt. 20.1–16) is
also made a parable for disciples by its insertion into its context. The same is
true of the parables of the treasure in the field and the precious pearl (Matt.
13.44–6; cf. Matt. 13.36), the parable of the unmerciful servant (Matt.
18.23–35; cf. 18.21; 18.1) and many others.

Here more has happened than just a change of audience. A basic
agreement has replaced the deep-reaching opposition which the
parable was originally intended to bridge by leading to agreement.
This has altered the whole structure of the parables. They have acquired a different character in their interpretation by the early Church,
and it is this character that has determined their understanding up to
the present day.

3(*a*) In the course of transmission the parables of Jesus were loosed from
their original historical situation. This situation cannot be passed down
in the same way as the actual words of the parable narrative. Only a
report of it can be transmitted; but for this purpose it must first be
detached from the situation, and abstracted, and that will as a rule take
place only when an historical interest is present. The men who passed
on the parables of Jesus were not historians. They were governed by
other interests. Accordingly they only transmitted what Jesus had said,
the "picture part" of the parable, and usually tell us nothing about its
original historical situation.

(*b*) In oral tradition the stories of Jesus and the sayings of Jesus,
including the parables, originally circulated singly,[32] since they had in
fact also been formed singly. In the early collections they were strung
together without connection.[33] It was the Evangelists who first produced the connections between the individual units of tradition. They
arranged the whole body of tradition as a "life" of Jesus. Topogra-
phical details, notices of times, typical transitional phrases, and a
number of schematized scenes, formed as it were the mortar with
which they stuck together the individual stories of the tradition to
make up the "Gospel".[34]

words something different from the words of a man long dead. But it would be
equally a misunderstanding to think that we could demonstrate our faith in
Jesus Christ by naïvely passing over the historical question put to us, and referring
Jesus' words immediately to ourselves.

Here it must be noticed that the Gospels do not owe their origin to an historical and biographical interest, but to a theological motive. They try to express that the one whom the Church confesses as its Lord and Saviour is none other than Jesus of Nazareth, and conversely that the one whom men have fastened to the cross has been by God "attested with wonders and signs" (Acts 2.22), "raised" (Acts 2.24), and "made both Lord and Christ" (Acts 2.36).

Theological motives are also at work in the arrangement of the material from tradition in the Gospels. They are decisive in whole or in part for the context within which a piece of tradition is placed, what pieces of tradition it is put in with, and what framework it is given.

The results of this for the parables of Jesus is that the context in the Gospels in which we find the parables of Jesus, tells us (as a rule)[e] nothing about the historical situation in which they have their origin; but it tells us a great deal about how the parables of Jesus were understood in the early Church.

4. The early Church did not transmit the words of Jesus from an historical interest, but for the building up of the Church, for use in preaching and teaching, for exhortation and proclamation. Accordingly it directly related the parables of Jesus too to its own situation, to its own problems and difficulties. For it expected answers and instruction for these from the words of its Lord. For this reason it is true in a narrower sense as well that the parables have been transmitted to us with a particular interpretation. This interpretation in the narrower sense, the "commentary" on the parables, is passed on to us by the early Church in various ways.

(a) Often the parables are interpreted by an application,[f] which was added to the text. The greater part of these later added applications, which in part had already grown on in the oral tradition, but in part only go back to the Evangelists, are generalizing sayings (*logia*).

Matt. 20.16 (labourers in the vineyard): So the last shall be first and the first last.

Matt. 22.14 (wedding banquet): Many are called, but few are chosen.

Matt. 25.29 (talents): To everyone who has will more be given, and he will

---

[e] Of course the question whether parable and context belong together must be asked about each parable separately.

[f] See above, pp. 17f.

have abundance; but from him who has not, even what he has will be taken away.

Luke 18.14b (Pharisée and tax-collector). Everyone who exalts himself will be humbled, but he who humbles himself will be exalted.

(Cf. Matt. 25.13; Luke 11.10; 12.21; 16.10; 16.13; etc.)[35]

"It is the voice of the Christian preacher or teacher, bent on interpreting the Lord's message, which we hear in the insertion of generalizing conclusions." The parables of Jesus, which originally referred to a concrete situation, were made "serviceable for the Christian community" by taking "a general instructional or parenetic [i.e. hortatory] meaning" from them.[36]

(b) Sometimes a parable was given a detailed interpretation.

Mark 4.14–20; Matt. 13.37–43; 13.49f.

(c) Occasionally the understanding of the parables was determined by a redactional statement of the situation.

The redactional verse, Luke 19.11, makes the parable of the pounds into the allegorical statement that Jesus is not yet entering on his Lordship at once, but will do so only at his return, his Parousia; that now is rather the time in which his servants should work and in which his enemies too have the opportunity for activity, until at the end of days he will reward the faithful servants but punish the unfaithful and his enemies.

The redactional verse, Luke 18.1, makes the parable of the unjust judge an exhortation to be persistent in prayer.

(d) Occasionally also a redactional verse and an application together show how the parable should be understood.

Luke 18.9 and 18.14b show that Luke has understood the illustration of the Pharisee and the tax-collector as a warning against pride and self-righteousness, and as an exhortation to humility.

(e) Frequently the interpretation of the parable is given only by its insertion into the context. Occasionally context and application supplement one another.

The parables of the hidden treasure (Matt. 13.44) and of the precious pearl (Matt. 13.45f), placed by Matthew between the interpretation of the parable of the tares among the wheat (Matt. 13.37–43) and the parable of the fish-net with its interpretation (Matt. 13.47–50), must in this context "illustrate the behaviour of those who hereafter as 'the righteous ones' (13.43) 'will shine like the sun in the kingdom of their Father', the behaviour of utter dedication, of radical obedience."[37]

To sum up the results of our discussion, as soon as we deal with the parables of Jesus in the context of the Gospels and of the New Testament, we are dealing with the interpretation of these texts by the Church's tradition. If we want to hear the parables as Jesus meant them and as his hearers must have understood them, we must use critical methods to go back behind the Gospels.[38]

This critical return does not mean that we regard what tradition has added to the parables as worthless wrapping material, which is thrown away as soon as we have unpacked the contents. It only means that we distinguish different layers of the text, each of which has a value of its own. The parables of Jesus in the sense which they have acquired in the early Church's interpretation are just as much part of the Bible for preaching and instruction in the Gospel, as are the parables of Jesus in their original meaning. The letters of the apostle Paul are re-used as texts for preaching in just the same way as are the words of Jesus.

Anyone who has the task of expounding a parable of Jesus in preaching or teaching must decide whether he wants to keep its original meaning or to follow the interpretation either of the Evangelist or of an earlier layer of the Church's tradition. Frequently both courses are equally possible and justified, but they must not be confused.[39]

It is so easy to confuse the point of reference that it needs great caution to avoid doing it. If we are asking what the parables meant on the lips of Jesus, this confusion has occurred the moment we forget that his original hearers were not already Christians. If we are looking for the meaning that a parable has acquired in the exposition of the Evangelist, there is already an illegitimate confusion at work when we uncritically take the situation to which the verses of the framework assign the parable as being the historical situation in which Jesus uttered it.

In this book we have confined ourselves to the question of the original meaning of the parables. The exposition of the parables by the Evangelists or by the tradition which went before them has been considered only in so far as it has left its mark on the framework or the (subsequently added) applications of the parables.

Our reason for this is that if the reader is not very familiar with the working methods of the science of exposition, he needs particularly for this question the help of technical theologians. A further reason is that the meaning the Evangelist gave a parable can often be more satisfactorily established if one already knows what Jesus meant by it. Accordingly the original meaning of the parable should be sought in every case, while the question of its exposition in the tradition of the early Church can be considered later. To answer both questions with equal thoroughness seemed to us, however, to ask too much not only from the author but also from the reader. This is so particularly because the meaning that the parables have in the context of the Gospels cannot be satisfactorily established without going into the composition of the Gospels and the theological motifs of the individual Evangelists.

But there is another reason too to seek particularly for the meanings of the parables of *Jesus*. These parables—words which were not addressed to disciples but to opponents, not to believers but to non-believers—can help us, especially to-day, when belief in Jesus as the Christ is beginning to lose the appearance of an obvious, generally shared assumption, to pass on the Gospel and to bring people to understand what is meant by it.

PART TWO

Expositions

1

The Story of the Good Samaritan

LUKE 10.25-37

The Question of the Scribe and
its Historical Background

Jesus uses the story of the good Samaritan to answer the question of a scribe: "Who is my neighbour?"[1]

He addresses Jesus as "Master", that is "Rabbi", and so recognizes him as of equal status. He puts a question to him, as was then customary to test a strange Rabbi's knowledge.[a] The question was not unusual, and it was important enough to be suitable for such a testing: Jesus is to express his opinion on the question who is to be regarded as a fellow man[b] and who is not. All ancient cultures draw a line between the insiders and the outsiders, and one set of laws applies for dealing with those inside and another for those outside.[2] It was no different in Israel. When for instance it was forbidden to charge interest in moneylending this prohibition of course only held good in respect of fellow men.[c]

In ancient Israel not only everyone who belonged to the people of

---

[a] The word that Luther (and A.V.) translates "tempt", "is a technical term for asking a difficult scholarly question, to establish by it whether the man questioned is a real scholar. A real scholar is one who immediately gives a correct answer to every question put to him in respect of the Halakhah, the rules for the conduct of life. What the law teacher does is called 'sniffing at the pots'" (Bornhäuser, p. 65). A better translation would therefore be "put to the test". Possibly the word "tempt" had a secondary meaning too in Luther's time. In any case the scribe's question has nothing to do with "tempting": this is neither allowed by the Greek nor appropriate to the situation. It remains, however, possible that a negative result was expected to such testing (cf. Bugge, p. 389).

[b] It would not be right to use the word "neighbour" here as yet, because "the Christian conception of the 'neighbour' is not the starting-point of the story, but that which the story was intended to create"(Jeremias, p. 202, n. 53).

[c] Deut. 23.19f.

c

God counted as a fellow man but also heathen aliens who lived in the land. The division between "inside" and "outside" was essentially a matter of common residence, and the question was no problem. It was different at the time of Jesus; gentiles had come into the land to a greater extent, Romans, Syrians, and Greeks. The question who was to be reckoned a fellow man had to be asked again. Apart from the Jews only full proselytes were now included, i.e. those gentiles who had been fully converted to the Jewish faith. There were in fact groups among the people who wanted to draw the limits still more narrowly. The Pharisees were inclined to exclude the mass of town and country dwellers who were ignorant of the law, who had neither time, opportunity, nor desire to learn and observe the many individual demands of the law, the various purity regulations and the tithe laws. The strict community of the Essenes only included members of their own order, and there was a widespread popular opinion that the requirement of the commandment to love did not need to extend as far as personal enemies.[3]

All the ordinances of the law that should govern a man's relationship to his fellow men were left up in the air if it was not clearly settled who counted as a fellow man. "What can be demanded of me?" is the question which lies unuttered behind the question about the neighbour, even when this is only put as an "academic question". The scribe finds what can be required of him presented very exactly in the six hundred and thirteen precepts of the law: at this point there is a gap, and— regardless of whether he is putting a genuine question to Jesus or not— his bias is towards closing this gap.

For to know "what can be required of me" is like a shell inside which one can live peacefully because everything inside it is familiar. For this purpose it is not so important whether this shell is perhaps too narrow and inconvenient—there existed at the time a large number of very inconvenient precepts! The main thing is the certainty that it gives. The effort to solve to perfection as far as possible even the last questions that remain unanswered is like striving to close even the last doors, so that nothing unusual and uncontrolled can enter. The ideal is to have everything cut and dried, though the demands that are made will be fulfilled seriously and with devotion.

The law puts the world in our hands as something perfectly laid out and so basically controlled. One only has to make this control one's own, just as every pupil has to make reading and writing his own, but does not have to invent them.

Jesus' Answer

This is the background to the question which Jesus answers with his story.[4] It is not a similitude but an illustration: the correct attitude does not have to be established in some other area of life, and then transferred to the problem at issue, but the subject that is in question is "brought to language" directly by a particularly well-chosen instance as an example.[d]

The road from high-lying Jerusalem to Jericho down the Jordan valley leads through an uninhabited rocky wilderness and is notorious even to this day for attacks by robbers. A man who had been robbed even of his clothes, seriously wounded, and left there to his fate by the robbers was bound to die miserably if he found no one to help him. A priest or a Levite, a temple servant[e] on the way from Jerusalem to Jericho or in the opposite direction was nothing unusual. Jericho was a priestly city, and every priest or Levite had to appear in Jerusalem when the course to which he belonged, of the twenty-four courses there were, was performing the temple worship, for eight days.[5]

Priest and Levite go by without bothering about the victim. Attempts are often made to find an excuse for this in some special precept of their order, but they cannot be upheld, and besides are out of keeping with the spirit of the story. For what matters is the contrast between the attitude of these cult officials and that of the Samaritan.[6] They belonged to the upper classes and were therefore particularly in the public eye. Nevertheless it did not surprise people that the story gave them the rôle of unmercifulness, because the priesthood was in bad repute at the time of Jesus.[7]

It was, however, surprising and offensive for Jesus' hearers that it should be a Samaritan that was given the rôle of the merciful man.[f]

---

[d] Cf. above, pp. 4f.

[e] "Within the priesthood the Levites were an order of lower clergy (cf. Num. 3.5ff; 8.5ff; 1 Chron. 23). 'They were the immediate assistants of the priest in sacrifices and in oversight of the temple area, but on penalty of death were not allowed themselves to come near the altar and the sanctuary (Num. 18.3). They skinned the sacrificial animals, and looked after the killing and the cooking, some of them prepared the shewbread for each Sabbath (1 Chron. 9.31f). Apart from this the Levites had charge of the purification of the temple' (Volz, *Die biblischen Altertümer*, p. 75)." *Die Christenlehre*, Vol. 3, 1950, Unterrichtshilfe, p. 21.

[f] "Samaria is the region of Palestine between Judaea and Galilee. . . . The population of Samaria was from the year 722 B.C. a mixed one, consisting of those Israelites who had not been taken into exile by the Assyrians, and of the heathen peoples who had been settled on the land. The religion of Israel was no longer

Between the Jews and this heretical mixed people there reigned implacable hatred. On the Jewish side it went so far that they cursed the Samaritans publicly in the synagogues, and prayed God that they should have no share in eternal life; that they would not believe the testimony of a Samaritan nor accept a service from one.[8] This hatred was fully reciprocated by the Samaritans. Between 9 and 6 B.C. they managed to prevent a Jewish passover by scattering dead men's bones on the temple area and so defiling it.[9] Why does Jesus mention a Samaritan here and not a Jewish layman—as his listeners were certainly expecting after a priest and a Levite?[10] The only thing the Samaritan had in common with the Jews in the eyes of the listeners was that he too was human. If it is he who shows mercy, this mercy is something that man as such shows to man. Any possibility of ascribing it to a common nationality or religion is excluded.[11] "By this means the limited question of determining one's fellow man by nationality or religion is converted into a question of the neighbour who can meet us in every man" (Weeber).

The act of the Samaritan finds its measure in the need of the neighbour; this is what gives it its simplicity. Everything that the helpless man needs is done, nothing more and nothing less. His wounds are cared for. (Oil and wine either mixed or separately were a usual treatment for wounds.) Because he is unable to walk the Samaritan puts him on his horse or mule, brings him away from the uninhabited wilderness, gives him food in the inn,[g] and accepts responsibility for his further care too, so that he is not turned out the next day. He gives two denarii to the innkeeper.[h] Beyond this, he promises that *he* will be responsible for all the other expenses, even if they turn out to be yet higher. The innkeeper is to lose nothing; on his return he intends to pay the rest.[12]

---

strictly observed (see 2 Kings 17). For that reason the Samaritans were not recognized as fellow countrymen by the Jews who returned from exile in the year 536, and were not allowed to take part in the building of the new temple. They then built a temple of their own on Mount Gerizim. The Jews still regarded them as inferior in the time of Jesus, and contact with them was avoided (John 4.9)." *Zürich Bible*, appendix to the NT, no. 119.

[g] This is to be inferred from the usage of this Greek word, which our translations render with literal accuracy as "took care of him" (v. 35) (see Jülicher, p. 591).

[h] This is two days' pay, as we know from Matt. 20.2. A further figure for comparison is the statement that the bread a man needed for one day cost one-twelfth of a denarius (Jeremias, p. 205).

At the conclusion of the story Jesus asks the scribe: "Which of these three, do you think, proved neighbour to the man who fell among the robbers?" "While the scribe's question (v. 29) concerned the object of the love (Whom must I treat as a friend?), Jesus in v. 36 asks about the subject of the love (Who acted as a friend?)."[13] This shift in the question gives rise to difficulties. But our difficulties only come because we ascribe a mistaken function to v. 36. We assume that here the question of v. 29 is to be resumed, so as to get a definitive answer. But the story itself, nothing else, is the answer to this question. We are not to expect a lesson to be drawn in vv. 36f from the story, which answers the question in v. 29, and leaves the story behind as a mere dressing up of this truth. Verse 36 belongs to the story as a signpost does to a crossroads. It is to ensure attention for what matters to the narrator in the story. Stylistically the question in v. 36 had to be so put that the answer could be formulated in close connection with the story (cf. Luke 7.43; Matt. 21.41). But in that case the question could scarcely be put or answered in any other way.[14]

The Meaning of Jesus' Answer

Jesus uses the story of the good Samaritan to bring the question of the neighbour to the right place. We should, however, be taking it too superficially if we were to understand it in the light of the demand "go and do likewise", as if Jesus were only recalling us from theory to practice. He does a great deal more: he calls man forth from the place where he views the world simply as one that is basically controlled by a law that is as complete as possible, and on to the movement of authentic living.[1]

[1] This does not invalidate the interpretation of the world which the law gives us. Without such a traditional comprehension of the world we should not be able to live at all. But this interpretation of the challenge meets us henceforth as an authentic demand to which we have to take up an attitude ourselves and on our own. We can no longer hide behind the fact that something is commanded or not commanded. The question "What can be demanded of me?" can no longer be put in that way. What is really demanded is revealed in the situation, whether I am adequate for it, or afterwards realize that I have failed it. Simply to hold fast to what the legal (i.e. purely general) demand requires (what anyone can require of me), is the same as to hide myself from the claim which the concrete situation addresses to me. By doing this, man banishes himself to a world of silence, to a wilderness, that offers him nothing to live from, so that he is completely thrown upon his own resources.

Cf. also the exposition of Schlatter: "This is the end of casuistry. By this Jesus

The story certainly leaves no doubt that what really matters is to act as the Samaritan did; and our conscience says a clear "yes" to this. But only in the same simplicity as he showed can we really act as he did, and let ourselves be governed completely by the need of the man who confronts us. And that is not a thing that can be "done". As soon as we let ourselves be called out of the shell we have made of the world into the unprotected life of real encounter, we shall unquestionably make the discovery that we are exposed to the possibility of failing in life, in fact are always doing so already. Then the question about our life makes us realize that we can no longer ourselves provide the answer to it. It is no longer this or that fault for which we need forgiveness; our whole life needs justification. Perhaps one must say that only when this question of our lives finds an answer does life truly continue in real encounter, and that in Christian preaching what is at stake is precisely the answer to this question.[15]

The History of the Text

The dialogue of the scribe with Jesus over the question "Who is my neighbour?", was linked in the course of tradition with another dialogue of a scribe with Jesus, in which the catch-word "neighbour" also occurred. Since the two dialogues were supplementary to one another in content it was possible for one of the two introductions giving the setting, which were the same or very similar, to be lost, and it then looked as if there was only one dialogue.[16] The other dialogue—Luke 10.25-8—underwent in the course of transmission various alterations. We read it best in Mark 12.28-34, where it has been preserved in its original form.[17]

A scribe sets before Jesus a question, such as was at this time discussed among the scribes, "Which is the most important commandment?" Six hundred and thirteen commandments were counted in the Torah, which was both secular and sacred law in one. This enormous number was reached by filling out the legal demands of the Old Testament with many juridical and cultic ordinances that went into particulars, in order to protect it from violations as if by a fence, and

has placed our dealings not under a precept, but under what real life shows, demands, and makes possible. The commandment receives its exposition, which governs its application, through what the movement of life sets before a man's eyes. *Behind this stands that idea of God which can say 'not one sparrow is forgotten before God'* (Luke 12.6)" (pp. 287ff, my italics).

to close up every hole that could arise through a change in historical circumstances. The Torah was valid right down to its letters as a divine demand, and it was held that all commandments had to be observed without differentiation, because it was God who had commanded them. Nevertheless the question was raised from time to time which of the commandments was the weightiest and most important.[18]

Jesus' answer is different from what the scribe must have expected. Jesus does not choose one of the commandments to give it a relative pre-eminence among the others: he puts together two texts as the "twofold commandment of love", and says of them that on them "depend all the law and the prophets"—as Matthew (22.40) rightly interprets the sense of the words of Jesus.[19] That means, however, that man is entrusted with the key to the *understanding* of what is commanded. Until now he had been directed to the immense number of individual commandments which he had to carry out because they were commanded. But now Jesus places him before the unitary will of God, and so makes him directly responsible to God.

In the course of the tradition and under the stamp of the first Christians' experiences it became harder and harder to understand the inquiring scribe as a man of good will, and the scholastic dialogue was turned into a controversy dialogue. It was typical of this stylistic form that the answer was given either by a parable or by a counter-question which sent the questioner about his business.[20] This counter-question is found in its Lucan version in 10.26. It does not mean that Jesus simply returns the question. Rather it shows the questioner that on this question Jesus agrees with the Bible and so answers it in the only possible and right way.[21] The assumption that as a matter of course in the entire Old Testament only one answer to the question could be found was of course only possible once it had become usual to summarize God's commandments with these words and in them to see the deepest meaning of all the Old Testament commandments. The reshaping of the Bible quotations as against Mark—the two texts appear in Luke as a single quotation—allows us to deduce a catechismal use of this group of texts. The reply of Jesus is not so much praise for the questioner as acknowledgement that he has hit upon Jesus' view.[22] The controversy seems to show the agreement of Jesus' teaching with the scriptures, a question which must have been important for the apologetic of the early Church.

Luke had to pass on this conversation for gentile readers, for whom such scribal disputations were no longer intelligible. He reinterpreted for them the question about the greatest commandment as the question about eternal life, which he found in the story of the rich young man.[23]

Does the demand in v. 28, which refers so well to this question, also come from him? He (or one of his predecessors?) understood the two disputes as one single one, and probably inserted in v. 29 the words, "but he, desiring to justify himself", because he believed he found there the reason why the scribe carries the conversation further after Jesus' answer. In this way vv. 25–8 lost their independence. They were made into an introduction to the story of the Good Samaritan, and the passage reached the form in which we have it to-day.

2

The Pharisee and the Tax-Collector

LUKE 18.9–14

Our understanding of the illustration[a] of "the Pharisee and the tax-collector" is determined in advance by the effect this story has had in the Christian tradition. The Pharisee has become the type of the pharisaical, hypocritical, proud pious man, while "the New Testament tax-collector has been for us covered with a religious patina, almost surrounded by a halo, the ideal type of the humble sinner".[1] If we want to understand the story aright, we must abandon this prejudgement and try to listen to the story as Jesus' listeners must have understood it.

Jesus' Listeners and the Pharisee

This figure, which we feel to be almost a caricature, was seen by Jesus' listeners with different eyes: an ideal of a pious man is here painted, in sight of which everyone must have confessed: "Yes, that is what one should be like!" This man can appear before God with thankful joy:[2] with God's help he has succeeded in avoiding any serious transgression

[a] See above, pp. 4f.

of God's commandments (v.11).[b] But more than that, he is one of those to whom it has been granted to fulfil God's Law completely (v. 12).[c] While the Law lays on every Jew one fast day a year as a day of repentance, he vicariously makes atonement for the sins of his people, by fasting twice a week.[3] To do this he has to give up not only food but also drink completely from sunrise to sunset, which in the heat of the East is a great act of self-denial.[4] Also with the tithe that the law lays on him this pious man prefers to do too much, rather than too little. "He gives tithes of everything he bought, thereby ensuring that he uses nothing that has not been tithed, although corn, new wine, and oil should already have been tithed by the producer."[5] He makes a great economic sacrifice, so that God may have what is his own undiminished.

It is not the case that the Pharisee whom Jesus describes holds out this pious life to God to base a claim on it. Nor may we regard it as proud scorn when he says, "I thank thee, God, that I am not like . . .".[d] Jesus' listeners will not have felt the prayer of the Pharisee to be hypocritical arrogance, but a genuine prayer of thanks for God's gracious guidance.[6] We see this from the very similar prayer of a pious scribe, which has been handed down to us in the Talmud. It runs: "I thank thee, O Lord my God, that thou hast given me my lot with those who sit in the house of study, and not with those who sit at the street-corners. . . . I am early to work on the words of the Torah, and they are early to work on things of no moment. . . . I weary myself and profit thereby, while they weary themselves to no profit. . . . I run towards the life of the Age to Come, and they run towards the pit of destruction."[e]

The Pharisee has therefore not only avoided transgressions of the

[b] "Unjust" is here to be understood as "swindlers".

[c] "He does not look for ways of evading the law. His boast is that he has fulfilled it completely" (Schlatter, *Lukas*, p. 399).

[d] For the Pharisee to include the tax-collector too here was for contemporary thought correct in point of fact (see below); it is, however, primarily to be regarded as a parenthesis of the narrator, which links the two parallel sections vv. 10ff and v. 13 to one another.

[e] b.Ber.28b; Jeremias, p. 142. Cf. with this the saying of another Jewish Rabbi: "R. Judah (c. 150) said: one must utter three praises every day: Praised (be the Lord), that he did not make me a heathen; for 'all the heathen are as nothing before him' (Isa. 40.17); praised be he, that he did not make me a woman, for woman is not under obligation to fulfil the law; praised be he that he did not make me . . . an uneducated man; for the uneducated man is not cautious to avoid sins" (T. Berakh. 7.18 [16]).

law and fulfilled more than his obligations, but he gives God the
praise as well—so it seems—and treats it all as his gift![f] The verdict of
the listeners on this figure which Jesus set before their eyes was bound
to be: "Here is a man after God's heart."

Jesus' Listeners and the Tax-Collector

The figure of the tax-collector, as Jesus paints it, also remains at first
within the framework of the attitudes and opinions of his contemporaries: for them the tax-collector was a sinner from the outset. He
not only collaborated with the Roman occupation powers, who
oppressed the people of God and continually hindered it in the fulfilment of its religious duties, but he belonged to a profession that as a
whole was regarded as being no better or worse than swindlers. The
tax-collectors, who had leased the taxes of a district ("farmed out
apparently to the highest bidder"), regularly made a profit for themselves. "Tariffs were no doubt fixed by the state, but the collectors
had no lack of devices for defrauding the public. In the general estimation they stood on a level with robbers; they possessed no civic rights,
and were shunned by all respectable persons."[7] In misappropriating
the property of their neighbour they were sinning at the same time
against the commandment of God. To obtain God's forgiveness was in
the eyes of Jesus' contemporaries very nearly impossible for a tax-
collector. Sorrow for sins was not enough for this. A visible and effective penance was necessary: he had to give up his profession, so as to
make an end of his sinful life, and to restore all that he had embezzled
in full, plus a fifth. But "how can he know everyone with whom he
has had dealings?"[8]

When therefore Jesus describes the tax-collector as one who "stood
afar off", pressed himself into the remotest corner and from shame for
his sins did not even dare to raise up his eyes,[g] in the view of his listeners
he has put him in the place where he belongs. Could there be any
doubt how the verdict must go when the Pharisee and the tax-collector
were thus placed side by side for comparison?

Jesus lets the tax-collector too utter a prayer, the only one that he has

---

[f] The wording given to the prayer by Jesus does not contradict this understanding, but it points beyond it and so allows the figure of the Pharisee *subsequently* to
appear in a different light.

[g] "He would not" means here in accordance with the sense "he dared not".
"Semitic has no word for 'dare'"(Jeremias, p. 141).

any right to: overwhelmed by the realization of his sins, he strikes him-self on the breast, on the heart which is regarded as the seat of sin,[9] and prays; "God be merciful to me a sinner!"

The Effect of the Contrast on the Audience

When the listeners hear this prayer, it must become clear to them that the place of the tax-collector is not a level far below the Pharisee, but the place in which the man who needs God's forgiveness stands. It is the place in which they have all already stood, and in which they will stand again and again. They must recognize what they have relied on in their own heart's need, when they have prayed in the same or a similar way as this tax-collector: that God forgives sin unconditionally.

The words of Holy Scripture in which forgiveness is promised are innumerable. Yet Jesus' listeners will perceive with horror that if God's mercy is not shown to this miserable sinner, all God's promises, on which they have themselves relied, fall down! And if it is shown to him, does the tax-collector still stand beside the Pharisee as the godless man beside the righteous? Is the one who has been forgiven not righteous? Has he not been justified by God? What is the position then of the righteousness of the Pharisee?

Who is righteous? Who can stand? Till then the answer to this question had been obvious: the Pharisee, of course! This obviousness is destroyed by Jesus' story.

Can they both be righteous then? No, that would not answer the question that is put here. The righteousness of the tax-collector and the righteousness of the Pharisee cannot be brought under a common heading: the righteousness which the Pharisee can show is unthinkable without an order of precedence, a scale on which, in distinction from others, he can be acknowledged as the righteous one. The righteous-ness which the tax-collector is given through God's forgiveness cannot be classified in any order of precedence, however arranged. Nor is it possible to understand it as an exception which breaks the rule. Every man who has been bowed down by the burden of guilt knows for sure that here not just *something* but *everything*, in fact he himself, has been called in question. If a man realizes what it means to need forgiveness, and that here the whole of his existence is exposed to a radical challenge, how could it occur to him to classify forgiveness as an exception?

The result is that in the Pharisee's order of precedence there is no room for a "righteous tax-collector", but in the place where the tax-collector stands, before God who forgives him, the sinner, the Pharisee's order of precedence loses its meaning.

An inescapable choice of alternatives comes to light here, which none of Jesus' listeners would have perceived without this story which Jesus paints for them. For man knows only too well how to hold apart what Jesus here sets before our eyes together. When man is at one with himself and can stand before what he has set himself as a standard, he makes this standard the final court of appeal.[10] But when his conscience declares him guilty, and when the world gives its verdict against his right to exist, he relies on something that can transcend it; he asks for a final court of appeal that can annul this verdict without denying it, and he cannot help doing so. Man is skilful at concealing this constant change of final appeal, which he always makes according to his particular needs. But now through Jesus' parable this ingenuousness is lost for his listeners. The change of final appeal is brought to their view, and that means it is revealed as a falsehood. One cannot *want* to assent to a lie. A basic decision is therefore inevitable. Each of Jesus' listeners must make it for himself, by deciding what he wants to count as the final court of appeal.

Jesus' Decision

Jesus' verdict runs, "I say to you, this man went down[h] to his house as a righteous man, not that one."[i]

"As a righteous man", we must translate the passage, so that it becomes at least roughly clear to us what Jesus said to his hearers. The usual translation "justified" is linguistically correct, but it does not take into consideration the change in meaning which the word has undergone. The meaning of the word "justified", in our language, is completely determined by the Pauline teaching on justification, so that we cannot help thinking of it in connection with "forgiveness", "gracious acceptance", and the like. But this inevitably conceals for us the meaning that it had for Jesus' listeners. Justification meant for them the

---

[h] Down: the temple at Jerusalem lay on a hill, cf. v. 10, "up".

[i] Linguistically it is just as possible to understand the words of the text as comparative ("more justified than the other") as it is to take them as exclusive. Materially, however, it would be meaningless, for how could one say that the one is "in a higher degree justified" than the other? (see Jeremias, p. 142).

judicial verdict in which God attests the integrity of the righteous man.[11] To them Jesus' verdict is quite outrageous: is the godless to be counted as the righteous man, and the righteous man as the godless?

But Jesus' verdict cannot be set aside as the incredible assertion of an individual. It has the authority of the truth behind it, a truth which each of the hearers knows. Jesus has captured his listeners with the truth; if the standard by which man must judge himself denies him the right to existence, then he knows well that this standard is not the final appeal. He knows it with all the despairing strength of his hope, which makes him ask for salvation. Should he not also know it when it concerns his neighbour? Should he not count on the grace of God for others too?

Behind Jesus' verdict stands Jesus' own decision. He does not allow the law to stand as the final appeal, and then count on God's grace for himself just when he needs it. He counts on the grace of God for his neighbour. In fact he stakes all on this. He directs his conduct accordingly, and holds table fellowship with tax-collectors and sinners.[1] To count on God's grace for your neighbour is something different from leaving him to himself and to God "whose business it is to forgive him".

Jesus wants to win the agreement of his listeners for his decision; that is why he tells them the parable. They cannot casually put his words aside, for he has gripped them with the truth; but they can allow Jesus to be right only if they go through a radical conversion, and let God's grace be the final appeal for their own lives. This means nothing less than to give up taking the law as the measure of self-judgement even when one can stand before the law, and in fact particularly then. It means no longer seeking one's life in "righteousness by the law".

If Jesus' listeners persist in their righteousness according to the law, they will not be able to put up with one who bears witness to the truth which they have resisted. They must accordingly strive to remove him from the world. If, however, they admit that Jesus' decision is right, then they are also ready to be their brother's keeper, to be responsible for him and to suffer alongside him. In the name of Jesus they will count on God's grace for him.

[1] Cf. Fuchs, *Studies*, pp. 161f: "Because he believed that God would honour his word, Jesus cast himself completely into the present—and was crucified. That was his self-surrender."

The Framework of the Story

The story of the Pharisee and the tax-collector has acquired an application[k] in v. 14b. This verse was originally an independent saying of Jesus: it is given also in Luke 14.11 and Matt. 23.12—each time in a different context.[12] It was probably the Evangelist who first inserted it here. In this way Luke supplies his commentary on Jesus' story. He understands it as a warning against pride and an exhortation to humility, and this is how he passes it on to the Church.

The redactional verse 18.9 seems to suggest a similar interpretation of the parable. Luke probably found it in his source;[13] it must accordingly have been created for the story by one of those who transmitted it. "Those who trusted in themselves that they were righteous" are people who are of the firm conviction that the verdict of God on themselves is bound to be favourable. To be righteous means, in the usage of the time, to be able to stand before the judgement of God. The description of the accused fits the Pharisees, and it may be correct so far as concerns the immediate hearers of the parables of Jesus. The periphrasis could have been chosen because such behaviour is not confined to the past. The Church of Christ too can fall into it. The story is passed on to exhort it and to warn it.

But Jesus' parable was more than an exhortation or warning. This interpretation does not do justice to its original meaning. This is not to find fault with it, for it was hard to ascertain the meaning which followed for Jesus' listeners from the original situation as soon as this was past. We must also remember that what his Jewish listeners could not help concluding immediately from Jesus' words was for the gentile Christian Luke a closed book, and that he was unacquainted with historical reflection such as we can and must employ.

k See above, pp. 17f.

3

The Similitudes of the Lost Sheep
and the Lost Coin

MATT. 18.12–14 / LUKE 15.1–10

The Similitude of the Lost Sheep in Matthew

While we find the similitude of the lost coin only in Luke, the similitude of the lost sheep is transmitted in two forms. We find the more original version in Matt. 18.12f.[a][1]

The similitude speaks of losing and finding, of things that happen every day and in which every man automatically behaves in the same way. It demands the agreement of the listeners: obviously this is how things happen. The narrator shows how sure he is of the verdict of his listeners by asking for it expressly with the words, "What do you think?" The formulation of v. 12b in the English as much as in the original text clearly expects the answer yes.

Now it would not in fact seem to be everyone's practice to leave behind ninety-nine sheep in the wilderness—that is, in the uninhabited desert land in the hill-country[b]—to look for the one that is lost. Some commentators have wished to conclude from this that the sheep will naturally have remained in the protection of a fold or in the keeping of a shepherd, while the owner went on the search. But the similitude says nothing of this; its effectiveness would be lost if this feature were introduced, and the contrast 1 : 99 would lose its significance. Another interpretation would understand the leaving behind of the ninety-nine to mean that here it is not man's but God's behaviour that is being spoken of. But the text does not speak of the divine shepherd, but of anyone. "A man", any man, is what Matthew says; in Luke the question is actually asked, "What man of you . . . ?" The language shows clearly that the similitude does not mean to describe an extreme case but typical behaviour.

[a] Cf. below, p. 67.
[b] "On the hills" (Matt.) and "in the wilderness" (Luke) mean the same. In Judaea the pasturelands lay in the hill-country.

The strangeness of the similitude is easily solved if it is understood as hyperbole, as an exaggerated representation to bring out what is at issue. The leaving behind of the ninety-nine to look for one lost sheep, this revaluation, "1 = more than 99", makes clear the emotion that is felt over a loss.

But the similitude does not stop at the emotion felt over a loss, but goes on to the emotion of joy which comes from finding again, and to this too applies the evaluation "1 = more than 99". The "1 = more than 99" is of course bound up with the situation. It is "correct" only at the moment of finding or of losing. The thing lost is an object of concern as long as it is lost; the thing found is an object of joy at the moment at which it is found. Our attitude to the object outside this setting is not an element in this general human situation which the similitude conjures up.

"Finding creates boundless joy"—that is the point of comparison of the similitude. The emotion felt over a loss, which is expressed in the search, is brought to our attention only in order to portray the emotion caused by finding again. The course of the story runs on clearly to the end of the similitude.[c]

The Similitude of the Lost Coin

Before we deal with the Lucan version of the similitude of the lost sheep, we ought to look at the similitude of the lost coin. For all its similarity it differs in some particulars from the similitude of the lost sheep, and to these we must give attention. The emotion felt over a loss is expressed by the housewife "turning the whole house upside down". She "lights a candle", "because the low door lets very little light into the miserable, windowless dwelling, and she 'sweeps the house' because in the dark the broom may make the coin tinkle on the stone floor".[2] The joy of finding is realized in this similitude by the calling together of the neighbours. Here is seen the general human trait that joy needs to be shared by the joy of others—it would be inhuman to refuse to share it.

The similitude is followed in v. 10 by an application.[d] The striking

[c] The way to test this is to retell the similitude without v. 12: "If a man who has a hundred sheep finds again a sheep that he had lost . . .". The story becomes pale and colourless, and the equation 1 = more than 99 no longer seems credible. The counter-test is that if the real subject were the love that seeks for what is lost, the similitude could and must have omitted v. 13.

[d] See above, pp. 17f.

phrase "before the angels of God" is explained thus: pious awe led men to avoid language speaking of emotions in God. For this reason it was not said that God rejoices but that there is joy *before* God. But uttering the name of God was also avoided, and it was paraphrased by "Heaven" or "the angels". We must probably ascribe it to a gentile Christian among the transmitters of the story that the name of God is in spite of this mentioned in v. 10.[3]

The Similitude of the Lost Sheep in Luke

Now we can turn to the similitude of the lost sheep as it is given in Luke.

If we compare it with the parallel passage in Matthew, some minor differences strike us at once. It is not significant that the question "What do you think?" is missing in Luke. It is covered by the "among you" of v. 4. More important is another divergence: in Matthew v. 13 runs, "And if he finds it" (the finding remains uncertain); in Luke, however, it reads, "Goes until he finds it . . . and when he has found it . . ." (the finding is counted on as certain). The Matthean version is closer to real life, and is certainly the original one. Luke on the other hand seems to have the "reality part" in view in his formulation of the similitude, and to be thinking of the "good shepherd", of him who searches for the sinner. This is why he has the finding appear as certain.

For the shepherd in Luke 15.5 to lay the sheep on his shoulders is a decorative accretion in comparison with Matthew's version, and so another sign that the latter is the more original. The action is commonplace, and not to be taken as a sign of special love and care. "When a sheep has strayed from the flock, it usually lies down helplessly, and will not move, stand up or run. Hence there is nothing for the shepherd to do but to carry it, and over long distances this can only be done by putting it on his shoulders, i.e. round his neck."[4]

The most important divergences of the two versions come in the conclusion of the similitude and in the application.

In the Lucan version the overwhelming joy of finding is not referred to the equation "1 = more than 99", but is expressed through the call to share the joy, as in the similitude of the lost coin. While calling together friends and neighbours is natural for the woman in the parable, who has her neighbours near, it fits badly the position of the shepherd.

Are we to assume that he carries the sheep from the wilderness of the hill-country into the inhabited area, instead of bringing it back as quickly as possible to the flock that he had left on its own? This feature cannot be original in the similitude of the lost sheep; it has been introduced from the similitude of the lost coin.[5] It is not difficult to understand how this came about. When the Christian Church passed on the words of Jesus, the similitude of the lost sheep, which at first circulated on its own,[6] was soon told together with the related similitude of the lost coin. In oral transmission it was then easy for both these similitudes, which are very like one another, to be assimilated still further.

The application in Luke 15.7 was also probably developed only in connection with v. 10. The original ending of the similitude, which was retained in Matt. 18.13, is still echoed in it.[7] The unqualified declaration, "So there is joy in heaven over one sinner who repents", is mixed up with the comparison, "More than over ninety-nine righteous persons". The "1 = more than 99" is here rendered in the manner of an allegorical exposition. The transference is not quite successful. It does not retain the reference to the moment of finding, which is necessary if the equation "1 = more than 99" is to be correct. There can of course be no suggestion that the penitent is of greater value than the righteous in the absolute. The Christian expositor who wrote these words naturally did not think, when he mentioned the righteous, of the problem which St Paul pondered, whether man can in fact be righteous before God. He used the word in the simple sense in which it was current in his Jewish environment, as a description of the man who has committed no gross sins and is not living an evil way of life of which he needs to repent. When he speaks of "joy in heaven" he means "joy with God", but he avoids uttering the name of the Almighty.

When we have said that the application of the similitude of the lost sheep in Luke 15.7 is an interpretation which was given to this similitude in the tradition, this still does not mean that the divergent application in Matt. 18.14 belongs originally to the similitude. It is shown to be a later interpretation by the fact that it does not keep exactly to the point of comparison; the point of comparison is the joy of finding again, and not the readiness not to abandon what has gone astray.[8] Besides, the wording of v. 14 ("one of these little ones") refers back to v. 10. This shows that Matthew has composed this verse. He expounds the similitude as Jesus' instruction to the Christian Church to despise none of its members (18.10f) and to help a member of the Church who has fallen into sin (18.15–18).[9]

The Historical Setting of the Similitudes

The context in which we find the similitude of the lost sheep in Matthew gives us no clue to what it meant in the mouth of Jesus. The Church Order of 18.1–35 has been put together by the Evangelist. 18.1 is not an historical report but a theological utterance: the Church awaits instruction from its Lord. The verse is not from the tradition, and does not inform us in what situation Jesus uttered the similitude.

The description of the situation in Luke (15.1f) also belongs to the redactional framework;[e] it too is not an historical report but a theological utterance. *All* the tax-collectors and sinners want to hear Jesus, but *the* Pharisees and scribes murmur.

How did Luke understand the words, "This man receives sinners"? We naturally think when we hear them of gracious acceptance and of the restoration of fellowship with God. But this usage is in fact a consequence of the pericope. Luke did not yet know it.[10] In his time the word could mean the reception of guests, or alternatively to have joy or pleasure in anyone. This last sense in particular he was familiar with from the Greek Bible.[11] Of course the Evangelist saw in Jesus' consorting with tax-collectors and sinners more than hospitality or a strange preference. But in fact he puts this saying in the mouth of Jesus' opponents; if he is giving their thoughts correctly, there can be no reference to the acceptance of sinners by the Saviour of sinners. Their protest is best expressed in translation by, "This man takes pleasure in tax-collectors and sinners and feasts with them".[f] "He feasts" fits the sense better than the literally correct translation "he eats", for a meal which brings together other people than just the members of the household is a meal with guests, in fact a feast.[12]

Though the verses Luke 15.1f are redactional and do not belong to the tradition, in this case there is no reason to doubt that the Evangelist with this introduction has correctly hit on the historical situation in which the three similitudes were spoken. The similitudes of the lost sheep and coin are Jesus' answer to the attacks of the Pharisees and scribes, who reproached him for his table fellowship with tax-collectors

[e] Cf. above, pp. 44ff.   [f] Cf. Luke 7.34.

and sinners.[13] Morality prescribed that one could not even approach a wicked man to teach him the laws of God; much more was the close company of a meal ruled out. Anyone who offended against the laws of God was expelled from the community, and the harshness with which this limit was drawn only reflects how strictly men subjected themselves to this law.[g] Jesus' opponents protest because he breaks the bounds of this proscription. Jesus is not in their eyes the saviour of sinners, whose company with sinners is as much a matter of course as the presence of the doctor by the bed of sickness.

Of course they too knew that man can fall, and it was the universal belief that God accepts the penitent, no matter whether he can look back to a life full of evil deeds, or only to one single lapse. No one attempted to deny fellowship to the man who had proved the seriousness of his penitence.[14] Clearly in the eyes of the Pharisees and scribes the table companions of Jesus were not penitents, otherwise they would not have raised their protest. They could not understand the coming of sinners to Jesus as repentance, as long as he was no more to them than a carpenter from Nazareth.[h] [15]

[g] One must here take note that as a consequence of the Christian faith, which is conscious (particularly in its Reformation form) of the hidden sins of man, such a visible delimitation between the ungodly and the righteous is to-day no longer possible just like that. We do not understand sin as transgression of a law, and therefore for us it cannot be tested and measured by the law. Nor do we still have a unity and synthesis of the law of God with the standards of justice of the community in a way that can be taken for granted. At the time of Jesus evident ungodliness led to expulsion from the people of God, which involved an exclusion from society of a sort that we can hardly now picture. To-day hardly anyone would take notice of an excommunication by the Church, and for all that we keep our distance, we still take it for granted that even a prostitute "is still human". "Each must see according to his lights." Tolerance, in the sense of not being shocked by the other man, is part of the basic structure of our society. Such a difference of situation must be kept in mind in interpreting the Bible.

[h] Cf. above, pp. 34f. If we have correctly determined the setting of the similitudes, the applications in 15.7 and 15.10 cannot come from Jesus. This was already likely in the case of 15.7 on other grounds. Jesus would have spoken over the heads of his hearers if he had answered their protest that he keeps company with the lost by saying explicitly, "So God rejoices over a sinner that repents." The verse must have been created by a Christian interpreter, because it only makes sense for the Christian Church which understands the coming of sinners to Jesus as being obviously repentance (see on this note 15). He renders correctly what the similitude has to say, but he obscures the "language event" that Jesus sets in motion by the similitude (cf. above, pp. 30–3).[16]

The Meaning of the Similitudes

Jesus answers the reproaches of his opponents that he holds fellowship with the lost, with similitudes whose climax is the joy of finding again. This must show his listeners that he regards his table companions as "lords of return", as the Hebrew puts it literally, not as lost but as found again. When he represents the joy of finding in the similitude, he is declaring that now is the time of finding again, and that his joy looks for them as human beings to share in the rejoicing.[17]

Can the Pharisees allow this verdict of Jesus to stand? We can only imagine hesitantly and conjecturally what a scandal it must have been to them. If they are to recognize Jesus' table companions as penitents—men in whom the pious Jew could discover absolutely no sign of repentance—then they must understand the nature of repentance in a radically new way. Because the seriousness of repentance is part of their innermost being and thinking, however, they would have to re-orientate themselves and all their thinking to allow that Jesus is right.

If anything is characteristic of the Pharisee, it is his seriousness about repentance. It is not works by which he stands or falls: "Many a man earns his (future) world in an hour"; and, "If a righteous man falls, he loses all, and if a sinner repents he wins all." But this seriousness which is shown in deeds, and proves itself in the avoidance of sin, is still the least that a man can show. And if a man is lacking in this seriousness which he can have, and therefore should have, if he so violates the holiness of God, then he counts as an ungodly man and a gentile, and has forfeited the company of men.

We can see how seriously the Pharisee takes repentance and what he understands by it, from the following legend:

"Nahum of Gimso, the pious teacher, was one day driving three asses, laden with bread and fruits, to the house of study. While he was following the beasts in the midday heat, more asleep than awake, a sick beggar, deformed with ulcers and half-dead of hunger, came up to him and asked him for some food.

"Nahum had never refused a beggar, but the heat of the day made him lazy, and he answered crossly: 'Just wait until I have found something for you.' With reluctant feet he followed the beasts that had gone on ahead, and began bad-temperedly to grope about in the panniers. But while he was still feeling about aimlessly, there struck his ear a weak and yet terribly urgent sigh, and when he turned round, the beggar lay stretched out dead in the sand.

"How quick were Nahum's hands to take bread and fruits out of the pannier, how swiftly his feet hurried back! He implored the dead man to eat, he threw himself on his ulcerated body to bring him back to life. But it was all in vain. Then Nahum cried to God and said: 'Lord of the world! Through my laziness a man's life has been lost! O ease my grief and punish me! May the feet that were slow to bring help to the needy become lame, the hands that were so negligent to serve him wither up, the eyes that looked askance at his need go blind, and my body bear his illness. Lord of the world, so punish me in this life and in my body, that thou punish me not in the next life and in my soul!' From that day on Nahum was sick. His feet went lame, his hands withered, his eyes went blind, and his body was covered with sores.

"Once Rabbi Akiba, his pupil, visited him, and when he saw him lying so wasted in his bed-sheets, he cried out for sorrow and said: 'Woe is me that I must see you like this, you pious man!'

"But Nahum smiled and said: 'Blessed are you, Akiba, that you can see me so, for this is a sign of grace to me, that God demands my sins from me in this life and in my body, and leaves me unharmed in the next life and in my soul.'"[18]

Note the seriousness about God's commandments, and the extreme readiness to repent. But repentance is here something that man sets at work, a last possibility that he grasps in a desperate effort to ensure his eternal future. But it is only a possibility, it goes no further than the hope: "Perhaps after all God will have mercy on us." Man here takes the first step; anything further he must hope for from God.

For Jesus salvation and repentance "have now changed places. While to the Jewish ways of thinking repentance is the first thing, the condition which affords the sinner the hope of grace, it is now the case that repentance comes by means of grace." "So little is repentance a human action preparing the way for grace, that it can be placed on the same level as being found."[19] Repentance for Jesus is not something done by man, but an event coming from God, the arrival of his kingdom. For this reason Jesus can set against the "perhaps" of hope an assertion of certainty.

In these similitudes Jesus tells his listeners that here and now in these objectionable table companions this deed of God has happened, and that his joy of finding expects their joy to share it, a joy that shares in

God's joy. He expects their assent to his table fellowship with the lost, with whom he celebrates God's joy.[1]

To come to agree with Jesus his listeners had to alter their ideas radically. They had to have faith in Jesus' proclamation of the arrival of the kingdom of God, and leave behind them all that had hitherto determined their life. On the other hand they cannot escape the truth of the similitudes. It was obvious to them that man is God's property. They lived out this idea in the seriousness of their repentance and in their piety towards the Law.[21] But how in fact does a man regularly behave with his own property?

It is breathtaking to see how Jesus, this carpenter from Nazareth, claims God as the one who is moved by men in losing and finding; how he claims him for ungodly men: not for man in general, who is "a sinner like anyone else", but for quite particular men with sins that one can point to with the finger, such as to make these men "impossible".

"Crucify him! This man blasphemes God!" This was the answer. But there was another answer too: "Truly this is the Son of God!"

4

The Parable of the Prodigal Son

LUKE 15.11–32

This parable is the answer of Jesus to the protest of the Pharisees against his table fellowship with tax-collectors and sinners.[a]

[1] For Jesus' listeners it must have been immediately clear from the situation that the similitude spoke of God, for losing and finding when spoken of in connection with sinful man can only refer to God. Of course the similitude is not to be understood as an allegory, as an utterance in cipher, in which it is really God who is meant by the shepherd and the woman, and the sinner by the lost sheep or coin. The similitude means the shepherd and the sheep to be really themselves, and an interpretation which explains it on the pattern of "the shepherd is God", etc., misses its meaning. The attempt to derive a direct utterance from the similitude of the form, "God behaves like . . ." also misses the basic nature of the similitude. In the interpretation of the parables the interplay of the parable and its setting in a discussion must be observed. It remains true that a similitude has only one point of comparison; but that does not mean that what it has to tell us is a simple utterance, which can be read off directly from it (cf. above, pp. 28f).[20]

[a] Cf. above, pp. 69f.

The Pharisees do not murmur because they understand the reception of sinners into table fellowship with Jesus as a pronouncement of the forgiveness of sins. Nor do they protest because sinners are forgiven and the grace of God is shared with them.[1] Their protest is for other reasons.

Jesus puts the world out of joint by what he does. He and his activity cannot be classified. Can a righteous man hold table fellowship with sinners and the scum of the earth, when it is even forbidden to meet them in order to teach them God's Holy Law? But is he then a sinner? Can his behaviour be disposed of with the proverb "birds of a feather flock together"? This is just as impossible. The great disturbance he makes is still there.

It is not sin and vice that disturb the ordering of the world. Certainly sin and vice are things that ought not to exist. But because sin is punished, vice condemned, sinners proscribed and avoided, the disturbed order is restored to balance. The more strongly the life of the individual is bound up with a community the stricter will be the proscription. Only societies in which the life of the individual has to a great extent become private, so that it affects the whole but little, can afford a far-reaching tolerance.

Because Jesus crosses the lines which have been drawn by the proscription he disturbs the order. He is the man who "does not co-operate", and so makes the conformity of the others no longer a matter of course. They cannot ignore him, they have to express their views. Their protest becomes open.

Jesus answers with a parable which sets what has happened in a new light, and by which he reveals to his listeners his view of things and helps them in manifold ways towards reaching agreement with him.

The threads that connect the parable and the situation with one another are numerous. Nevertheless the parable remains all the time pure narrative which bears its own weight. In no place does it become an allegory in which "picture part" and "reality part" are identical.

The parable as its listeners understand it

A Son goes to a Far Country   The first sentences of the parable do not yet reveal to Jesus' hearers in what direction he is going.

For the younger son of a large-scale farmer to come to his father and ask him to pay him his legal share of the inheritance was nothing unusual.[2] A farm was by the law of the time a family possession, and together with all that belonged to it passed to the eldest son.[3] But the younger son had a right of inheritance to the disposable property, that is, to the possessions that did not belong directly to the farm. However, he did not get all of it; according to the law two portions of it went to the firstborn (so two-thirds when there were two sons), while the younger received a third (cf. Deut. 21.17).

Again, to Jesus' listeners the words of the younger son really did sound like a request, not like an impertinent demand.[4] They are not surprised when the father complies with it and divides up the property for his sons. While the younger is paid, the elder, no doubt, receives only a reckoning of what is due to him.[5]

It is again nothing out of the ordinary when the second son after a short while packs up all that belongs to him—or, as the passage can also be understood, turns it into cash—and emigrates. "He wants to build himself a life abroad", think Jesus' listeners. Thoughts such as one finds in many commentaries that it was "rebelliousness against his father" or "the wish to get away from parental control" that drove the son abroad,[6] could not occur to them. Palestine, visited by frequent famines, was not able to support the people of Israel, and anyone who wanted to get on had a better chance in the great trading cities of the Levant. Emigration was the order of the day. While the Jewish population of Palestine amounted to no more than half a million, four million Jews lived in the Diaspora.[7]

The Son becomes a Prodigal But the young man, so the story tells, gets on to the wrong track while in the far country, and squanders the inheritance he has had from his father in prodigal living.

Here it is perhaps already becoming clear to the listener what Jesus is getting at—that the parable is really concerned with the point that is in dispute between him and them. The loose and ungodly life of the son— is it not basically the same thing that enrages them in the "tax-collectors and sinners"?

The son has just squandered it all when a famine hits the country and redoubles his misery. "What the thoughtless boy does now, however, is to the listeners the worst thing he can possibly do. It must not be forgotten that the parable is told to pharisaic scribes. We are tempted to say, 'What else should the man have done other than what he did when he was destitute? When he went to a citizen of the land at least he wanted to work.' The pharisaic scribe would say, 'He should have worn his feet sore until he came to the nearest Jewish community, and should have asked there for help and work.' This way he adds apostasy from the faith of his fathers to his immoral life, since for him, living with a citizen of a foreign, gentile country, there can be no Sabbath, no ritual eating, etc." [8] Even the work which this gentile employer gives him means for him a sin. "Cursed be the man who keeps swine", runs a Jewish saying.[9] "He was forced to be in contact with unclean animals (Lev. 11.7) . . . he must have been . . . practically forced to renounce the regular practice of his religion." [10]

The picture of the son is here painted in gloomy colours. He really is a lost son. The allusion to the tax-collectors, to those who have renounced the laws of their fathers' religion and gone into the service of the gentiles, is now obvious. But not in such a way that the son "means" the tax-collectors. We must understand how Jesus here allows something to his listeners in order the more certainly to win acceptance for what his parable is saying. Whatever is to be said about the reality in the case of the "tax-collectors and sinners", the verdict cannot turn out worse than it must be here for the "prodigal son". To this extent the parable can claim to be saying something relevant to the reality.[b]

What was Lost is Found   This sinful job hardly gives the son the poorest of nourishment. He even envies the swine their fodder, the dried-up husks of the carob-bean tree, which are only eaten by men in direst need. How gladly he would have filled his belly with this food, which is scarcely edible, just simply to satisfy his hunger. But he does not get it. The stranger must stand back for the beasts, which are the property of his master.[11]

A Jewish proverb says, "When the Israelites stand in need of carob-beans, then they return (to God)." [12] It is like this for the prodigal son. He compares his lot with that of his father's day-labourers, to whom their kind master gives more bread than they can eat. It does not stop there, though. He realizes how he has sinned against God and his father by his dissolute life, and he knows that he no longer deserves to be treated as his father's son. He decides to go home, confess everything, and try to induce his father at least to treat him like one of his day-labourers.

For a man to come to recognize his sins and repent under the pressure of self-incurred misery is not unusual, and is credible in its effect. What the parable next narrates, however, is far from commonplace.

[b] Cf. above; pp. 26f.

Even if he is in a great hurry, for an aged oriental it is beneath his dignity to run.[13] When the father falls about his son's neck, he is stopping him from going down before him on his knees to him and humbling himself. When he kisses him this is not only a sign of over-flowing affection from joy at seeing him again at last. "We must remember the symbolism of the kiss to grasp fully the meaning of the text. The servant, the slave, kisses the feet. Even the kiss on the hand, for which one bends the knee, still expresses that the man kissed is being honoured as a superior. The kiss on the cheek is for an equal."[14]

When the father embraces and kisses his returning son, he has "shown him without a word that 'you are to be my son, in spite of all that has happened.'"[15]

Everything too that the story tells in the following sentences about the conduct of the father follows the same pattern. The son is to be marked out as an honoured guest by a garment of honour. The giving of the ring, which is to be thought of as a signet ring, as excavations show, means the bestowal of authority. The wearing of shoes (a luxury at the time) distinguishes the free man from the slave who walks barefoot. The killing of the fatted calf "means a feast for the family and the servants, and the festal reception of the returning son to the family table. The . . . orders given by the father are the manifest tokens of forgiveness and reinstatement, evident to all."[16]

To Jesus' listeners the conduct of the father will hardly have seemed a matter of course. But neither could what the parable relates of the father be unintelligible or simply incredible to them. Fatherly com-passion was for them so proverbial that it could serve as a standing image of the compassion of God for the sinful. So they prayed with the 103rd Psalm: "As a father pities his children, so the Lord pities those who fear him."[c] Moreover, the father's words in v. 24 display a strength of their own. (When one can again count as an asset what one had had to write off, when what had been lost is found, that really must be ground for joy!)

The listeners cannot help noticing that with what happens here be-tween father and son, Jesus again alludes to the situation on which they disagree with him. They reproach him that he keeps company with sinners, and he tells a story of a sinner, but of a sinner who repents. And in this story repentance appears as something very simple. Misery drives a man to realize that turning back is the only road left

---

[c] Verse 13, cf. also Isa. 64.7.

on which there is still something to hope for. His confession of guilt is
answered by abundant mercy. No test of genuineness is demanded of
him; in uttering his confession of guilt he is already received back as a
son in his father's house. Now if this turning back were repentance,
could not a lost soul look confusingly like a penitent soul? If this were
repentance . . . ! Jesus must know the strict demands that were made
of the penitent. He knows that he was expected to show very clearly in
his life that something different had come of it, while at the same time
there was no want of readiness to receive him fully into the community
again when he had sufficiently proved himself. Jesus knows all this. If
in spite of that he tells the story in this way, he obviously means to see
repentance in the light of this story. Can he succeed in bringing his
listeners to do so too? If it is possible to make such compassion
credible in an earthly father, how much more can it be asserted of the
heavenly father!

Although the conduct of the father in the parable, as we have said, is
by no means an everyday one, the proverbial nature of a father's
compassion must prevent any of the listeners from dismissing it as improbable and so avoiding the force of the parable. All the more so,
because its proverbiality is charged with energy by the patriarchal
society of the times, and fed by the analogy not infrequently made
between human and divine fatherhood.[17] This feature of the parable is
not one that is a matter of course; but it does not derive its credibility
from the "reality part" either. It expresses something basic which goes
deeper than the psychologically probable or the mean average.[18]

Finding must be Celebrated   With v. 24 the real theme of the parable is
reached. As in all "double-edged" parables the emphasis lies on the
second half.[19] The *reader* of the parable, who has the text before him,
gets the impression that v. 24, which occurs again with minor variations in verse 32, like the refrain at the end of a strophe, divides up the
story into two equal parts.[20] For the *listeners* to the parable, this
division must have been concealed by the dynamic of the flow of the
story: v. 24 ensures the right attitude to what follows. We have here a
narrative device. The listener has already heard in v. 24 what is first
said to the son in v. 32, so that the attitude of the elder son appears to
him from the start in this light, and he agrees all the more surely with
the words of the father.

This saying of the father justifies the feast. But the rest of the story
must make it plain to the listeners that it is the feast that is at issue,

nothing else. The narrator has the elder son come to the house only when the feast is already in progress. Even the dance of the men, which usually follows a festal meal, must already have begun, so that the rejoicing and the din can be heard outside, and the protest of the son against the feast is expressed as a refusal to go in. This is not a reflection of real life but stage-management by the narrator.[d] Only in this way can the point be added that the father goes out to the elder as he ran to meet the younger, so that the same gesture of love is again repeated. The father speaks to the son. When he answers with reproaches, he does not intend to complain of a life of narrow servitude. It is not correct that he disparages his life with his father as slavery, as some commentators say.[21] Nor does he reproach his father that he has kept him short of money. Not even a lamb! The comparison must reveal what a scale this feast is on. All these years—and never a feast! But now! What upsets him is the reason for it. Such a feast for this reason! That is what the elder son is protesting about.[e]

It is part of the masterly art of the narrator that he lets this protest be so explicitly put into words, only to cut it short and the more surely prove the rightness of the feast. "Everything that is mine is yours." The elder son is not short of money! No more than the owner in the parable of the labourers in the vineyard is the father in this parable unjust. "You are always with me": this answers the words of the son, "All these years have I served you", but it is contrasted to what must be said of the younger brother, "He was lost and is found again"; just as in the parable of the lost sheep the ninety-nine in safety are contrasted to the one that is lost. So the listeners can hardly disagree when the father says "this is an event that must be met with a feast". It is a sacred necessity that obtains here (cf. below, pp. 110f).

What the father says can be variously translated. It must mean either: "It was simply necessary to hold such a feast for this reason";[22] or alternatively: "You ought to be glad and make merry".[23] Both really come to the same thing. If in the first version the father shows the

---

[d] Cf. above, pp. 10f.

[e] Some commentators take these verses as meaning that here the elder son too shows himself to be a lost son who has gone away from his father, although outwardly he has stayed by him (Schniewind, p. 81; cf. Bugge, p. 425, Schlatter, p. 357). Such a thought could not possibly occur to Jesus' listeners, first because they could not identify their protest against Jesus with the protest of the elder brother (see below), secondly because the son in the parable did not regard his life with his father as "slavery", nor did the Pharisees so regard their obedience to the law.

necessity to hold the feast, this also shows the son's duty to take part in it. In the second version, however, the saying is more than just a reproach; it points out what the demand of the moment is, which the elder son ought to have respected.

It would be a misunderstanding of the situation in which the parable was told to identify the Pharisees with the figure of the elder brother.[24] The protest of the elder brother against the feast is not the same as theirs. There is here an interlocking such as we often find in the parables of Jesus. The reproach brought by the Pharisees was, "How can you celebrate with such people?" Jesus' answer runs: "The lost is found. This must be celebrated. I am joining in celebrating God's feast. And what are you doing?"[f]

Certainly Jesus alludes to the Pharisees in the figure of the elder brother. It is not for nothing that v. 29 is put: "I have never disobeyed a command." When Jesus so characterizes this figure in its positive traits that it is like the image of the Pharisee, he gives his listeners the same rôle.[g] Precisely because the protest of the elder brother is here only a foil against which the rightness of the feast is brought into relief, the Pharisee can be connected with the elder brother, though his protest is not the same as the elder brother's. This allusion makes sure, however, that the parable is listened to by Jesus' hearers as a word that awaits their response.[h]

Jesus' Word and the Response of his Hearers

Jesus announces what hour has struck, and wants to persuade his hearers to agree he is right in so fixing the time. Will they agree with him and recognize that now is the time in which the lost comes home? Will they join in the joy of this finding and no longer protest against the company in which Jesus celebrates the feast of the return as the beginning of the greatest of the works of God, as "the proleptic celebration of the kingdom of God"?[25]

Jesus' action turns the world upside down, because it disturbs its order, as we said at the beginning. What matters is how this action is received. Is this disturbance understood as destruction, which must be put out of the world as quickly as possible before it does any more

---

[f] Cf. above, p. 27.

[g] Cf. above, pp. 26f.

[h] "Jesus' hearers were in the position of the elder son who had to decide whether he would accept his father's invitation and share his joy" (Jeremias, pp. 131f).

damage? Or is it a response to an event in which the might of him who is greater than the world and its order breaks in?

The man who would hold the latter to be true must leave concern about the world staying "in order" to him whose action he responds to—which does not mean that by this he can contract out of the responsibility entrusted to him.[1] He must also be ready, however, to suffer it that people will "put him out of the world" for the sake of the order of the world.[26]

5

The Parable of the Labourers in the Vineyard

MATT. 20.1–16

The Introduction to the Parable

The parable of the labourers in the vineyard is introduced by a formula of comparison. This means only that the parable has some connection with the kingdom of God. We must not be misled by this introduction to understand the parable as a timeless revelation about the kingdom of Heaven put into picture form, but must look for the connection between the parable and the historical situation in which it was spoken.[a]

The Parable Narrative

. . . who went out early in the morning to hire labourers . . . Jesus' listeners were familiar with the situation which the parable presupposes. An owner of a vineyard goes off at break of day[b] to the

---

[1] Cf. on this subject Gogarten in *Der Mensch zwischen Gott und Welt* and in *Verhängnis und Hoffnung der Neuzeit*.

[a] Cf. above, pp. 16f.

[b] In the original the passage runs literally "together with early", i.e., at the beginning of the (working) day.

market-place (cf. v. 3) where the day-labourers that are looking for
work are regularly to be found. He takes on a number of workers for
his vineyard, after he has come to an agreement with them about the
day's pay. A denarius was "by the standards of the time a generous
wage".[c]

The working day lasts from sunrise to sunset. It is divided into twelve
"hours" which are counted from sunrise on.

The conversation of the owner of the vineyard with the day-
labourers whom he still finds idle in the market-place at the eleventh
hour is scarcely meant to represent their lack of work as undeserved,
for the parable does not connect the payment of full wages to them
with undeserved want. Probably it has only a formal function in the
construction of the story: by mentioning it explicitly it emphasizes
the hiring of the last workers to an extent that corresponds to their
significance in the narrative as a whole. Whether the excuse of the
labourers in v. 7 should be taken seriously or only thought of as a poor
evasion which "conceals their characteristic oriental indifference"[1]
can hardly be decided.

It is unusual that the householder goes out several times in the day,
for the last time only shortly before the evening end of work, to look
for workers. Normally an owner estimates how large a labour force
he needs and engages the corresponding number of day-labourers in the
morning. This unusual feature depends on the intention of the narrator
to contrast the labourers who worked all day with those who worked
for the last hour only.[d] It is based on the reality to which the parable is
pointing, not on the material of the story.[e]

It is not to the point to understand the strange conduct of the householder from, for instance, a pressing harvest situation. The story gives
no support to this,[f] and it would also ruin the point of the parable if it
allowed thoughts of this kind to occur to the hearers. They would

---

[c] Michaelis, *Gleichnisse*, p. 172; cf. Billerbeck, I, p. 831. It contributes to the
effectiveness of the parable if the listeners get the impression that the wages
agreed upon with the day-labourers were completely fair.

[d] "In the parable of the labourers in the vineyard there are five groups of
labourers; *it is only the first and last groups that matter for the story*, but the sharp
contrast of the extremes has to be mitigated by some sort of intermediaries;
otherwise the story would sound grossly improbable" (Bultmann, *HST*, p. 190,
my italics). Cf. above, p. 14.

[e] Cf. above, pp. 28f.

[f] The absence of motivation in the presentation is a feature of the style (Bultmann, *HST*, p. 190; cf. above, p. 14).

then not understand the generous treatment of those who came last as an act of goodness, as the parable intends it to be, but as the thanks owed them by the owner of the vineyard because they did not leave him in the lurch in a critical situation.[2]

But neither does this unusual trait compel the listeners to look behind the parable and seek the explanation in the fact that here not an earthly householder, but God, is spoken of. Since the engagement of labourers at a later hour of the working day could occur, the trait has in fact enough probability not to ruin the story. Besides, because the strange conduct of the owner is told without any explanation, a strong tension is built up, which keeps the listeners' attention on the progress of the story, and does not let the question of the reason for the owner's strange conduct arise.

. . . *whatever is right I will give you* While the story explicitly mentions the day's pay for the workers who were hired at dawn, it has the master say to those hired later: "Whatever is right I will give you", and with the last ones it makes no mention of pay at all, if we follow the better manuscripts. None of Jesus' listeners, however, would be given the idea that meets us in some interpretations: that by going without an agreement on pay the labourers hired later had shown the owner special trust, and proved that they had a personal relationship with him and were willing to work for his sake, while those hired first were only concerned with their own advantage.[3] In respect of a day-labourer relationship such thoughts are absurd. The reason that the narrator speaks here so imprecisely or not at all of pay agreements lies in the flow of the narrative.[g] It would in fact spoil the parable if he let it appear already at this stage that the master intends to pay them all a full day's pay.[4]

The guarantee of the owner to pay what is "right and proper" must have been understood by the listeners as meaning that the pay of the labourers hired later would amount to the appropriate fraction of a denarius.[5]

. . ."*pay them their wages*" "The paying of wages in the evening is such an obvious occurrence (Lev. 19.13; Deut. 24.14f) that the issuing of a special order suggests some definite purpose in the mind of the owner. This special intention was certainly not . . . that the last should be the first to receive their wages, but that all, without exception, should receive the full day's wages."[6] That the first receive their

[g] Cf. above, pp. 11f.

pay last is not meant as an affront, but is a device of the narrator, who in this manner lets "the first be witnesses of the extremely generous payment of their comrades".[7] It is part of the narrator's staging too that the owner is thought of as present at the payment of wages, for this was not usual when a steward paid out the wages.[8]

To be made equal with those who worked for the last hour is felt by the labourers who had worked all day as a double injustice: "(1) They have been obliged to toil for twelve hours, while the others have only worked one hour; (2) they have worked in the burning midday heat, the others in the cool of the evening. . . . In their indignation they omit the address."[9] The answer of the owner makes one of the grumblers the representative of the whole group. When he addresses him as "friend", this is not to be taken as a sign of special friendliness. The Greek word, which could also be rendered "my dear sir" or "my good man", is generally used in addressing someone whose name one does not know.[10]

The owner shows the grumbler in two ways that his indignation is not justified:

1. No injustice has been done to you; you have got what was agreed on.

2. You cannot anyway deny that I have the full right of disposal over my possessions, and this allows me to give the other exactly as much as you.

This argument has a double function:

1. It forms the starting-point for the attitude of the owner being understood as one of goodness. Justice forms a background against which goodness can appear as goodness, without being misinterpreted as caprice. Goodness would not be goodness if it gave to one at the expense of the other.

2. Because the owner is clearly in the right, the question is thrown back at the grumblers. The final sentence of the parable is not, however, to be understood as a rebuke. It counts on the agreement of the man addressed. "You cannot very well be jealous because I am generous." Goodness demands approval, and no one can escape its demands. If goodness is understood as goodness, it must also be approved. One cannot grumble against goodness![h]

[h] "Here it must be understood that . . . goodness not only grants freedom (from need) to the man concerned, but gives fellowship to everyone who understands" (Fuchs, *Studies*, p. 155, with a correction to ET).

Literally translated, v. 15b runs: "Or is your eye evil, because I am good?" We cannot catch the unprecedented sharpening of the language, because "good" in our language means a quality, not a relationship with or attitude to another. We must replace it by the word "kind", to get the intended sense more exactly. The phrase "evil eye" can refer to envy, but it is not confined to this concept, which is ill suited to grasp the causal connection between the kind conduct of the owner and the "evil eye" of the grumbling day-labourer. Envy includes the idea of coveting, and one could have some such phrase as, "Are you envious, because they had less work than you?" The question, "Are you envious because I am kind?", however, offends against the nature of language. The opposite of the "evil eye", "the good eye", can be rendered as "goodwill", being well disposed. We have in English no corresponding single word "evilwill". What is meant would best be conveyed by the term "disapproval". But even then we have not yet caught all the nuances that matter. The description "evil eye" also contains an evaluation of what the eye does as it looks. The expression Luther uses, "Does your eye see cross-eyed?" perhaps best expresses fully what is meant in the original text by the expression "evil eye". Only we must then not narrow it down to the meaning "envy".[11]

The Framework of the Parable

The parable of the labourers in the vineyard has acquired an application in v. 16. This verse picks up 19.30 and makes the parable appear to be an explanation of the saying about the first that become the last. In this way the parable is made to strengthen the warning that is given to the disciples along with the promise in 19.27–30, that their position of precedence should not mislead them into exalting themselves.

But the application does not fit the sense of the parable. That the first become the last is only an unemphasized minor feature of it. Furthermore it can be shown that the connection of the parable with the saying of Jesus in 19.30 cannot be original. This saying is transmitted not only in Mark (10.31) without the parable, but also by Luke (13.30) in a completely different context from that in Matthew and Mark, and must accordingly have once been independent. In that case 20.16 too cannot originally have belonged to the parable, because this verse is dependent on 19.30. It must have been devised by the Evangelist, in order to insert the parable at this place into its context in the Gospel. It is only the context that makes the parable into one addressed to disciples.[1]

The Parable in relation to its Situation

The historical situation from which we must understand the parable is the same as we have met in the parables of the lost sheep and the coin in Luke 15: Jesus is answering the protest of the scribes and Pharisees against his table fellowship with tax-collectors and sinners.[12]

Jesus stands before his listeners as one who disturbs God's order. He ignores the difference which the law erects between the righteous and the sinner. He keeps company with notorious sinners, although he himself is no sinner, as his opponents know well. If he does not observe the boundary between sinners and righteous, it is as if the dam which is to protect society against the overflowing of sin has been breached. This must infuriate serious, responsible, and devout men, such as the scribes and Pharisees were, against Jesus. It is not envy nor loveless self-seeking that impels them.[13]

Jesus answers with a parable that sketches out an alternative picture of the situation to that which determines the verdict of his opponents.[1]

In the parable too an ordered system is violated. Not because the owner is still taking on workmen in the late evening; nor because those who came last receive a whole denarius for one single hour's work. The expectation of those who worked the whole day that they would receive correspondingly more rests on the confidence that the ordered system of pay would in all cases be followed. But since the householder pays them only the stipulated denarius, this system is infringed. This is what calls forth the protest of the day-labourers ("You have made them equal to us . . ."). The master of the house is able, however, to show that justice has been satisfied: what appeared as a breach in the ordered system of justice was in truth the appearance of goodness, and goodness cannot be disapproved.

Their immediate and natural attitude to busy and lazy labourers, to production and pay, must move the listeners to take the side of the grumbling day-labourers. But precisely by this means they are compelled to join in making the change of verdict which the words of the owner bring about.

Of course nothing would have been achieved for the narrator if his

[1] Cf. above, pp. 42f.   [1] Cf. above, pp. 22f.

listeners did not also make this change of verdict in respect of the matter that is in dispute between him and them. For this reason he has so arranged it that "picture" and "reality" correspond to one another extensively. The parable contrasts the whole-day labourers with the labourers of the last hour in the same way as in the reality the Pharisees, zealously and patiently concerned their life long for the fulfilment of the law, are contrasted with open transgressors of the law. By taking into the parable the ratio of values which in the judgement of his listeners exists in the real situation, the narrator makes sufficient allowance to his listeners to be able to be sure that they will connect the parable with the situation.[k]

After they have heard Jesus' story, it must be clear to them that Jesus would have them understand the event against which they have protested as the appearance of goodness, and expects from them the approval which one can hardly refuse to goodness.[1]

Is Jesus speaking of his own goodness? The introduction of the parable connects the appearance of goodness with the kingdom of God, which Jesus proclaims is now arriving.[14]

There lies hidden here an enormous claim if Jesus answers an attack on his behaviour with a parable which speaks of God's action![15] It is not as if Jesus wants to claim for himself a special honour, or to say of himself that he is the Messiah, or the Son of Man, or the Son of God. It is the claim that Jesus with his behaviour answers up to the action of God![m] But that means for his listeners the demand in understanding

---

[k] Cf. above, p. 27.

[1] The phrase, "the appearance of goodness", which perhaps sounds strange, has been chosen for its echo of the idea of epiphany. For it is a question here of an epiphany, of an appearance of God. This goodness is not the effect of an attribute of God that is unchangeable and always there. It is unforeseen and comes into play miraculously.

[m] Cf. Fuchs, *Studies*, p. 36: "We can hardly be mistaken in concluding that Jesus' meal—or his entire conduct towards tax-collectors and sinners who did 'penance'—comprised in Jesus' eyes anyway a specific act of God's goodness, or that his conduct was at least comparable with such an act (Matt. 4.17). This also means that sinful man is dependent on God's goodness. In particular it means that Jesus in any case held out as a prospect this act of God's goodness and ordered his conduct towards sinful man accordingly. . . . He appeared not simply as the preacher of some possible goodness of God, of which all stood equally in need. Instead Jesus held to this goodness, as to an event known to him; and he did not shrink from demonstrating the correspondence between this event and his own conduct towards those under judgement. Jesus acted in a quite concrete way as God's representative, and said himself of this, 'Blessed is he who takes no offence

and behaviour to answer up to the appearance of the goodness of God, which Jesus sees in his companionship with tax-collectors and sinners. As the grumbling day-labourer could recognize the goodness of the owner only when his eyes were turned from himself to the other who received this goodness, they are to see the appearance of goodness in the neighbour who had need of this goodness. And in view of this goodness, which goes far beyond the law, they are to go beyond the barriers which the law is constantly erecting between men.

Any of Jesus' listeners who ventured on this would understand Jesus as the one who has proclaimed God's time of grace with full authority (2 Cor. 6.2). But those who remain closed to his word must raise the demand: "Crucify him, this man blasphemes God."

6

The Great Supper

LUKE 14.15–24 / MATT. 22.2–14

The Great Supper

The parable in Luke 14.16–24 tells of a man who arranges a great banquet and invites many to it.

The listeners can assume from what Jesus says that it is an evening meal. This was usual for a great banquet, because the chief meal of the day was eaten in the hours of the late afternoon—usually it was the only one, apart from a meagre breakfast in the morning.[1]

The host observes a polite custom which had been adopted particularly in the fashionable circles of Jerusalem. At the time of the meal he sends his servant again to those invited with the message, "Come, because it is now ready." But all the guests to a man begin to excuse themselves. Suddenly they have no time. One is in the act of buying a

at me' (Matt. 11.6). A declaration of this kind relates, however, not to Jesus' personal qualities, nor to a dogmatic assessment of his person, but to his conduct and to his proclamation."

field, another five yoke of oxen, and they want to inspect their purchases at'once.ᵃ

Such deals were for preference carried through after the real work of the day, but before work ended for the evening.³ It had of course to be finished at the latest shortly after sunset. In the East the day is followed by the night almost without transition, and at night one can neither inspect a field nor judge the performance of a team of oxen.

A banquet that begins in the late hours of the afternoon usually goes on far into the evening, often till after midnight. So at sunset it has really only just begun. Since the excuses of the guests are not typical "weak excuses" nor bear the character of a deliberate slight, Jesus' listeners will hardly have understood them as refusals, but as excuses for coming late.⁴ The guests want first still to use the remaining hour or two of day for business before they come to the banquet. They think it is still early enough to arrive at sunset, for—so we must understand their attitude—the banquet will not run away.

> Verse 20 admittedly does not fit this pattern; it can only be understood as a refusal. The request to be excused is also missing here. Since, however, there are reasons to think that this verse was only inserted into the parable later on,ᵇ we can here leave it out of consideration.

To a certain extent etiquette allowed for arriving late at a banquet; guests could appear up to the end of the first course. It was then (according to the custom of Jerusalem at least) that a sign which had been set up at the entrance of the host's house was removed, to show that any further latecomers were unwanted.⁵ But the host realizes what is the attitude of the guests. He is furious at the rudeness and disrespect with which they have treated him, and decides to teach them a lesson. He quickly sends his servant in to the streets to invite to his house the first people he can find.ᶜ When the servant tells him that there is still room,

---

ᵃ This is usually translated, "I have bought". But to get the sense, and to suit our own usage, we should do better to put it, "I am in the act of buying"; for the field must in fact first be valued, and the team tested by a sample of its work, before the deal is complete.²

ᵇ Cf. note 16.

ᶜ Both in Matthew and in the parallel passage in the Gospel of Thomas (see note 15) it is not the poor, etc., that are named in the invitation, but the first people to be found in the streets. The mention of the poor, crippled, blind, and lame in v. 21 may be the work of Luke, who wanted to assimilate this verse to v. 13 (see Jülicher, II, p. 418; Hauck, p. 192; Jeremias, pp. 44f). It does not make a great difference to the sense, because those who can be invited at a minute's notice

although he has collected all he can find, the master sends him outside the city too, to look for quickly available guests.[6] The word used for "invite" here is "compel", because "even the poorest, with oriental courtesy, modestly resist the invitation to the entertainment until they are taken by the hand and gently forced to enter the house".[7]

The house is to be filled to the very last place. The intention behind this is that when the original guests at last turn up at sunset, they will have to learn that there is no more room for them. They will not manage to taste of the meal, which they imagined they would not miss. They thought that it was still early enough, but it is too late.[8]

It is not to the servant that the owner explains in v. 24 the real meaning of his measures; the "you" is in the plural. He steps as it were on to the apron of the stage and addresses the audience. The solemn manner of speech shows that this is the concluding verse of the parable. It still belongs to the "picture part", but points forward to the "reality part" (cf. Matt. 18.13; Luke 11.8; 18.14).[9]

"Now is the Acceptable Time"

Jesus uses the parable of the great supper to answer the exclamation of a pious Jew who calls blessed the man who will take part in the feast in the kingdom of God.[d] [10] "How well it will be one day for those who have been invited to the banquet that God will prepare for the righteous at the time when he will reveal his kingdom!"[e]

When God fulfils his promise and finally comes out of concealment, when it becomes visible that he alone controls all that happens in the world, and all powers and authorities are subject to him, this is bound to be so great a joy that the pious Jew cannot but see it under the image of a joyful banquet.[f] Blessed is the man who can take part in it! To this end is directed all the pious zeal of the Pharisees. "To have a part in the community that is freed from need and death and brought to eternal life, they bore happily and diligently the burden of the law, and were intent on breaking not a single commandment." Among them was to

without more ado will in any case be this sort of people. Only the situation can easily be concealed by Luke's version. The master of the house is not concerned to invite the poor, but to collect the guests needed as quickly as possible.

[d] To eat bread stands for taking part in a meal (the part for the whole).

[e] Schlatter, *Lukas*, p. 336. On the Jewish expectation of the kingdom of God, cf. above, pp. 35ff.

[f] Cf. Matt. 8.11.

be counted the man who turned to Jesus and uttered this beatitude. By it he declâres what the measure of his life is; by it he measures his life and by it he would wish to be measured.

The pious Jew who utters this beatitude believes that he is conforming to the will of God with this attitude, and yet at the same time thinks that he is in agreement with Jesus.[11] Jesus' parable shows that he was mistaken. It claims that he and those like him are people who still will not come, although the banquet has already begun. "Blessed is he who *hereafter* shall eat bread in the kingdom of God"—so the content of the beatitude of the Pharisee is to be filled out. Jesus' answer runs: "For him who does not arrive for it *now* it will hereafter be too late." He proclaims in fact that the kingdom of God is already arriving (Matt. 12.28), that God stands at the door (Mark 1.15). With tax-collectors and sinners he holds the proleptic celebration of the feast that all Israel is expecting to enjoy in the kingdom of God.[g] [12]

In this parable too we must pay attention to the interlocking.[h] The Pharisees do not believe that the kingdom of God is beginning *now*, and see no connection between this event and Jesus' table fellowship with the lost. But Jesus places the situation in the light of a parable in which some people are not prepared to respect the fact that the meal has already begun, and have to put up with the consequences. Anyone who is not willing to be summoned to the first course, does not get to taste of the meal proper. There is a tension between the evaluation of the situation by Jesus' audience and Jesus' own understanding of it, as it is expressed in the parable. This does not mean that Jesus is at cross-purposes with his listeners, but indicates the change in understanding which he wants to bring them to through his parable. We can hardly discover now what help the parable gave them on particular points so that they could make this change. But we can say what the change consists in. It is to come to have fáith in the Gospel which invites to God's feast *now*, and to act accordingly.

The whole future depends for each man on his taking seriously this "now"; this the parable shows. But Jesus' saying is more than a threat. He chooses for what he wants to say the form of a parable, i.e. he is concerned to help his hearers to a right understanding. While the fate of the unwilling guests in the parable is already decided, it is left open for Jesus' listeners. They still have the decision before them.

[g] On Jesus' proclamation of the arrival of the kingdom of God, cf. above, pp. 37ff, and below, pp. 101f.

[h] Cf. above, pp. 27f.

This decision must be correctly understood. It is not a question of
"mustering up our energy", of "deciding wholly for God". In that
case we should not find the tax-collectors and sinners but Pharisees and
scribes in the company of Jesus. They applied a considerable degree of
energy to such moral and religious efforts. It cannot be said of them
that "they do desire the Kingdom, but they desire it along with other
things—riches, and the respect of other men; they are not ready for
repentance. When the invitation to the Kingdom comes to them they
are claimed by various other interests." How much the kingdom of
God could stand "above all else" for a Pharisee is shown, e.g., by the
Rabbi Akiba (died 135), who in the awful tortures of a martyr's death
still made his confession to God in prayer.[13] By this decision no
renunciatory preparation for God's kingdom is meant. It is not without
reason that the parable chooses precisely the image of the banquet
and shows the banquet as already begun. Any exposition that does not
do justice to this "Now is the acceptable time" (cf. 2 Cor. 6.2), has
missed the sense of the parable.

The Exposition of the Parable in the Early Church

In the course of its transmission Jesus' parable has been expounded in
varying ways, and each new understanding of the text often led to a
reshaping of it. None of these expositions which we can read off from
the different stages in the history of the passage was able to grasp what
was the decisive point of the parable as Jesus told it. The opposition
between Jesus and his listeners over the fixing of the time, on which the
parable of the great supper is built, could no longer be understood in
the early Church. This is not to say that the early Church had aban-
doned Jesus' faith that the time of salvation is breaking in now, that
God is already standing at the door. But it spoke of it with different
words from those Jesus had used. For the Church what mattered most
was that it was *Jesus* who had announced this nearness of God with
authority. The actuality of salvation lay for it in the certainty of sharing
in this salvation through what Jesus did on the cross, through his death
for many (Mark 10.45; 14.25), and of belonging to the community of
the time of salvation that was called together by the risen Lord. It only
spoke of the kingdom of God, however, as future,[14] and differed very
little in its language about this from the Pharisees. The climax of the
parable, which came in the disagreement over determining the time,

was therefore inevitably lost for them. Instead, other things said in the parable came to the fore.[15]

Earthly Interests and Heavenly Calling

Originally the parable was meant as an argument to convince opponents through the power of analogy. Now, however, it was heard and read as the instructions of the Lord and Saviour.[1] It was no longer understood as an independent narrative which contained its own meaning and precisely by this meaning pointed to a deeper context of significance, but was listened to from the start as containing a deeper significance.

Such a listener or reader was able to see the decisive point of the parable in the contrast between "earthly interests" and "heavenly calling". "This is how men behave when God's call meets them. Their earthly interests are more important to them than God's invitation. But when this earth passes away, God will exclude them from the only thing that remains, which they have now so little regarded."

In such an understanding it must have been noticed how one-sided the chosen examples were. It is certainly not only possessions that hold men captive in this manner! It may be for such a consideration that v. 20 was inserted into the parable.[16] It contains a refusal, and accordingly at that time the other excuses were also no doubt understood as refusals.

"Those invited were not worthy!"

But the contrast between those invited first and those invited later could also catch the eye. Then the parable would look like an answer to a question which troubled the Church considerably in those days: how could it happen that Israel rejected the preaching of the apostles, while the gentiles received the gospel of the crucified and risen Jesus? Did not this mean that those whom God had called from of old were excluded from salvation, while those whom God had once called "not my people" stepped into the place of the elect people?[1]

It was as an answer to this question that the parable was understood by the later narrator to whom we owe the version of the story that we find in Matthew 22, if we ignore verses 6f, and 10-14, which were

[1] Cf. above, p. 42.   [1] Cf. Rom. 9.25.

added only later.[k] He too regarded the excuses of those invited—he probably found in front of him only the first two—as refusals. He could therefore no longer understand the original flow of the narrative, and could make no sense of the doubled invitation of the substitute guests. He set about telling the story again and more effectively. We must not think here of a conscious rearrangement, but of something which is found frequently in the oral transmission of narrative material: a practised narrator will always shape the material handed down to him in his own way, without intending to alter it.[1] It must of course affect this if he no longer sees the point of comparison of the story in the same place as did its original author.

The course of the story in its new form goes as follows:

A king on the occasion of his son's wedding orders a great feast and invites many to it. The private citizen has unobtrusively become a king. The king was already in the parables of the scribes a favourite key word for God; but there could be another reason for the intrusion of the metaphor. If the verdict in v. 8 is to stand, the worthiness of the host must be established beyond doubt.[18] The polite, repeated invitation, which we have already found in Luke, is reported in detail.[19] The message with which the servants—there are several, not one, as is only to be expected with a king—are sent at the time of the feast to the guests is phrased even more invitingly than in Luke. But while in the original version those invited at first accept the invitation, here from

[k] For the invited guests to disregard the invitation and instead go to their work is certainly unusual, but not inconceivable. For the messengers of the King to be slain, on the other hand, falls completely outside the framework of the narrative. This is even more the case when the King—whose banquet is already prepared—wages a campaign first before he invites the substitute guests to table. These verses can only be understood as an allegorical expansion.

Verses 10–14 also cannot originally belong to the parable. Where is someone who has been brought in from the highway to get a wedding garment from? "The favourite explanation, that it was customary to provide invited guests with a festal garment (cf. 2 Kings 10.22) breaks down here, since there is no example of the existence of such a custom in the time of Jesus" (Jeremias, p. 65). Apart from the logical difficulty, considerations of style also demonstrate that these verses, which have no parallel in Luke, were only later combined with the parable.

Verse 10 should not be regarded as the last verse of the parable of the royal wedding (Matt. 22.1–9). It does not fit the style of the parable to recount the carrying out of the command, and "bad and good" refers on to the following verses. Verse 10a is a transition, which links vv. 1–9 with 11 (or 10b)–14.[17]

[1] See Fiebig, *Der Erzählungsstil der Evangelien*, throughout. In contrast the tradition of the sayings usually preserves the actual words very carefully.

the very start "they would not come". With the second invitation at the time of the feast they show their refusal so clearly that they simply leave the messengers of the king standing, and go off to their business.[m] They do not even think of sending excuses for themselves. The contrast between the behaviour of the king and that of his guests is glaringly demonstrated. After what has gone before no one can refuse assent to the king's verdict: "Those invited were not worthy of it."

This verdict is the focal point of the parable. The unworthiness of those invited first is accentuated, the subsequent invitation appended as a mere sequel which clarifies the meaning of the verdict.[n] It is not thought of as a measure to exclude the guests invited first, because there is no longer any question of their coming. They have excluded themselves.[20]

As already mentioned, the parable in this form answers the question, "Why has the Gospel, the invitation to the kingdom of God, passed from the Jews, the chosen people, to the gentiles?". The answer is, "They were not worthy of it, they have proved this by their rejection of the Gospel of salvation. It is not God's fault. Like the kind and courtly host, he has done everything that was possible."

"Mind that you are prepared!"

A later reader—probably it was the Evangelist—read the parable as an allegory. Right down to individual details it seemed to him to show forth the history of God's dealings with his people. They would not listen even to the first messengers of God—the prophets—and when God sent out other servants[o]—the apostles—with the message "Now everything is ready, the time of salvation is here", it went no better with them.

One who read the parable in this way must have felt that it needed supplementation. Israel did not just ignore the messengers of God; it treated them shamefully and killed them (v. 6). But God could not let himself be so treated; he sent out armies, destroyed the murderers and

---

[m] The king's banquet, to go by the wording of the Greek, is not to be thought of as an evening meal but as a meal earlier in the day. Such meals were held occasionally in Jewish circles in imitation of a Roman custom, and took place at about noon.

[n] For a formal parallel, cf. Matt. 18.23–35. In this parable too the real climax is the verdict of the king, and v. 34 only draws out the consequences of v. 33.

[o] The word "other" in v. 4 was probably inserted by the Evangelist in connection with this allegorical interpretation of the verse.

burned their city (v. 7). The Evangelist who inserted these features
into the narrative as best he could, was thinking of the recent destruction of Jerusalem, which he could only understand as a judgement of
God on the people that had crucified his Anointed. In the later invited
guests he saw those gentiles who had come to faith in Christ. But then
the question inevitably arose for him, Is the new people of God really
worthy of God's invitation? Is the message of the Gospel not such that
both good and bad respond to it (v. 10)? Even the Church is not yet the
community of the elect saints (v. 14). Through the Church too the
division will one day go (cf. Matt. 13.36–43; 49f). Only those who
have in truth been obedient to God, who wear the white garment of
righteousness, will then be able to stand.

These thoughts the Evangelist expresses by supplementing the parable
narrative with another parable from his tradition: the parable of the
guest without a wedding garment. The beginning of this parable had
to be omitted to join it on here. Its conclusion too underwent some
alterations when it was read in its context after the parable of the royal
wedding as an allegory.[21] The original text of the parable may have
run somewhat as follows:

> The kingdom of heaven is like a king who made a wedding for his son. And
> the wedding hall was filled with guests. But when the king came in to see the
> guests, he found there a man who had no wedding garment on, and he said
> to him, "Friend, how did you get in here without having on a wedding
> garment?" But he was left speechless. Then the king said to the attendants,
> "Seize him by his hands and feet and cast him out".

The "wedding garment" that the king notices the guest has not got is
not a special garment, but "to be understood as a . . . newly washed
garment. The soiled garment is an insult to the host."[22] The guest
who is found in it is left speechless, or as the forceful Greek expression
actually puts it, "His mouth was stopped!" There was nothing that he
could say in answer to this question. We go completely astray if we
try to guess why the guest appeared in this attire. It is not just a point
of the style that the motive is not given.[p] The want of motivation here
greatly assists the effectiveness of the story and shows that there is no
answer to this question. Any excuse is ruled out—this is meant to be
demonstrated by the king's question. The casting out has to be seen
on the strength of this as an obvious consequence.

[p] See above, p. 14.

The meaning of the parable is, "If you are invited to God's banquet, mind out that you are prepared."[23]

The Evangelist has not just taken over this basic idea but has also interpreted the parable allegorically in its individual points. Exclusion from the feast of the kingdom of God is more than casting out, it signifies eternal damnation. For this reason Matthew elucidates it by letting the "reality part" press into the "picture part". The unworthy guest is thrown out "into outer darkness", where there is "weeping and gnashing of teeth", that is into eternal destruction, which the Evangelist regularly describes with these words (cf. Matt. 8.12; 13.42, 50; 24.51; 25.30).[q][21]

The allegory has acquired an application in v. 14. This application cannot be (and no doubt is not intended to be) an interpretation of the narrative, "since the truth that only a small number will be saved is not portrayed either in Matt. 22.1–10 (the guest-room is full) or in 22.11–13 (only one unworthy guest is rejected)."[24] We must probably understand this application as a piece of preaching. It is a warning to sharpen the conscience, which was added to the allegory to fill in a point that was not expressed clearly in the parable.

7

The Unique Opportunity

MATT. 13.44–6

The parables of the "treasure in the field" and of the "pearl of great price" are so similar that we can best consider them together.[1]

"The kingdom of Heaven is like . . ."

Both parables have the same introduction: "The kingdom of Heaven is like . . .". "The kingdom of Heaven" is what the Jew said at the time

---

q "'Wailing and gnashing of teeth' is . . . a symbol of despair, a despair caused by a salvation forfeited by one's own fault" (Jeremias, p. 105).

of Jesus when he meant the kingdom of God. Men avoided uttering the most holy name of God and therefore used such periphrases.[a]

Some will perhaps be surprised that the kingdom of God is compared in the first similitude to the treasure, but in the second not to the pearl but to the pearl-merchant. This discrepancy calls attention to the position of such parable introductions. They are imprecise and are not to be taken literally. They do not mean to say that the kingdom of Heaven is like a treasure or a pearl-merchant. If it was only a matter of such a direct comparison, all the rest of the story would in fact be superfluous. Rather they are abbreviated forms for a fuller expression: It is the case with the kingdom of God as with the following story of a treasure . . . or of a merchant.[b]

". . . *a treasure that was hidden in a field* . . ."

Finding buried treasure was a great piece of luck on which all the same thoughts and hopes centred in antiquity as to-day surround the pools or the Derby winner. Of course such a lucky find happened only rarely, but the possibility could not be ruled out. There were as yet no banks, and burying was in fact the safest protection against thieves. Besides it was the only way to escape plundering in the frequent disturbances of war. If the owner died before he could tell his heirs the hiding-place, the treasure lay hidden and forgotten in the earth and waited for a lucky finder. In our parable this is probably a day-labourer. He works on someone else's land, and is so poor that he has to sell all his possessions if he wants to acquire the field.[2]

Jesus' listeners will probably have pictured the finder as striking a pot or vessel filled with gold and silver coins while ploughing, through the ploughshare coming against it in the ground. Possibly, however, their ideas were also influenced by a well-known story of a Rabbi, a Jewish scribe, who was ploughing one day when his cow sank in and broke a leg, and discovered a great treasure when he went to help it out.[3]

The finder leaves the treasure for a while in the field. It is only as the owner of the field that he can remove it without anyone being in a position to question his possession of it.[4] All efforts to evaluate morally the conduct of the finder of the treasure or to measure it by the position in law are idle. If it is not morally a hundred per cent unobjectionable

---

[a] On the meaning of the phrase "kingdom of God" cf. above, pp. 37ff, below, pp. 101f.

[b] Cf. above, pp. 16f.

this is as unimportant as is the question whether the finder's "action was formally legitimate"[5] or not. It is part of the stage-management of the narrator that the finder does not simply remove the treasure, but buries it again, so as to acquire it together with the field. Only so can the point of comparison which the narrator has in mind be brought out from this material (see below).

"... *a pearl of great price* ..."

The second parable tells of a merchant who is in search of fine pearls.[c] The Greek word shows that we have here a large-scale dealer, a travelling merchant, not a small trader.[6] He will try to buy pearls from the pearl fishers.[7] Even for him it is a great piece of luck to discover an extremely valuable pearl.[d] Admittedly he is looking for pearls in the course of his job, but he was not looking for the pearl of great price. It just comes his way.[e] Even when he has sold all he has he will not be paying its real value, but only the price at which the present owner is ready to sell it.[8]

Of course Jesus' listeners will not have imagined that the merchant keeps the pearl only to suffer hunger from now on while enjoying his possession, but rather that he will sell it at a great profit.[9] Such a situation, to risk everything for the sake of an exceptional profit, does indeed occur, however, in business life.

"... *sold everything that he had and bought* ..."

The point of comparison of both similitudes[f] lies in the behaviour of the lucky finder.[g] This behaviour is so determined by the special

---

[c] The pearl played something of the rôle in the luxury of the ancient world that the diamond does to-day (Jülicher). It had become proverbial for a treasure.

[d] So it must be translated. The translation in AV (cf. RSV) "*one* pearl of great price", rests on a failure to recognize a Semitic idiom which underlies the choice of words in the Greek (cf. Jeremias, pp. 199f).

[e] The similitudes therefore do not differ in the manner of the discovery—unsought, as against after long wearisome search. We still have, however, the contrast between poor and rich (see Jeremias, p. 200).

[f] Cf. above, pp. 23f.

[g] If the *value* of the thing found or the *event* of the discovery were the point of comparison, the similitudes would not mention the behaviour of the finder at all. But in fact they give it the place of emphasis at the end.[10] Nor can the value of the thing found be the point of comparison, because for Jesus' listeners "the kingdom of God" was "the great object of hope and prayer", so that "they did not need to be assured of its value" (Dodd, p. 85).

situation that it cannot be characterized correctly without giving consideration to the main features of the situation, the accident of the discovery, and the value of the thing found, which is what lends significance to the discovery. If our formulation of the point of comparison is not to degenerate into a complete reproduction of the parables, we must try to grasp exactly the situation portrayed, and to describe it correctly.

What do the lucky finders do? They *buy*. The words, "He sold everything that he had", do not in fact mention an independent transaction, but describe how high the purchase price is in the graphic manner of popular narrative. The behaviour of the pearl-merchant and of the finder of the treasure is generally understood as a sacrifice. But these men are not making a sacrifice; they are paying a purchase price. There is a basic difference between a purchase price and a sacrifice. Purchase is directed towards acquiring an object of equivalent value. Sacrifice on the other hand is a giving that expects no reward. Its profit consists only in its being to the benefit of whoever it was made for. Then "it has paid". Otherwise it is "meaningless".[h]

The purchase by the finder has, however, a distinctive nature. It is almost an extreme case of what buying is: it is a striking instance of a "unique opportunity". Only a fool could hope to find such a treasure a second time in his life. Even if there are fine pearls to be had every day, an extremely valuable one is not found again so quickly. It is precisely its rarity that gives it its value. The man who does not seize the opportunity is a fool, who if it rained porridge would still not have a spoon. In such a situation men are in fact ready to risk everything without hesitation if it is necessary.

It is part of the stage-management of the narrator that the parables take such a course that the lucky finders need to sell everything in order to acquire possession of the treasure or the pearl. This does not

[h] Cf. Fuchs, *Studies*, p. 94. "There is no mention of a sacrifice. The gain corresponds instead to the stake, and even exceeds it considerably." Similarly Jüngel, p. 143.

The reason that the idea of sacrifice has become so fixed an element in the exposition of these similitudes is no doubt that the treasure in the field and the pearl of great price were allegorically identified with the kingdom of God. The kingdom of God cannot be bought—only a sacrifice would be adequate for it. So the first mistake of method was necessarily followed by a second. Conclusions were drawn from the (supposed) reality part to the picture part, instead of the problem of the reality part being answered by careful observation of the phenomena portrayed in the picture part.[11]

in fact follow from the value of the thing found, as is often said.[12] The treasure could have been inconceivably valuable—but if a man were to find it on his own land he would not need to pay a penny. And whatever value the precious pearl has, the price demanded will never come to the exact limit of all his possessions. It is the narrator who arranges it that the merchant can only acquire it if he gives up all he has for it. He sets this limit to the wealth of the merchant, he lets the finder discover the treasure in someone else's field and be so poor that the purchase of the field (not of the treasure!) exhausts his whole means. So to him it is a question of "selling all", of risking everything.[13] We can in fact best formulate the point of comparison as risking all in view of a unique opportunity.

The Unique Opportunity

Risking all in view of a unique opportunity is the "turning point" that binds together the "picture part" and the "reality part".[1] If we work back from the parable to the historical situation in which it was told we can say that Jesus reckons that this sort of resolute risking of everything is necessary, and that such a unique opportunity is present. In the "reality part" too the risking of all and the unique opportunity of which advantage is taken must stand side by side if the parables are to be effective. The behaviour of the lucky finders would otherwise not be comparable, and the parables would be at cross-purposes with the reality. Jesus wants to use the parables to set in the right light what the situation demands in his judgement. His listeners are to recognize the situation as the unique opportunity that is offered them and to direct their behaviour accordingly.

The introductory formula of the parable, "The kingdom of Heaven is like", shows us what this "unique opportunity" is. Jesus proclaims that "the kingdom of God is at hand" (Mark 1.15). The moment has come for which the whole people of Israel was waiting, God is coming out of his hiddenness, and it is becoming obvious that it is he alone who holds sway over the world. To him the empires of the world and their kings are as much subjected as are death and all the other powers of corruption.[1] But Jesus had not, like some of his contemporaries, the

---

[1] Cf. above, pp. 24f.

[1] This is the meaning of the expression "the kingdom of God is at hand" (Mark 1.15), so Professor Jeremias informs me, if one goes back to the underlying Aramaic.

apocalyptists, worked out a fixed time. He was not giving information about when in the near or immediate future this revelation of God would happen. If God stood at the door, then what mattered was not to have correct information, but to make oneself ready, to turn about, to repent.

But God's nearness not only makes the present a challenge, it already reaches itself into the present. Satan, the ruler "of this world", has already been cast out of heaven (Luke 10.18). The power of the demons has been broken, they have to yield before the approach of God (Matt. 12.28; Mark 3.27). Now is the time that the promises of salvation come to fulfilment (Matt. 11.5f). It is the wedding time, the time of joy (Mark 2.18f). "Blessed are the eyes which see what you see, and the ears which hear what you hear", Jesus cries to his listeners (Luke 10.23f). This nearness of God cannot simply be "taken cognizance of". Jesus has to say: "And blessed is he who takes no offence at me" (Matt. 11.6). And in truth there was reason enough to take offence at his message. People were expecting the reversal of the whole of life. Was the decisive event now to turn out to have happened already, so that conversion was the only thing still necessary?

Certainly Jesus' expectation too was directed towards the future. He expected the resurrection of the dead, and the future judgement, and the time in which those for whom God had prepared it would enter the kingdom of God: the poor, those who hungered after righteousness, the peacemakers, those who had become like children (Matt. 5.3–9; 18.3). Yet for him there was no longer a basic difference between present and future, they belonged together. But in that case one could not simply wait until the nearness of God had become visible in the reversal of the whole of life, so that it could let itself be "taken cognizance of". What mattered was to take seriously this nearness of God here and now. And the conversion that Jesus demanded meant precisely this.[k]

[k] Cf. above, pp. 37ff, and Bornkamm, *Jesus*, pp. 92f: the utterances about the present and the future are "in Jesus' preaching . . . related in the closest fashion. The present dawn of the kingdom of God is always spoken of so as to show that the present reveals the future as salvation and judgement, and therefore does not anticipate it. Again the future is always spoken of as unlocking and lighting up the present, and therefore revealing to-day as the day of decision . . . The future of God is salvation to that man who apprehends the present as God's present and as the hour of salvation. The future of God is judgement to the man who does not accept the 'now' of God, but clings to his own present, his own past, and also to his own dreams of the future. . . . In this acceptance of the present as the present of

Deliberate Risk

The nearness of the kingdom of God is the unique opportunity that these parables of Jesus allude to.[14] But what is the risking of all, by means of which advantage can be taken of this opportunity?

Although the parables, with their "sold all that he had", remind us of the story of the rich young man, we are not entitled to draw the conclusion that the sale of all one's goods is intended. Reality and parable must be comparable, but they do not need to be the same.[15]

Is Jesus speaking of discipleship, of following him?[16] In the sayings of Jesus which speak of this, the thought is similarly of risking all: "Whoever does not bear his own cross and come after me, cannot be my disciple" (Luke 14.27). "If anyone comes to me and does not hate his own father and mother and wife and children and brothers and sisters, yes, and even his own life, he cannot be my disciple" (Luke 14.26). "No one who puts his hand to the plough and looks back is fit for the kingdom of God" (Luke 9.62). "Follow me, and leave the dead to bury their own dead" (Matt. 8.22).

But none of these sayings helps us further than this. They teach us to recognize the seriousness of the demand, but they do not make clear precisely what is demanded. What does it mean to "put the hand to the plough"? What sort of cross are we to bear? When is it necessary to put second even father and mother for the sake of being a disciple? Is it what James and John did when they left their father at the nets and followed Jesus? But what has this literal following, this wandering after Jesus on the highways of Palestine, to do with the kingdom of God? How is this the way to seize the unique opportunity of its nearness? This remains hidden from us. The texts are ciphers whose meaning we cannot read.

The Secret of the Parables

What the texts mean to say cannot be expressed in language without the concrete reference for which they were coined. Only when the word meets the situation in which it belongs does it become intelligible and the puzzle is solved.

Does this mean that we cannot find the meaning of the parables of

God, as we have tried to make clear, pardon and conversion are one in the word of Jesus."

the treasure in the field and of the pearl of great price, because we cannot ascertain in what situation Jesus uttered them? No! Rather we must realize that it would help us relatively little if the concrete reference of these parables were known. In its concreteness it is unique and not identical with our situation. We should in any case have to translate. But the passages do at least give us what we need for this translation of the word of Jesus.

This is not to say that this translation can be carried out every time. The key to the meaning of the parables can only be revealed to us by our own actual circumstances. We possess this key when those things which are juxtaposed in the parables, and which produce an effect because they are put together in this way, are present for us too: that is, when we are confronted with the possibility of risking everything, because that which is worth more to us than anything else has come near to us, with all its promise, and demands that we should risk everything.

But when Jesus announces the time, when he says that God is now near, is this not just as true to-day? Is it not the faith of Christianity that God has committed himself through the resurrection to this Jesus and his announcement of the time? Is it not this that enabled Paul to proclaim, "*Now* is the acceptable time" (2 Cor. 6.2)?

But this announcement of the time on its own does not seem to help us. It does not set us free to risk everything. It is obviously necessary that an announcement of the place should be added to it, telling us *where* we can count on the nearness of God.

Jesus has also made an announcement of the place. He has claimed the saving nearness of God in those and for those who had need of God. He expected God's coming in the possessed, the sick, the poor, and sinners.

This announcement of the place has not lost its validity any more than has the announcement of the time. But it is only true in a concrete situation. Otherwise it loses its original meaning. If it is made into an announcement of a general truth, which can be taught and learnt, it has lost its connection with the words of Jesus. Because the announcement of the place is true only in a concrete situation, it must be repeated. Jesus' words and actions give us directions for this repetition, but we must make it ourselves—in the name of Jesus.[1]

---

[1] This does not mean an "imitation of Christ". Jesus is not turned into a teacher. For we can dare such action only in the trust that we have Jesus at our side as the one who intercedes for us, and that Jesus' action and will are well-pleasing to God.

The claim laid to the saving nearness of God really demands the risking of everything, if it is to be made concrete. It is perhaps, for instance, not difficult to say in general that God forgives sins. But to say to my neighbour in the name of God: "Your sins are forgiven you", can only be done so seriously and responsibly that one is ready if need be to die for it. (Jesus has realized this claim to the nearness of God at the price of the cross.)

The position here is circular. The concrete claim to the saving nearness of God demands the risking of everything. But only where it does demand the risking of everything can it be made effective.

For this reason we are still left with the question where and when we can achieve it in the name of Jesus, the question what we have the power to do. But this question does not simply remain an open one. Rather, faith in Jesus drives us to it with all its might, and makes it the sort of question that we wait daily for an answer to. For faith in Jesus means holding fast to the promise of this nearness of God. Without Jesus this question could not be put. He brings us to the point that we wait for the coming of God, in fact so wait that we pray God to open our eyes, so that we do not culpably miss his nearness.

8

The Parable of the Unmerciful Servant

MATT. 18.21–35

The Framework of the Parable

The parable of the unmerciful servant is handed down to us by Matthew in his 18th chapter. At first sight it seems to be the answer to Peter's question in v. 21. But this question has in fact already received its answer in v. 22, and the parable is only loosely joined by the word "therefore" to the saying of Jesus with which it is connected by its subject-matter.[1] In Luke it is absent from the corresponding passage. Besides, this saying of Jesus does not match the point of comparison of the parable, in which there is no mention of repeated forgiveness. So the parable is an independent piece of tradition, and was first put in this context by Matthew.[2]

We must also get away from the idea that v. 21 gives the situation in which Jesus told the parable. This little scene has in fact been created by the Evangelist. To understand this we must become acquainted a little with his manner of working. We know that the tradition about Jesus lay before him in various sources. He had the Gospel of Mark, which gave him primarily stories about Jesus, and a Sayings Source (Q), which contained the words of Jesus. Furthermore various individual pieces had come into his hands, his so-called special material, to which our parable belongs. He linked together these various strands of tradition in his Gospel, giving careful thought to how best it could be done. In chapter 18, for instance, he put together a number of pieces of tradition in such a way as to make a Church Order. "At that time the disciples came to Jesus", says 18.1; in other words the Church awaits instruction from the words of Jesus. The question who is greatest in the kingdom of Heaven is dealt with, and how one should behave towards the little ones and the weak. In the parable of the lost sheep the right attitude to take to a member of the Church who has fallen into sin is shown, and vv. 15–17 discuss in detail how everyone ought to behave towards such as person. Verses 18–20 promise the Church the authority for such action. Verses 22–35 enjoin that this action must stand as a sign of readiness for limitless forgiveness, and that judgement will inexorably come to everyone who lacks such readiness.

A continuous context could of course be made out of the individual sections transmitted to Matthew only if he treated them with a certain freedom. In v. 15, for example, he takes up a saying that Luke gives in 17.3f. Because he particularly wants to fill out the general admonition of Luke 17.3 (entirely relevantly) by specific regulations, he must now postpone the verse that corresponds to Luke 17.4. He cannot yet use it after v. 17 either. Since, however, it was impossible simply to attach it to v. 20, he has made an introduction for it by Peter's question. Peter must, as it were, give Jesus the cue for his utterance.[a][3]

It is only from this necessity in the construction of the Gospel that Peter's strange question can be explained. For how could one try to establish in advance quite theoretically how often a man should forgive? There could be no thought of forgiveness at all if we were counting whether it was the fourth, the fifth, or even already the

[a] Cf. above, pp. 43f.

seventh time. We should only be saving up the sins in order to go on punishing them still when the total had been reached.[b]

The saying of Jesus in v. 22 means that forgiveness should have no limit. However often our brother has transgressed against us, he should still receive our forgiveness. If Matthew has seventy-seven times and Luke seven times on one day, this is not a real difference. Both numbers mean the same: an infinite number of times. They are round numbers, which exclude any counting up. It was probably Matthew who introduced the proportion seven times—seventy-seven times into the saying of Jesus. He could well use this contrast for his little scene, and besides in this way he achieved a delicate allusion to the Old Testament, as this Evangelist loves to do. All of his readers who knew the Scriptures must have remembered that the same pair of numbers could be found in Gen. 4.24. There it says, "If Cain is avenged sevenfold, truly Lamech seventy-sevenfold." What was said in the Old Testament of blood feud is now in the New Covenant to be true of forgiveness.[5]

Since the connection of the parable with vv. 21f is not original, we cannot use these verses to discover what Jesus wanted to say to his listeners by this parable. The realization that the little scene in v. 21 has been put together by the Evangelist rules out for us the obvious assumption that the parable was spoken to the disciples. A tendency can be observed in the tradition of the parables to turn those that were originally directed to a different group of listeners into parables for the disciples, because the Church continually referred to itself the words of its Lord.[c] So we shall do better to suppose the opposite development here.[6]

The application[d] in v. 35 does not in any case belong originally to the parable, but is an interpretation which Matthew has added to it.[7] It does not quite fit the meaning of the parable, because it makes v. 34 the point of comparison (see below) and makes the parable appear as a threat, which is exactly what it is not. Since we are primarily interested in understanding the parable as a saying of Jesus, we shall not try to

[b] See Schlatter, *Erläuterungen zum Neuen Testament*, p. 209.

The attempt has been made to explain Peter's strange question from a rule of the scribes at the time of Jesus, that a man needs to forgive the same offender only three times. Peter's question has been seen as indicating a readiness to go far beyond this number. But in fact there never was an unnatural rule of this sort. The idea arose from a misunderstanding of a passage in the Rabbinic tradition, a mistake which has been corrected by the specialists.[4]

[c] Cf. above, pp. 42f, and Jeremias, pp. 33–41.

[d] Cf. above, pp. 17f.

show what the (quite understandable) reasons were which led Matthew to his particular exposition.

The introductory formula[e] too probably goes back to Matthew. He has a preference for this turn of phrase, and uses it in places where it is missing in Luke (cf. Matt. 22.2 with Luke 14.16). Naturally this cannot be said for certain with a piece of his special material.

The Parable Narrative

The parable tells of a king[8] who wants to hold a reckoning with his servants. He is an absolute ruler, who can fix such a day of reckoning whenever he pleases. Of course Jesus' listeners knew that the "servants" of the king are not slaves, although the same word is used which serves to describe slaves elsewhere. The position of the great men of an oriental king, his governors and high officials, was not very different from the position of a slave in relation to his master. They were unconditionally subject to him; there was nothing they could not fear from him, and nothing they could not hope for.[9] This was not quite true of Israel, but they had for centuries lived among the great empires, between Egyptians, Babylonians, Assyrians, Syrians, and Persians, so that they knew by hearsay the sort of conditions presupposed in the parable.[10]

Jesus' listeners will have pictured the man with the great debt as a governor.[11] The amount of taxes that he has to pay is extremely large—10,000 talents. A talent was 10,000 denarii, and a denarius was worth about 1/6d.[f] So it is a question of millions. When one considers that the annual income of Herod the Great was not more than 900 talents, and that the whole of Galilee and Peraea only paid 200 talents tax in the year 4 B.C., this sum must appear fantastic. But we need not be surprised at this. The story is dealing with a realm in which extremely large figures are conceivable, with kings and with princes. As the listeners and the narrator are unfamiliar with this realm, the chosen figure need not be a real one. For a man who only called 10 or 20 denarii his own, 200, 2,000, or 10,000 talents are all equally fabulous sums. In such a case one usually takes the highest imaginable figure, and this has the meaning of "infinitely much". "Ten thousand is the highest

[e] Cf. above, pp. 16f.

[f] Others give the total as about £3,000,000, which is also possible, for the value of the talent fluctuated. Our statement is based on the figures given in Jeremias (p. 210). The value of the denarius is given by Klostermann, *Matt.*, p. 153.

number used in reckoning, and the talent is the largest currency unit in the whole of the Near East." [12]

The governor is unable to pay, and the king thereupon orders him, his wife and children, and all that he has to be sold to get what compensation is possible.[g] It was quite obvious that even the sale of the whole family could not defray the debt, "since the average value of a slave was about 500 to 2,000 denarii".[h]

The governor throws himself in the dust before the king to evoke his generosity by this abasement, and to obtain a delay in payment.[i] "He promises to work out the debt." [13] When he promises to pay all, that is only to be regarded as "a promise given in fear and need". The king has pity on him, however, and not only lifts the order to sell him into slavery,[14] but lets him off the debt as well. "The king's goodness goes far beyond the plea of his servant." [15]

Immediately after this, so the story would have us believe, the governor accidentally meets one of his fellow-servants, who owes him 100 denarii. Jesus' listeners will have pictured him as a minor official or a tax-lessor. He must obviously be a subordinate of the governor; he is called fellow-servant because like the governor he too is a servant of the king. His creditor grasps him by his collar, so that he cannot escape. He must pay what he owes now, at once, on the spot.

The story takes great pains to picture this second scene as like the first as possible, so that the differences stand out all the more clearly. Here too the debtor is completely dependent on the will of his creditor (cf. v. 30, "but he would not"). Here too the debtor throws himself down and promises to fulfil his obligations, if he can get a delay in payment. He

[g] The parable presupposes non-Jewish legal ideas, which were probably familiar to Jesus' listeners by hearsay:

(a) The sale of the wife (Matt. 18.25) was forbidden in Jewish law. A man could only be liable for his own person and his children.

(b) There was no institution of slavery for debt in Israel.

(c) Torture (Matt. 18.34) was not allowed by Jewish law (see Jeremias, pp. 212f).

[h] Jeremias, p. 211. Yet against Jeremias I would not understand the action of the king as an expression of his anger, because the parable does not demand it, and this would conceal the fact that the king demands what at that time was lawful and usual, so that the contrast is not one of anger and grace, but of justice and grace.

[i] AV translates "and worshipped him"; the Greek word underlying this is in fact usually used in the sense of the worship of God or gods, but also describes prostration before a king. Here it is "the gesture of fervent supplication of a humiliated man" (Lohmeyer, *Matt.*, p. 279).

uses the same words as his creditor did before, with the difference that he will for certain be in a position to carry out his promise, which was unthinkable with the huge sum that the governor owes. The difference in the debt is striking, but the difference which matters most lies in the attitude of the creditor. While the king lets mercy prevail, the governor remains hard. He throws his debtor into the debtors' prison, from which he will only be released when his dependants have raised the sum of the debt, and can ransom him. He cannot sell him into slavery, because the total of the debt is a great deal lower than the price of a slave.

Full of indignation—the more obvious translation "distressed" is here unsuitable—the "fellow-servants", who are probably to be thought of as high officials, report to the king what has happened. He summons the governor to himself, reproaches him for his wrongdoing and cancels the remission of debt. He hands him over to the torturers, until he has paid all—that is, the 100 million denarii. The punishment of torture was "regularly employed in the East against a disloyal governor, or one who was tardy in his delivery of the taxes, in order to discover where they had hidden the money, or to extort the amount from their relations or friends".[j] After what has been said in v. 25 the hearer of the parable cannot receive the impression that the torture is here meant to serve as a means of extorting the sum of the debt. In view of the magnitude of the debt a full payment is inconceivable. "Till he should pay all" can therefore only mean that the punishment will never end.

The point of comparison of the parable lies in v. 33. This can easily be demonstrated. If v. 34 were the point of the parable the king's words in v. 33 would not have needed to be told. They are without significance for the course of the story, and it is quite obvious that in the way the parable is told the king's question expects no answer from the wicked servant. It is spoken as it were over the footlights, for the listeners of the parable. It is no objection to this that the last verse of a parable as a rule bears the weight. Verse 34 is the necessary completion of v. 33. It shows that the "must" was intended as the exclusive meaning of the situation, for to fail in it would have inevitable consequences. There is such a thing as "too late".[16]

The seriousness with which the words of the king are meant to be taken is shown too by the word used. Unfortunately our word

[j] Jeremias, p. 212—cf. footnote g.

"must" is much too colourless to be able to render fully what is meant here. The Greek word that it is used to translate conveys the deep solemnity of a sacred law. It is used for instance in the prophecies of the passion (Mark 8.31 and parallels). The risen Lord explains to the disciples on the way to Emmaus, "Was it not necessary that the Christ should suffer these things and enter into his glory?" (Luke 24.26). "The son of man must be lifted up", says John 3.14. "It must take place", is said of the predicted events at the end of the world (Mark 13.7). The day has come on which the passover must be sacrificed (Luke 22.7). These commandments of the law one must do and not neglect the others (Matt. 23.23). These are some examples of this usage, which could easily be multiplied.

The Meaning of the Parable

The parable compels us to agree with the verdict of the king. When we hear how the wicked servant is handed over to the torturers we think, "He is getting his deserts, he ought to have been merciful!" But the sureness with which the parable reaches its goal should not conceal from us that this agreement is far from being a matter of course. Has the wicked servant after all done anything different from what we are used to doing every day? He has taken his stand on the principle of justice, and helped himself to recover his own property according to the laws in force at the time. How can this seem so reprehensible?

The reason why it does must lie in the contrast between mercy received and unmercifulness shown. If the attitude of the wicked servant had been told without the preceding generosity of the king, it would never have evoked our protest.[k] The parable makes it become clear that this contrast is more than a mere sequence of events in time which have no inherent connection with one another. Clearly mercy is essentially not something which is granted us on a single occasion, not something which we can accept with a feeling of relief at having got away with it once more, only to let things go on again just as we used to. It appears to have the character of an ordinance, just as justice is an ordinance.

By this the parable brings to light something that is usually concealed from us. We normally assign a quite different rôle to mercy. For us it is the great exception, the possibility of giving up a claim that one can

[k] The immediate temporal sequence is unimportant. It is an artifice of the story-telling, to strengthen the effect even more.

make "by rights". To make use of this possibility is regarded as honourable and admirable—but the norm is still that one insists on one's rights. For us mercy is contained within the ordinance of justice, or it would be more correct to say within the ordinance of claims, for justice is in fact still more than claims. A claim is as it were the reverse side of justice; justice is primarily the limit that puts people in their place, and not a principle of justice on which one can take up a stand.

While the parable shows that mercy has the character of an ordinance, it so opposes mercy to the ordinance of claims that a radical opposition is forced open, and only a choice of alternatives is possible. If mercy by its nature has the character of an ordinance, it cannot be an "exception", but only the "norm". In this case it is obvious that everything that now diverges from this norm cannot be an admissible exception, but can only be a failure. Here mercy is not put at our discretion as one possibility among others, but meets us as a demand.[1] This certainly does not mean that there is no longer any such thing as justice. But it does mean that there can be such a thing as "my rights" only so far as mercy permits it. The limit of this permission is not drawn by a principle, but by the needs of one's neighbour. Otherwise it would no longer make sense to talk of mercy. The behaviour of the wicked servant can appear to us to be as reprehensible as it does only because the parable introduces us to a way of looking at things that fits the ordinance of mercy. But how is it possible for us to engage in this way of thinking involuntarily, although we are used to keeping to the ordinance of claims? Someone to whom I put this question answered: "This ordinance is natural, as natural as the sun and the earth, as birds or trees!"

Can it be that the original ordering of reality becomes visible here?[m]

Our assent to the parable means that we have fallen into contradiction with ourselves. But the parable not only makes this contradiction obvious, it can also help us to overcome it. The meaning of Jesus' words is: We should risk our lives on the ordinance of mercy.[n]

---

[1] Only in this context does it make sense to talk of a *commandment* of love!

[m] Those who are used to it and feel they can, may speak here of creation by God. But no one is compelled to do so, and no one may be compelled to do so. The words do not matter; the reality appears of itself, and every word that conceals this appearing is a pernicious hindrance to the faith of my brother, which cannot be defended.

[n] At this point an objection from historical exposition would be possible. It is true that Jesus' parable did not first of all have this general sense. Jesus uttered the parable in argument with his contemporaries, and it refers to a particular indi-

There is the truth, in front of us—this we have admitted ourselves by our involuntary agreement. Now we must afterwards match this truth with our lives—or we should have to give up the truth for our lives. After the word of Jesus has reached us, we cannot leave everything as it was and still think everything is in order.

Now here it is important to clear a misunderstanding out of the way. To venture on the way of mercy does not mean to erect a law over oneself that demands, "Thou shalt be merciful, thou shalt forgive, etc." It means rather to commit oneself to the belief that reality matches this ordinance, although appearances seem to suggest that the opposite is true. It means to question reality on whether it does not itself point a way for mercy in the place where it is needed, a way that is a way of life for the merciful, not only a list of prohibitions. Forgiveness for instance here means something other than "saying no more about it", or as it is so nicely put, "letting the grass grow over it". It means the confidence that for the other man and for me a common future is possible.

Only experience can show that mercy is the way the world is ordered, and I can get this experience only if I commit myself to it. "If you would believe", we read, "you would see the wonders of God."

But experience is never unequivocal, and not till the end will it be shown what the meaning of reality was. Faith must be risked. But it may and can be risked, because the words of Jesus have prevailed on us as the truth. We have in fact no choice, for how could we live in untruth! We are in the position of Peter, who declares, "Lord, to whom shall we go? You have the words of eternal life" (John 6.68).

vidual case, in which Jesus and his listeners were basically of a different mind. This situation has not been passed down to us. On the strength of the parable, however, we may assume that Jesus' listeners were willing to (or already in the act of) conducting themselves in relation to fellow men who needed their mercy by the ordinance of claims, according to their custom. If Jesus' listeners let themselves be moved by the parable to respond to the truth, then meanwhile more had happened to them than that their attitude had altered in a particular single case. A life opened up for them under the ordinance of mercy, a new life, which was unmistakably different from life under the ordinance of claims. And to this extent we are justified in the exposition given above.[17] To say that the word of Jesus, spoken in a long-forgotten moment to long dead and forgotten listeners, concerns us too, rests on no other presupposition than that the truth apprehended by the parable convinces us too. When, however, we venture in faith to accept this truth, Jesus becomes for us "the faithful witness" (Rev. 1.5) and we move on to the praise of Jesus. But this is the consequence, and must not be smuggled in as a presupposition.

9

The Parable of the Sower and its Interpretation

MARK 4.1–9,14–20

The Framework

The parable of the sower is told by each of the three synoptic gospels. We will confine ourselves to the Marcan version, which may for good reasons be regarded as the oldest.[a]

The parable is preceded in v. 1 by a description of the scene. It is not an historical report, with the intention of telling us on what occasion Jesus uttered the parable. It is a "symbolical" scene, created by the Evangelist, pregnant with theological utterance.[b] It is one of the pictures that faith paints of Jesus to show how it sees him.[c] The Evangelist shows Jesus as the teacher to whom the whole people flocks to hear his saving teaching. He expresses the size of the crowd that presses in on Jesus, by having Jesus compelled to get into a boat. Jesus' authority is seen when it says that he *sits* on the boat. For this is appropriate to a teacher, while the listening multitude remains on the shore—standing, as Matthew makes clear. As already said, here the significance of Jesus is being portrayed, and not the historical situation reported in which Jesus told the parable. Verse 2 also is still a part of the framework, and gives the connection between the elements from tradition in the chapter.[1]

The demand, "Listen", which introduces the parable does not only mean listening with physical ears, as is clear from v. 9; and the word "see" is not used to call on the imagination. This usage, which is

---

[a] We can omit a comparison of the synoptic parallels, because we are inquiring into the original meaning of the parable. For this question the parallel texts are no help. They can only tell us about the history of the interpretation of this parable in early Christianity.

[b] Cf. above, pp. 43ff.

[c] Cf. above, pp. 34f.

frequent in the Old and New Testaments, means nothing more than a full colon. It indicates, "Here it comes"!

The Parable

Though the parable mentions the sower first, he does not stand at the centre of the story.[d2] The words, "a sower went out to sow", are a sort of introduction to the story. The real course of the story begins with, "and it happened". We could not understand it if we did not have some knowledge of the peculiarities of Palestinian farming. After the harvest in June a field is left as it is until the sowing time in November or December. Even if it is ploughed soon after the harvest once or several times—though this by no means always happens— it is never ploughed immediately before the sowing.[3] "The whole summer has gone by over it, the stubble", if it has not been ploughed in, "has been grazed bare or destroyed by the sun and the wind, here and there thorny summer plants, various kinds of thistles, have grown and withered again, so that they now stand there, parched and tough as wood. If there are many of them, they will perhaps be burned. If they are only found sporadically, one knows that the plough will turn them over and cover them."[4] The field is divided into strips for sowing, and as soon as the sower has scattered the seed out of the sowing-cloth hung about him, or out of his outer garment, which is gathered up high, in a wide swing over one of the strips, it is ploughed in, "so that the interval between sowing and ploughing does not become too long".[e] Often, apart from the sower, a ploughman is at work in the same field. If they tried to sow the field as a whole, the birds would not leave much of the seed over. But what has unavoidably fallen on the thin path which winds through the field, in spite of all the care of the sower, is certain to become their prey. It would be pointless to plough the path. It is trodden hard, and by prescriptive right it would very soon be trodden out again in the same place by men and beasts of burden.[5]

It is a peculiarity of the Palestinian hill-country, and also of the region of Capernaum in Galilee, that the rocky substratum reaches up almost to the surface of the field, and in places is only covered by a thin crust of earth. Such places are not easily recognized—at least in an

[d] Any more than the "rich man" mentioned in the parable of the unjust steward in Luke 16.1 is the central figure in it.
[e] Dalman, *PJ*, p. 121. Harrowing in the seed is unknown in Palestine.

E

unploughed field—and since in any case they are only small, they can hardly be left out in sowing. The seed that falls on them springs up especially quickly, either because "the thin topsoil is completely saturated by the strong rain-like dew of Palestine"[6] or because it is warmed right through by the sun.[7] Perhaps it is also dependent on the plants having no deep layer to force themselves through,[8] and being able to develop in only one direction, upwards, into the stalk.[9] But as soon as it pushes up it is already all over for such a plant. The story seems to suggest that even the sun of the first morning after the sowing scorches it, so that it withers away. But this can hardly be true. It is a sign of a graphic narrative style, which is not concerned with the passing of time.

The sun in this land really has a devastating strength—even in the early morning—and the choice of the word "scorched" in the original text is fully justified. "One can picture that the hot sun, the dry air and the want of nightly dew on the East wind days of April and May must bring a particularly quick end to the life of these plants, which in their isolation are completely unshaded. Leaf and stalk stand there, first yellow, then white, and the ear is missing."[10]

It fares little better for the seed that falls under the thorns—the word is here a comprehensive expression for all sorts of thorny weeds. They are "often huge plants, up to six feet tall, with beautiful yellow, red, or blue flowers."[11] "The falling of the seed on the thistles, which only later spring up, indicates that the thistles have sown themselves in this spot. They are invisible. One could, however, in Palestine also picture the situation as being that thistles and thorny plants were now visible . . . ; during the summer thistles have in places shot upwards, and now the seed falls among them. Ploughing of course turns the surface of the earth. But the thistle seeds and the roots of perennial thorny plants remain in it, and are awoken to new life by the winter rain that soaks into the earth, just as is the wheat seed. Here the wide-spreading thorny plants have the advantage."[12] Slowly they deprive the stalks of wheat completely of food and light, and even if they manage to grow, they will no longer succeed in bearing fruit.

So in each sowing seed gets lost in various ways. Of course it is only a little, for "he would indeed be a strange sower who sowed so carelessly that the bulk, or even the half, or even, in fact, any considerable portion of the seed, fell on unprofitable soil."[f]

[f] C. W. F. Smith, p. 63. Though the description of the causes which stop part of the seed from bearing fruit occupies three times as much space in the story as

The rest, that fell on good ground, bears "thirtyfold, sixtyfold, and a hundredfold." It is not the yield of the whole field that is meant here—this is calculated after the threshing from the proportion of seed to harvest—but the fruit produced by the individual grain.[13] In that country each ear bears thirty-five seeds on the average, but up to sixty are often counted and occasionally even a hundred on one ear.[14]

The Interpretation

The parable of the sower had already had quite a long history before Mark took it into his Gospel, and however faithfully its actual language has been passed down to us, through a long oral and written tradition, its original meaning has in the process been lost.[15] We can no longer ~~- Dodd~~ discover on what occasion Jesus uttered it and what he meant to convey by it. The Gospel-writers and the men who transmitted it were not historians. They were not concerned to establish what Jesus had said once for a particular reason at a particular moment, but passed on his words because they found in them an answer to their own questions. But if the original meaning can no longer be ascertained, we can still ~~+ Jeremias~~ discover how the early Church understood this parable.

When the earliest Church proclaimed the joyful gospel of the resurrection of Jesus, it made the perplexing and distressing discovery that only a few will believe the message. The others pass by heedlessly what for us is the great gift of God. This experience did not indeed make them doubt their faith, but it raised what was for them a great and burning question. How could it happen that in this matter, which concerns all men alike, such a difference, such a very deep gulf exists between us and the others? They found an answer in the words of the parable. The answer ran: Do not be dismayed by this experience, it

the description of the success of the harvest, no one hearing the parable who was familiar with farming could think of connecting the proportion of three to one with the *quantity* of fruit-producing seed. Since the parable does not mention this good land till the end, it lays the stress on the success of the sowing, not on its failure.

The concrete description of several causes which can prevent a grain of seed from bearing fruit is obviously likely to strengthen the impression that it was natural and obvious that not every grain should ripen to harvest. The power of the parable as an argument lies precisely in the obviousness that the events described must have had for the listeners. Those occasions which cause disturbance and give anxiety to the listeners (or awaken their mistrust), are meant to appear to them in the light of the parable as something that must naturally so happen.

cannot in fact be otherwise. Just see what happens when the sower scatters his seed. It is not every grain that bears fruit. Much is lost for one reason or another.[g]

Once this understanding had been kindled by the parable, it was noticed that it not only illuminates the question as a whole, but also throws light on many individual points.[h] [16]

Just as it is with the seed which is sown on the path, which the birds pick away, without it even reaching the earth, so it seems to be with many men. The word of the preaching does not enter them. It is as if they had never heard it, as if already at the moment they receive it with their ears the devil were tearing the words out of their hearts.

But there is enough, too, of the luxuriant growth, which in the end bears no fruit. Many men are ready enough to receive the Gospel, but they have no persistence. It does not go deep enough with them. It grows without resistance, and has therefore not grown up equal to any resistance.

Like the seed sown under the thorns is the word with those who hear, but are so full of cares and desires that the word loses its effectiveness.

As with the seed on the good land, however, so it is with those who hear the word, receive it, and bring forth fruit.[i]

It is noteworthy how very much the whole interpretation of the parable remains "in the picture", precisely as if the outline were being

---

[g] In 2 Esdras 8.41, which was written about the end of the first century A.D., a similar thought is connected with the image of sowing: "For just as the farmer sows many seeds upon the ground and plants a multitude of seedlings, and yet not all that have been sown will come up in due season, and not all that were planted will take root; so also those who have been sown in the world will not all be saved."

[h] The interpretation of the parable of the sower (Mark 4.14–20) came into existence first in the primitive Church (cf. n. 16); it does not go back to Jesus. Nor correspondingly do verses 10–13 give the situation in which this interpretation was spoken. This permits us to pass by these verses in our exposition. They are burdened with difficult exegetical problems, and if we wished to go into them more closely we should have to take our investigation far beyond the task of exposition of individual pericopes which we have set ourselves. We can only say here that Jesus' parables are not veiled riddles, which needed subsequent decoding (cf. v. 34). What we find in vv. 10ff is a theological conception of the Evangelist.

[i] It should not cause surprise that the interpretation of Mark 4.14ff does not make comparisons, but says, "These *are* those on the way", or that men are at one time compared to the seed, at another to the ground. This is the abbreviated, inexact oriental way of saying it. More explicitly it would have to be put: "Just as it happens when the seed . . . it is the case with men, who . . .".

retraced. It is said of men that they "have no root", and "bear fruit" is left as a metaphor. The blaze of the sun suggests the thought of affliction and persecution (cf. 1 Pet. 4.12). In our language too we can still talk of "the heat being on". Like thorns and thistles, cares and desires leave room for nothing else. They fill a man completely.

But now we have to reflect that with man, unlike grains of wheat, it is not only the mass that matters, but the individual. The realization, "not all bears fruit", becomes the anxious knowledge that a man can fail in his life, and forces him to ask, "How does it stand with me?"

This question is not answered by my knowing to which group I belong. The only answer it can obtain is if at the end of my life it can be said, "It bore fruit".

But such fruit-bearing does not consist of any specific thing. It is not an achievement nor something we bequeath to those that come after.[1] It means that the life of a man has become what it ought to be. But this can happen, our passage says, only when the "word", the Gospel of Jesus Christ, is heard and received.

10

The Unjust Judge

LUKE 18.1–8

The Judge and the Widow

The leading characters in the parable are an unscrupulous judge and an unprotected widow.

The judge, although he ought to pronounce justice in the name of God (2 Chron. 19.6ff), does not fear God, nor is he restrained by any regard for men. He is called the "unjust" judge, because he is the exact opposite of a righteous man. We should go wrong if we took the

---

[1] It is to be noticed that the text keeps the metaphor here. Nor is the fruit-bearing made more precise, in the ways we find this done in the Old Testament: "fruit of repentance, fruit of righteousness", etc.

word only to refer to his deficient sense of justice. It expresses much the same as "godless" or "impious".[1]

The widow, without a husband to protect her, often in want, belonged together with the orphan to the "socially weak". Their helpless position was very often shamelessly exploited. For that reason it was regarded as the chief duty of the judge to give justice to widows and orphans. But what can a poor widow hope for if "the judge is an unjust man, who is not bothered if she has to suffer injustice"?[2]

The widow comes to the judge with the request that he should help her to justice against her opponents. Obviously it was a money matter, because this was the only sort of case that an individual judge could decide on his own. "A debt, a pledge, or a portion of an inheritance, is being withheld from her."[3] The justice of the case is apparently so clear that the widow will be quite certain to get her rights if only she can get a hearing.[4] But it lies within the power of the judge to fix whatever date he likes for the trial. "And an experienced legal expert even then still had many possible ways of postponing a case that was inconvenient to himself."[5]

The Victory of Persistence

The only means that the widow can employ is her persistence. Again and again she goes to him and begs him: "Give me justice." The Greek of v. 3 clearly implies that she keeps on coming.[6]

So much persistence in the end becomes too much for the judge. He decides to give in. It is very important to the narrator to show that it is her persistence alone that leads to his change of mind, and that all other motives are excluded. For this reason he lets the judge in the soliloquy of v. 4 pick up the characterization of v. 2.[7] Many translations give the impression that besides this the fear of acts of violence by the desperate woman brings the judge to this step. This, however, is probably a mistranslation, which spoils the conclusiveness of the parable.[8] It should be translated: Though I do not fear even God, and do not dread any man—because this widow is pestering me I will give her justice, "so that she does not keep on coming whining to me" "It is not the fear of an outburst of rage on the part of the woman that makes him give way, but her persistence. He is tired of her perpetual nagging and wants to be left in peace."[9] Verse 5b is meant to illustrate what the trouble is that the judge wants to avoid, so that this point, which is particularly important for the parable, may be brought out clearly. A very strong expression is intentionally used, which could easily mislead the translators into taking it literally.[10] The words that most translators render by "at last", "in the end", can just as well mean "for ever", a usage for which there are many parallels.[11]

The Interpretation of the Parable

The Lord's demand, "Hear what the unjust judge says", moves the listeners away from the story to its meaning, and lets the words of the figure in the parable become a transparent expression of what is meant to be said through the parable.[a] Verse 7 draws from it the conclusion, "If even so unjust a judge gives in to the obstinacy of a woman to whom he is indifferent, how much more will the righteous God listen to his elect . . . who cry to him incessantly!"[12] The first question of the verse is formulated in the Greek in such a way that only one answer is possible.[b] The listener is not expected to give the answer to this question himself.[13] The speaker gives it himself with his, "But I say to you". This answer does not rest, as it seems to, just on the authority of the Lord; it is borne fully and completely by the parable. It rests on the contrast between the unjust judge, who puts off the case of the defenceless widow unduly long, and God who is just. If persistence can defeat even a godless judge, how much more must an answer be granted it by God. This "how much more" is the basis of the "soon".

The Parable and its Audience

In the parable of the unjust judge we are certainly not dealing with a parable of the "historical Jesus", but with a word of the ascended Lord, that is, a prophetic word that was spoken in the name and spirit of Jesus to the community of believers.[14]

The parable is a saying that is spoken from faith and intends to restore the confidence of faith. It is directed to a Church that is suffering under oppression and persecution, whose situation is like that of the widow. The only thing that lies in the power of the disciples is to pray. "No one can reveal that they are right except their Lord alone. He

[a] It "is parallel to 'he who has ears to hear, let him hear!', 8.8; 14.35." (Jülicher, p. 284).

[b] This is correctly rendered in the RSV: "And will not God vindicate his elect, who cry to him day and night? Will he delay long over them?"

alone can give proof of the truth of what they say when he reveals himself, and he alone has the power to give them what they hope for, by leading them into his kingdom."[15] This Church looks longingly for the day on which God will vindicate it against its oppressors and come to its help. It cries day and night to God: O Lord, help us, and let thy day of judgement come!

Early Christianity shared with its Jewish contemporaries and the apocalyptic sects the expectation of the end of the world. Jesus had proclaimed that the kingdom of God was in process of arriving. The faith of his Church, that God has raised up this Jesus (Acts 2.22–4) and made him Lord and Christ (Acts 2.36), that the really decisive event has already happened, was expressed at first in the expectation that now the fulfilment of all the promises must soon be seen, until increasingly it found a new language more its own.

The character of this language of faith cannot be missed in our parable too. Persecution and troubles must have made the expectation still more fervent; but as one day followed another, a doubt could gnaw at the heart, will the day of the Lord never come? It was a scarcely admitted, anxious question, because those who asked it did not cease to cry to God. It is in this situation that the joyful certainty of the parable belongs. With the help of the image of the godless judge it conjures up the father-like counter-image of God, which is of course not new to the listeners, so that they can grasp again the courage of faith. If so much persistence forced the judge to give in, they too can be certain of being granted their petitions for their persistence in prayer. It is not that God's will first has to be overcome; rather that God, who is ready to listen to the prayer of his elect, will not, like that judge, keep them waiting for his help. He will soon give them their right.[16]

An Unfulfilled Promise?

It could be said that the narrator promised something that has not been fulfilled, that the parable is an unfulfilled promise. But in that case has faith been deceived of its fulfilment? Has it been cast away by him on whom it cast itself? Was the courage with which it went ahead into the future mistaken, because the future turned out differently from the way in which faith had represented it? Only faith itself has the right to answer these questions.

But faith dares to repeat in the name of Jesus what the unknown narrator of the parable did. When faced with what disheartens us, it dares to recall us in the name of Jesus to the courage of faith, in trust upon God.

The History of the Text

The parable later had a question added on in 8b which was meant as a warning: Will the Son of Man, the Christ, when he appears "on his day" (Luke 17.24, cf. also vv. 20–37), revealed "in his glory" (Luke 21.27), still find faith on earth? [17]

This probably does not mean, "Will Christians still exist then?" Nor is it likely that the word "faith" is meant to suggest the idea of the firm hope that God will do justice for his elect. Rather we shall be reminded by this verse of 2 Tim. 4.7, "I have fought the good fight, I have finished the race, I have kept the faith", and of the warning that in the oppressions before the end of the world many will fall away (cf. Mark 13.22). In the context of the parable the question in 8b means, "God will not fail, but how does it stand with you?"

Next, Luke with his introduction in v. 1 gave his own interpretation of the parable. [18] The exhortation "always" to pray does not mean that one should stay at prayer day and night without a break, but is a call not to weary in prayer even when we are kept waiting a long time for our prayer to be granted. [19] Probably Luke is here thinking primarily of prayer for the coming of the kingdom of God, for he makes the parable follow the sayings about the day of the Son of Man (17.22–37). [20]

The stresses of the parable have shifted for Luke. This was almost inevitable, as soon as it lost its connection with its original situation. Perseverance in prayer was originally so bound up with its sure success that present perseverance was a pledge of the certainty of the prayer being granted. Now, however, an exhortation was given to perseverance in prayer because it was bound to have success, as the example would show. The parable admits of both possibilities of application. Only we must not be led astray by the generalization of v. 1 to make a neat and logical sum out of it. One cannot reckon up before God the total of one's prayers, and conclude from it that it is time for them to be granted. God is not a slot-machine in which one only needs to insert the coin of persistent prayer to get what is wanted! The declaration that the parable makes about the granting of persistent prayer is true only when it is repeated as a promise, that is when it is spoken responsibly as an exhortation or a consolation, and where a faith answers it which, on the strength of what is said, relies against all appearances on God.

11

The Parable of the Wise and Foolish Virgins

MATT. 25.1–13

The Parable Narrative

. . . ten Virgins, who took their Lamps . . . The parable tells of some virgins who set out with lanterns to escort the bridegroom with a festal procession and conduct him to the wedding house. Ten are mentioned: this is a favourite round number to describe a fair-sized group of people. They set out and then wait on the road along which the bridegroom has to come.

Is he coming with his friends from his parents' house to the bride's house to hold the wedding there? This was not the rule, but it could happen. Or has the bride already been escorted to his parents' home, or to his own, and does he have to wait outside until he is led ceremoniously to the bridal chamber? This too is conceivable. Our knowledge of the wedding customs of the time is not sufficient to give a clear answer to this question.[1] Moreover, there are grounds for the assumption that the narrator is not starting from a well-established custom at all, but to suit his purposes has put together individual features that were a part of the image of every wedding, to make a course of events that could happen, even though it was not the rule.[2]

The storm-lamps with which the ten virgins set out to provide the bridegroom with an escort were oil-lamps. The wick was drawn through a ring or spout, and burnt as long as the oil in the lamp lasted, just like our own paraffin-lamps.

. . . Five of them were Foolish The precise proportion of one to one is not important to the story: the numbers are brought in only to express graphically the division into two groups. The wisdom of the wise consists just in their bringing with them another jug with oil to refill their lamps, and the folly of the foolish consists just in their ignoring this precaution. This is clearer in the original text than in the AV, but is brought out in the RSV.[a]

The verdict of v.2 is explained in v. 3. So it has nothing to do with intelligence and stupidity. The original meaning of the word that we translate "wise" is "to keep the eyes open".[3] The wise were "sharp", they grasped what mattered at this moment. They allowed for the possibility that the bridegroom might come late. In fact the whole story depends on this delay of the bridegroom.

. . . the bridegroom delayed . . . The bridegroom keeps them waiting; the story illustrates how long by the fact that all the virgins become sleepy and finally fall asleep. They leave their lamps burning meanwhile, "since if the bridegroom comes unexpectedly it is not easy to kindle the lamps in a hurry".[4] Kindling a flame, before matches had been invented, was a laborious and lengthy process. At a later hour, about midnight, they are woken by a loud cry: "The bridegroom is coming." They stand up and make their lamps ready. "They snuff the lamps, removing the burnt wick", and the wise ones "fill them with oil, so that they may burn brightly again".[4] But the foolish now discover that their lamps are just going out. The oil in them has been burnt up during the long wait, which they had not allowed for.

Their omission cannot be made good. The careful ones rightly refuse to give up some of their store of oil. There could not be enough for all, and the wedding procession would end in shame and disgrace if the lights went out too soon. The suggestion of going to the shopkeeper "is not meant ironically; in fact the foolish virgins act on it".[5] But it serves the dramatic flow of the narrative. At the decisive moment the foolish ones are not there—so it becomes clear that they have excluded themselves from great joy through their own folly.

. . . I do not know you! The bridegroom refuses admission to the wedding hall to the virgins who missed the procession through their

---

[a] "For when the foolish took their lamps, they took no oil with them; but the wise took flasks of oil with their lamps" (RSV).

folly. They have forfeited their right to take part in the feast, because they did not fulfil their duty as bridesmaids.[b]

The words, "I do not know you", must be understood in the sense, "I do not want to know you", i.e., "I do not want to have anything to do with you."[c]

The solemn tone of the refusal goes far beyond the occasion for it and makes it clear that v. 12 is the key verse of the parable. It still belongs to the "picture part", but points ahead to the "reality part" (cf. Matt. 18.13; Luke 11.8; 14.24; 18.14).[6]

The Parable and its Audience

The parable of the wise and foolish virgins is certainly a creation of the early Church. A Christian prophet or teacher unknown to us uttered it in the name and in the spirit of Jesus. If we are to understand it rightly, we must picture the situation in which the Church was addressed through this parable, and heard it as a saying of its exalted Lord, so that it could henceforth include it among the sayings that Jesus had uttered in his lifetime.[7]

The early Church shared with late Judaism the expectation of the end of the world. But for the Church the end of the world meant not only that it would be shown that God has the last word in everything that happens in our lives and in the world, that the ancient promises of God would find fulfilment, and that all godless existence would come to an end in the judgement of God. For the Church it meant also the day on which Jesus would be revealed in his majesty as the Christ, the "Son of Man", as Lord of the world and saviour of those who believe. The faith that God had raised this Jesus and made him the Christ, and that in this the decisive event had already happened, was expressed in the expectation that the day was near on which Jesus would come again as "Son of Man", as judge of the world.[d]

This expectation was the expression of this faith, the historical form

[b] Possibly we should picture the situation as being that the girls had not been entrusted with the rôle of bridesmaids by the bridegroom or bride or their respective families, and so invited to the wedding, but had taken on this position of honour on their own initiative, to get themselves an invitation to the wedding by this means. (See Burkitt, p. 269.)

[c] The Jewish scribe, for example, used these words for the reproof "forbidding his scholar access to him for seven days" (Jeremias, p. 175).

[d] Cf. Matt. 10.23; Mark 13.30, cf. 9.1; Luke 18.7; Matt. 24.30f; 24.37–41; 25.31f.

of it, but it was not the faith itself. This is shown best by the fact that this faith was not lost as day by day, year by year went by and the expected end of the world did not come. It learnt to understand and express what was important for it in other terms. It had to free itself from the expectation in which it originally took shape.

The parable of the ten virgins belongs to one stage in this history of faith. The attempt artificially to preserve the expectation of the return of Christ in its original high tension is met here with the objection that it is foolish not to reckon with a longer waiting period. True readiness for the Lord does not mean holding fast to the expectation that he must come "shortly", but it means prudently taking into consideration the possibility that he "delays".

For the narrator who addressed his Church with this parable in the name of Jesus, the material for his imagery lay ready to hand. The wedding was familiar to him and his hearers as an image of the bliss of the end. If the Church expected the coming of its Lord, that would easily suggest the coming of the bridegroom, and the thought that the return of Christ was keeping them waiting would suggest the delay of the bridegroom. But these points of contact between parable and reality do not mean that we are dealing with an allegory. The narrator has used them only to secure the connection of the parable with the situation. The narrative is completely independent, and so planned that the listener is compelled to agree with the verdict of v. 2, that those who thought it superfluous to prepare themselves for a lengthy period of waiting were foolish. They are rightly excluded from the joy of the feast. The allusions to the reality ensure only that the claim of this verdict to hold good in the reality too is immediately granted.[8]

The Framework of the Parable

The parable is introduced by the formula: "The kingdom of Heaven is like . . .". This introduction is not to be taken literally. The kingdom of Heaven is not compared with the virgins; what it means is: "With reference to the kingdom of Heaven, the case is as in this story of the ten virgins".[e] When the Evangelist says "then",[9] he is referring back to the previous chapter (cf. 24.30f, 39ff, 44, 50); when the Son of Man comes these will "enter into the joy of their Lord", and the others will have to admit that they have excluded themselves by their own foolishness.

e Cf. above, pp. 16f.

It is possible that the introductory formula is also an explanatory "Matthean addition".[10]

At the end of the parable we find for an application[f] the exhortation: "Watch therefore, for you know neither the day nor the hour, in which [so the later manuscripts explain it] the Son of Man comes." This application does not come from the narrator of the parable; it is a later explanation of the passage. Does it fit the meaning of the parable? We need not wonder that in v. 13 wakefulness is demanded, while according to v. 5 all the virgins are asleep. The word has here the transferred sense of "preparedness". The parable speaks of preparedness; but this general exhortation only renders incompletely what the parable is trying to say. It does not make us realize that real readiness should consist precisely in taking into account a lengthy period of waiting. The generalization certainly gives the passage a timeless meaning, but it does not in the last analysis render it correctly, or express fully its intention.[11] If, however, we listen to the passage as it ties in with its unique historical situation, it contains for us the promise that faith is not shattered by changes in its historical situation, and that the word, which makes it possible for it to remain faith, comes to its help again and again.[g] The passage, which denies us any general truth that we can take hold of, refers us back thereby to the living God.

[f] Cf. above, pp. 17f.

[g] "Theologically it becomes clear in the case of this passage too that the Word of Jesus to his Church can never be limited to the *ipsissima verba* [the words quite certainly spoken by Jesus himself, i.e. "genuine" sayings] of the historical Jesus, but includes the word of the exalted Lord, uttered to meet each new situation. What critical research has described in the history of the tradition as 'inauthentic' or 'a creation of the Church' acquires in this way a strongly positive sense." (Bornkamm, "Verzögerung", p. 126; my additions in brackets.)

Notes

The Basic Principles of
Parable Interpretation

1. The "classification of the parables according to categories" should not be described as "a fruitless labour" on the ground that the Hebrew *mashal* and the Aramaic *mathla* include "figurative forms of speech of every kind" (Jeremias, p. 20). For although the concept *mashal* includes a rich variety of meanings, in each individual occurrence it is used throughout in a single sense. As Eissfeldt (*Der Maschal im AT*, BZAW 24, 1913) has observed, "it is not a general concept under which the individual *genera* are brought together. *Mashal* is a technical term now for one type, now for another" (p. 33).

Jülicher has often been criticized for applying the categories of Greek rhetoric to the parables. This criticism would be justified only if he had done violence to the material through his classification of the parables (it is only the classification that comes into consideration here—this needs to be said against Jüngel, p. 95, n. 1) and clothed it in a scheme foreign to its real nature. But the differences between the individual forms of parable discourse are quite obvious in the parables of the New Testament. Jülicher has merely applied to the material the categories needed to understand the differences which are there in conceptual terms.

Though there can be hesitation in individual cases in which category a particular passage should be placed, this does not eliminate the differences in principle (cf. Bultmann, *HST*, p. 174).

2. Bultmann, *HST*, p. 174.
3. Jülicher, I, p. 93.
4. Jülicher, I, pp. 97f. Words in Greek have been translated, and the word fable has been replaced by parable in order not to introduce yet another new idea. This is justifiable because Jülicher says, "The majority of the *parabolai* of Jesus which are in narrative form are fables" (I, p. 98), and so himself makes the equation of fable and parable.
5. Cf. Jülicher, II, p. 585.
6. Weinel, p. 2.
7. Fuchs, *Hermeneutik*, p. 212.
8. Ibid., p. 213.
9. Bultmann, *HST*, pp. 188–92, a little abbreviated. Greek words and unfamiliar foreign words have been translated and some references supplied in brackets. (One or two alterations or corrections of the English translation have been made. Tr.)
10. Jeremias, p. 102.
11. Ibid., p. 102.

12. Eichholz takes a similar view: "The person addressed . . . belongs . . . to the structure of the parable" ("Das Gleichnis als Spiel", p. 319).
13. Billerbeck, I, p. 654. Additions in brackets are by me.
14. Ibid., p. 878.
15. A full and literal version of the text, which has here been rendered very freely, and heavily abbreviated, is given with a list of references in Fiebig, *Gleichnisreden Jesu*, pp. 10f.
16. A.Z.54b; Bultmann, *HST*, p. 43.
17. Livy, *History of Rome*, translated from the version in *Römische Prosaiker in Neuen Übersetzungen*, vol. 2, Stuttgart, 1926, pp. 176f, by C. F. Klaiber, ed. G. L. F. Tafel, C. N. Osiander, and G. Schwab.
18. Fiebig, *Die Gleichnisreden Jesu*, p. 11.
19. Cf. Fuchs, *Hermeneutik*, §6: "Das Problem der Wirklichkeit und die Sprache".
20. The proof of this has been given by Madsen.
21. Heidegger, *Unterwegs zur Sprache*, pp. 20 and 33.
22. Bornkamm, *Jesus*, p. 65.
23. Ibid., pp. 65–6.
24. Ibid., p. 67.
25. Ibid., p. 67.
26. The tension between the sayings of Jesus which proclaim the arrival of the kingdom of God and those which assume it as future cannot be removed by ignoring one of the two groups of sayings or declaring it unauthentic, or by trying to divest the sayings of their temporal character. This no longer needs to be proved expressly (see on this Kümmel, *PF*, throughout).

It must, however, be made clear that this tension is no better removed by arguing that Jesus expected the kingdom of God in the immediate future, so that present and future are connected as coming and fulfilment. There is admittedly almost a general consensus in favour of this assumption of a "near expectation" in the thought of Jesus. It is reckoned one of the "assured results of Biblical criticism" that Jesus expected "the kingdom in the future, and in fact in the very near future" (Grässer). An examination of the passages cited in support of the "near expectation" seems to me, however, to show that this assumption has no adequate support in them. In my opinion there is not one saying of Jesus that speaks expressly of the nearness of the kingdom of God the authenticity of which is not at least disputed.

Mark 1.15 and parallels are generally regarded as a secondary summary of the preaching of Jesus. Whether it is an appropriate summary can be settled only after a comparison with genuine sayings of Jesus.

Matt. 10.7 is not an independent logion and cannot be detached from its context (which is generally regarded as secondary). Though Jesus according to this saying gives the disciples the same Gospel that he is preaching himself, this repetition is still no evidence that the early Church, which formulated both sayings, was rendering Jesus' Gospel correctly. This is all the more true since tendencies can be demonstrated which *necessarily* led to the obscuring in the tradition of the knowledge that Jesus preached that the kingdom was already arriving (see Otto, *Kingdom*, pp. 150ff).

Mark 9.1 is treated as a "community formula of consolation in view of the delay of the Parousia" by Bultmann (*HST*, p. 121), Fuchs (*Aufsätze*, II, p. 67), Bornkamm ("Verzögerung", pp. 116 ff), Conzelmann (*TSL*, p. 104), Percy (p. 172), Grässer (pp. 131ff), against Kümmel (*PF*, pp. 25–8). "The usual argument, that it cannot be a community creation, as the non-fulfilment of this prophecy would give rise to difficulties, is a strange one" (Conzelmann, *TSL*, p. 104, n. 1). For, to put this more fully, whoever uttered such a consolation-saying to the Church in the name of the ascended Lord was counting on its fulfilment, and therefore could not possibly be thinking about the difficulties which would result from its non-fulfilment.

Mark 13.30 cannot "be separated from its context as an isolated saying" (Grässer, p. 129), because the verse is incomplete. It says nothing about what the *tauta panta* refer to.

It is of course possible that the verse lost its complete wording when it was inserted into its context; but this cannot be proved. The verse could just as well have been created from the start (incomplete) for the context. It is not shown to be an independent saying by the *amēn legō hymīn* (against Kümmel *PF*, p. 59, cf. Matt. 8.10; 10.15; 13.17; 18.13; 21.31; 23.36; 24.2; 24.47; 25.12; 26.13; 26.21).

If nevertheless the verse is claimed to be an independent saying just as it stands, it must be admitted that the original sense remains obscure. To connect the *tauta panta* of an isolated saying with the events of the last days is not the "nearest course to hand" (Grässer, p. 129), but is exegetical caprice. A reference to eschatology is not ensured by the *panta*! (against Kümmel, *PF*, p. 60).

It is only in its context that Mark 13.30 predicts "that the end will come during the lifetime of the present generation" (Kümmel, *PF*, p. 60). But the context does not vouch for the verse as an original saying of Jesus. Its connection with the parable of the fig-tree is secondary (Bultmann, *HST*, p. 123; Kümmel, *PF*, pp. 59–60; Grässer, p. 129), and an original connection with v. 27 would mean that Mark 13.30 was "the original conclusion of the Jewish apocalypse" (Bultmann, ibid.).

So Mark 13.30 does not provide a proof for the "near expectation" of Jesus.

Matt. 10.23: We must first of all ask whether this logion is a unity, or whether 23b originally stood on its own, as Kümmel (*PF*, pp. 61–4) assumes.

1. Kümmel's arguments are: (a) "*telesēte* can hardly signify 'to come to the end of anything'; it connotes the completion of a task ('to bring to an end, to discharge', cf. Luke 12.50)" (p. 62).

(b) 10.23b also was not originally connected with 10.24f.

On (a): Kümmel fails to give any evidence for this view, which is not shared by e.g. Bauer, *Greek-English Lexicon of the NT* s.v. (Grässer does not give this evidence either, although he considerably increases the number of passages for comparison. If the word means to "accomplish", or "conclude", in many places, this is not to say that another meaning is impossible.)

On (b): from this it certainly follows that v. 23 is an independent saying, but not that 23b is.

Even if it were assumed that Matt. 10.23b was originally independent, its meaning would have to be left completely open. Kümmel has no justification

for connecting *telesēte* with the "completion of the missionary task", because the context cannot be taken into consideration to determine the
meaning of an isolated logion. With a saying of which the meaning is obscure,
one can hardly decide whether it is to be ascribed to Jesus or not.

2. If the unity of Matt. 10.23 is assumed and an attempt made to understand the verse independently of its context, then it will at once be noticed
that Jesus does not include himself with those addressed. This would certainly
be completely intelligible in the context of the sending of the disciples on
their mission; but can the fact of the sending out of the disciples in Jesus' lifetime be demonstrated historically? And is there any other situation in the lifetime of Jesus which presupposes the absence of the disciples from him?
Furthermore there is still the question whether the situation was already so
critical in Jesus' lifetime that a flight from one city to another was necessary.
For this reason it is definitely better to take the logion "as a consolation-
saying uttered by a prophetically inspired Christian to his brethren in a persecution situation. . . . One might think of the persecution of which we
have legendary traces in Acts 6–9" (Vielhauer, "Gottesreich", p. 60).

The *amēn* in 23b is not a proof of authenticity (see Vielhauer. p. 60). Nor is
the distinction between the speaker (Jesus) and the Son of Man. It has according to Iber "the purpose of delimiting the activity of one and the same person in the two ages" (Vielhauer, "Jesus und der Menschensohn", p. 146), at a
time when the Church could not yet directly equate the *earthly* Jesus and the
apocalyptic Son of Man.

Mark 14.25: Granted that this verse is a vow of abstinence, the conclusion
of Kümmel ("From this it follows that Jesus expects the coming of the Kingdom of God to be in the near future, and that he feels it to be so near that he
can impress its proximity on his disciples by limiting his abstinence to the
dawning of the Kingdom of God", *PF*, pp. 31f) seems to me inadmissible, for
one would otherwise have to suppose that such abstinence is only possible for
a short duration! This conclusion is all the stranger in its result if, as Kümmel
thinks (p. 32), "Jesus foresees between his imminent death and this eschatological 'coming' a certain interval of time", for then it is the death of Jesus
that is the limit of the pledge of abstinence, and not the coming of the Kingdom of God.

Mark 13.28f: Against Dodd (p. 102) Kümmel may be right in saying that
the similitude does not demand recognition of the significance of the present
situation, but that rather "*tauta* must signify some kind of premonitory
signs of the end, whilst as the subject of *engys estin* the end, the parousia, the
entry of the Kingdom of God must be presumed" (*PF*, p. 21). But the conclusion Kümmel draws from this seems to me untenable, that "this gives us a
reliable proof of the fact that Jesus expected the eschatological consummation
in the near future and knew its imminent coming to be announced by premonitory signs in the present" (ibid.).

1. Verse 29 only says that *when* the premonitory signs are there, the end is
near, but not *that* they are there. The presence of the premonitory signs was
not at all obvious for Jesus' listeners; for that reason Jesus would have had to
say so explicitly.

It cannot be argued, "Of course it is presupposed that the signs are already

there; the disciples can now recognize them" (Conzelmann, *ZTK*, 54, p. 287).
The condition for the possibility of recognizing the signs of the time is not
discipleship, but a word of Jesus that claims these signs as signs of the time,
and lays a claim to them. It is not that the recognition comes about through the
preliminary condition of discipleship, but that faith comes about through the
word of Jesus, and only through this does discipleship come about. But
whether there is a word of Jesus that refers to the preliminary signs of the
near end is still the question.

2. It is furthermore far from certain whether the similitude of the fig-tree
goes back to Jesus, or whether it did not rather originally form the conclusion
of the Jewish apocalypse reworked by Mark (cf. Mark 13.4).

Luke 12.54–6: Although the material would have suggested it, the application
does not refer to the temporal connection between the premonitory sign and
what is signified by it. The application does not even refer to the character
of the premonitory sign which is found in the material of the picture part. It
only reproaches those addressed that they are able to judge the appearance
of sky and earth, but cannot value this *kairos* rightly.

It is not methodologically permissible to combine Mark 13.28f and Luke
12.54–6 and in this way to produce a reference to the "near expectation" in
Luke 12.54–6 and to claim authenticity for Mark 13.28f (against Kümmel,
PF, p. 22).

The "general exhortations to watchfulness" (Grässer) in Mark 13.33 and
37; Luke 12.35 (cf. Matt. 25.13); and the so-called parables of watchfulness,
Mark 13.33 6; Luke 12.36 8; Matt. 24.43–51 = Luke 12.42–6, Matt. 24.43f =
Luke 12.39f, probably have their "setting in life" in the problem of the delay
of the Parousia (for evidence I would refer to Grässer, pp. 84–95).

The similitude of the thief in the night would not be an argument for a
"near expectation" even if the application is (correctly) regarded as secondary
(Fuchs, *Hermeneutik*, p. 223; Jeremias, p. 49). A burglary is an event that is in
any connection unpredictable, both the fact of it and the time of it. The
parable of the burglar has its point of comparison in the impossibility of
making provision against it. Jesus cannot possibly have meant to say by this
parable, "Prepare yourselves! Soon it will be too late" (Jeremias, p. 49).

Luke 18.1–8 and Matt. 25.1–13 also probably first arose in the early Church
to meet the problem of the delay of the Parousia. For the evidence see my
exposition of these parables, esp. pp. 187f and 190ff.

Apart from the passages mentioned, Jesus' connection with the Baptist is
produced as an argument that Jesus stood for a "near expectation" of the
Kingdom of God. The argument is strong. The assumption is obvious that
Jesus shared the "near expectation" of the Baptist. However, it seems to me
to be just as possible that Jesus did not continue the "near expectation" of the
Baptist, but changed it into the certainty that the Kingdom of God is now
arriving. (This cannot of course be understood as a simple reversal of an
extremely tensed-up expectation, because such a simple reversal could
historically never have been effective.)

Cf. on this Fuchs, *Studies*, pp. 122–3: "The proclamation of the *nearness* of
the Basileia [Kingdom] more probably belongs to the Baptist and the early
Church. The problem of the delay of the Parousia arose from this proclama-

tion. We find no trace of this problem in Jesus, when we read without pre-
judice such passages as Luke 11.20, par. Matt. 12.28; Luke 6.20f, par. Matt.
5.3ff. These passages assume the efficacy of the Basileia, but not the question of its relationship within time to the present . . . Even the distinction
between a beginning and its continuation is precarious, because it assumes a
definite, though it may be very small, distance between the beginning and
the continuation, that is, between Jesus and the Basileia. It is questionable
whether a temporal problem exists here at all. The *prōton pseudos* of our scholarly position to-day might well consist of the fact that from the outset we
accommodate the *nature* of the Basileia within a secondary temporal context.
But there is a difference between the time in which a person moves—whether
something passes into the future, or arrives from the future—and a time
which is defined and imprinted by a definite content and thus always already
'filled' (this applies also to Gal. 4.4.)."

27. So that Ebeling can rightly say that in Jesus "faith came to expression in
language" (*Word and Faith*, p. 206).

28. Cf. Fuchs, *Hermeneutik*, throughout; but especially p. 156.

29. The proposition that "the coming of the kingdom is indissolubly linked with
his [Jesus'] person" (Frör, *Hermeneutik*, p. 294) cannot in my view be maintained. Matt. 12.28 par. speaks of Jesus' action, but not necessarily of his
person. Nor can the reference of Luke 17.21 to Jesus' *person* be proved. There
is accordingly in my opinion no demonstrably genuine saying of Jesus, in
which he reflects on his own position in the coming of the kingdom. (Mark
8.38 par. too is secondary, according to Käsemann, "Sätze heiligen Rechts
im NT", *NTS*, 1 (1954/55), pp. 248–60, and Vielhauer, "Gottesreich",
pp. 68–70, "Jesus und der Menschensohn", pp. 141–7).

30. This is not to overlook the historical question of the causes of the crucifixion
of Jesus and the share in it of the Romans, who were certainly not the audience he had in mind in his preaching.

31. It has not been overlooked that the title "Son of God" was not possible on
the lips or in the thoughts of the Jewish contemporaries of Jesus. For the
reality intended, it does not matter in this connection what titles are used to
express it. The title "Son of God" was chosen to make the point, because in
our language it alone brings the intended meaning to mind immediately.

On this subject, it should be added that it need not be assumed that Jesus'
preaching found no response of faith in his own lifetime. The "misunderstanding of the disciples" is a theological construction. Nor is it to be maintained on the other hand that we have to allow for a thoroughly thought out
Christology among the disciples of Jesus. Only this much should be said,
that from the agreement with Jesus which was effected by his word the recognition of his unique God-given authority must have grown as a natural consequence, independently of the extent to which (and of the—already exist-
ing—forms in which) it could be put into language (see on this Ebeling,
Theologie und Verkündigung, throughout).

This recognition of the authority of Jesus is independent of whether Jesus
ascribed to himself a specific title (Messianic consciousness) or whether he
reflected at all on the meaning of his person in connection with his message
(self-consciousness).

This means, however, that faith has its origin neither in the event of the resurrection (however that is to be understood), nor in a special self-consciousness of Jesus; faith has its origin in the word of Jesus. Jesus has put faith into language, faith which against appearance puts its trust in the true word.

This is not to say that faith could not occur before Jesus. "There has always been the 'moment', but God wanted the 'moment' to become communicable" (Fuchs). Only since Jesus has there existed the Word that asserts its truth as against the visible not only in this or that concrete situation (Isa. 7.1) but always.

32. In this connection it makes no difference that smaller groups of texts were already sometimes collected together in oral tradition (for instance under a catchword).

33. The nature of this stringing together can be studied in the Gospel of Thomas.

34. Cf. Bultmann, *Erforschung der Synoptischen Evangelien*, pp. 17ff; *HST*, pp. 321–67.

35. See Jeremias, pp. 110ff.

36. Ibid., pp. 112–13.

37. Bornkamm, in *Tradition and Interpretation in Matthew*, p. 19, n. 6.

38. In view of the changes in form that the parables of Jesus inevitably underwent in their transmission in the early Church (cf. Jeremias, pp. 23–114) the necessity for the critical return "from the early Church to Jesus" and for the question of the "setting in the life of Jesus" of the parables can no longer be open to question.

As for the *possibility* of this return: 1. Cadoux is right in saying that "this method is not so haphazard as may appear at first sight: in any case, the only and commonly employed alternative—to seek for what is most commonplace in the story and regard it as inculcating a commonplace of morals or religion—is more certain only in being more certainly wrong. And the risk of mistake will seem smaller when we consider that the concrete uniqueness of the point of the story leaves us without great choice as to the occasions of its applicability" (*Parables*, p. 55).

2. Obvious mistakes in determining the original situation of a parable or far-reaching differences between the various commentators are no evidence that such a determination is in principle impossible. They only show that we have not yet perfected a method by which we can establish the original historical situation of a parable with a degree of certainty. Once this has been achieved, a consensus of the commentators will follow naturally. Of course in such historical questions much depends on the judgement of the individual scholar. But that does not mean that the whole thing dissolves into uncertainty.

3. Of course one must also respect the limits that apply to any inquiry into the historical situation. Biographical details, the precise occasion that led to Jesus telling a particular parable, cannot be ascertained. The situation can be illuminated only in its basic features. But in any case more than this is not necessary.

39. Cf. Frör, "Gleichnis und Parabel in Predigt und Unterricht", *RGG* (ed. 3), vol. 2, coll. 1619–21.

Exposition

1. THE STORY OF THE GOOD SAMARITAN

1. Since the connection between the question about the greatest commandment and the story of the good Samaritan is secondary (cf. n. 17), v. 29 must either be a transitional verse formed by the Evangelist or else—at least in its basic core—belong originally with the narrative.

The way v. 36 is phrased assumes that the neighbour has already been mentioned (or else this concept did not originally stand in v. 36 either). If v. 29 were a redactional transition, v. 36 (at least in its present form, which contains the term neighbour) would also belong to the redaction. Luke would have linked the story of the Good Samaritan to the question, "Who then is my neighbour?" without even the connecting word "neighbour"!

This could not be explained from redactional motives. The redactional work of the Evangelist is contained within modest limits, as can be seen from Bultmann, *HST*, pp. 334ff. Luke has usually taken his theme from the words that he wanted to pass on or from other pieces of tradition. To bring the story into the scene of 10.25–8 the question of v. 29 was not needed. The words, "and he told him a parable", would have sufficed.

It can therefore be assumed that an independent interest already existed in the question, "Who then is my neighbour?" This interest has its "setting in life" in Palestinian Judaism (as Jeremias, pp. 202–3, makes probable), much rather than in the Christian community of Luke.

If v. 29 is not a redactional transition, the connection of the question with the story must be understood as being "apophthegmatic". As a "scholastic dialogue", however, 10.29–37 was doubtless not first composed by Luke, but must already have originated in Palestine.

Although it would be possible that it was the early Church that first answered the question, "Who then is my neighbour?", with Jesus' story of the Good Samaritan, I regard it as at least equally possible that it was Jesus who did so. We should then owe the fact that the narrative has been transmitted in connection with its original question to the circumstance that the early Church too was interested in this question. Cf. on this question Michaelis, *Gleichnisse*, p. 205: "Although we must have before us the work of the Evangelist in the sequence, words of exhortation by Jesus in 10.28 and question by the scribe in 10.29, the question in 10.29 as such can have belonged originally to the parable. It is quite possible that Jesus was once asked who was to be regarded as one's neighbour, and that he answered this question with the parable, which also, according to 10.36f, had the task of answering the question when the command to love one's neighbour has really been fulfilled."

2. See Manson, p. 261.
3. See Jeremias, p. 203.
4. More than once the assertion has been made that Jesus' story is based on an actual occurrence. But so long as no grounds are given for this I cannot but regard it with Jülicher, Klostermann, and others as an invented story. Possibly 2 Chron. 28.5–15 has had some influence on its formation. In style it is constructed by means of a well-known and widespread fairy tale motif: two respected persons turn out to be heartless, and only the third, despised man, is merciful. See on this Bultmann, *HST*, p. 204.
5. See Billerbeck, II, pp. 55–68 and p. 180.
6. So Billerbeck, II, p. 183, and Schmid, p. 192: "Any . . . ground of excuse would impair the lesson of the story."
7. Billerbeck, II, p. 182: "But the reason that Jesus takes a priest and a Levite as representatives of human heartlessness is hardly that one would in his days have expected from them as servants of God a quite specially active love of neighbour. That sort of expectation was certainly not cherished of a profession whose members were branded in a writing of the time [Testament of the Twelve Patriarchs, Testament of Levi 17] as 'idolaters, adulterers, lovers of money, proud, lawless, lascivious, abusers of children and beasts'. The reason is much rather that the profession of the priests and Levites was in common opinion the leading and privileged profession." Priests and Levites are in no way representative of Jewish piety, as is often asserted in this connection. This is shown by the whole of Billerbeck's material, especially the excursus "Pharisees and Sadducees in Ancient Jewish Literature", IV, 1, pp. 334–52. Only Pharisees and scribes could count as such representatives in the time of Jesus.
8. See Bugge, p. 395.
9. See Jeremias, p. 204.
10. Ibid., p. 204.
11. See on this Bugge, p. 395: "It is precisely a non-Jew that Jesus needs in the narrative here. Otherwise the compassionate love could be ascribed to their common nationality." Schlatter, p. 286: "Jesus places the Samaritan in the parable to unfreeze the term 'neighbour' and to make it live."
12. See Jülicher, II, p. 592.
13. See Jeremias, p. 205.
14. Jülicher sees "no possibility of clarifying the deficient 'logic of the conversation' other than to say that the story was first inserted here by Luke from another context . . . the shift from the neighbour that is to be loved of v. 29 to the man that loves his neighbour of vv. 30–7a . . . is psychologically easily comprehensible as soon as we assume this subsequent combination" (II, p. 196).

Bultmann explains the formal discrepancy between vv. 29 and 36 by saying that the previous conclusion of the story has left its traces in Luke's formulation. "Apart from this, I believe that originally the passage ended with a question and answer, like Luke 7.41–3; Matt. 21.28–31. For it is clear that the beginning of the question in v. 36, *tis toutōn tōn triōn*, and the answer in v. 37, *ho poiēsas to eleos met' autou*, were given to Luke, and from this the question in v. 36 was prepared with a degree of artificiality. Luke was obliged after his introduction so to construct his question and answer as to make the attacked man the 'neighbour'" (*HST*, p. 178).

But Luke could not have been given just "the beginning of the question in v. 36"! He must then have ignored its *content* and at the same time have kept so slavishly to its *form* that to do so he put up with logical discrepancies! Such a process would in my view be without analogy in the history of the synoptic tradition.

According to Klostermann, "the inconsistency between the question of v. 29 and the answer given in the parable was meant to be hidden" by v. 36.

Jülicher, Klostermann, and Bultmann are at one in the assumption that the framework of vv. 29 and 36 does not fit the story and was only connected with it later. The point of the story according to Jülicher is that "the self-sacrificing practice of love has the highest worth in the eyes of God and of men. No advantage of position or birth can replace it. The merciful man earns blessedness, even if he is a Samaritan, rather than the Jewish temple-official, who is a slave to selfishness" (II, p. 596). Similarly Klostermann says: "A merciful Samaritan is nearer to the kingdom of God than an unmerciful representative of Judaism" (p. 119). According to Bultmann, "the point of the story lies in the contrast of the unloving Jews and the loving Samaritan" (*HST*, p. 178).

There is no mention in the story of "blessedness" or the "kingdom of God". And a reference to Luke 18.9-14 is no justification for introducing these thoughts here.

Nor can the contrast of Jews and Samaritans be the point of the story, any more than the point is in Luke 15.11-32 the contrast between the elder and the younger son, or in Matt. 25.14-30 the contrast between the servant who doubles his master's property and the one who buries it uselessly. Bultmann leaves completely open what is meant by this contrast anyway, although a satisfactory explanation can be given for the contrasting of the Jews with the Samaritan in connection with v. 29.

According to Conzelmann, the story was created by particular circles in the early Church to justify their mission to Samaria (*TSL*, p. 72). But how can one suppose that an invented story of the mercifulness of a Samaritan could play this part? And what grounds are there to deny the attribution of the story to Jesus?

In contrast to the commentators mentioned above, Jeremias holds firmly to the authenticity of vv. 29 and 36. The shift in the question is only a matter of "a formal inconsistency" (p. 205). He says that the scribe is certainly "thinking of himself", when he asks: 'What is the limit of my responsibility?', while Jesus says to him, 'Think of the sufferer, put yourself in his place, consider, Who needs help from me?'"; but at the same time he gives a warning against eisegesis.

Gollwitzer does not make the assumption of an inconsistency in the editing, and thinks that the scene is to demonstrate to the lawyer "that it could very well be the case that he would, and should, spontaneously greet even a Samaritan as neighbour" (p. 63), by bringing him to see himself "in the most miserable condition on the stage of the narrative", so that he is no longer capable of fulfilling the law, but only of thankfulness (p. 61).

But how could the lawyer, who in the context of the law asks about his neighbour, come to identify himself with the man that has been attacked? The shift between the question in v. 29 and the counter-question in v. 36, which the hearer first experiences after the conclusion of the narrative, cannot possibly effect this—if only because the word which we translate by "neighbour", or "fellow man", is in Aramaic a reciprocal concept (see Gerhardsson, p. 7).

15. For Jüngel (pp. 172f) the illustration belongs with the parables of the kingdom of God, because Jesus uses it to tell his listeners how the "near future" of the kingdom of God, which is near in the event of the love of God, refers men to their own present time as the place for the love of neighbour. "The kingdom of God is as near to you as the Samaritan was to the man threatened with death!"

But how it could appear to Jesus' hearers from this illustration—which explicitly does not speak of the kingdom of God—that the kingdom of God is near to them in such a manner, is a question Jüngel does not ask. Thereby he fails to put his exposition to the decisive test.

I should like at least to refer here to the exposition of Leenhardt, with which I am in agreement.

16. This interpretation of the history of the passage seems to me the only possible way of dealing with it correctly, inasmuch as vv. 25–8 must be regarded as a parallel to Mark 12.28–34 (see n. 17), while vv. 29–37 must be taken as a unitary piece of tradition (see n. 1 and n. 14).

The connection of Luke 10.25–8 with 29–37 should be understood with Klostermann as a linkage by catchwords. For the loss of an introduction when similar pieces of tradition are being connected, cf. Matt. 22.1–14, where the introduction to the parable of the wedding-garment must have been lost when this unit of tradition was connected with the parable of the royal wedding (see Jeremias, p. 65).

If the two sections, Luke 10.25–8 and 29–37, do not originally belong together, and if there are compelling grounds against understanding v. 29 as a redactional transition, the motivation "he desired to justify himself" must be a later addition. In any case it must be understood in the light of its literary function and not of the historical situation. The psychological observations of some commentators on the thoughts and feelings of the scribe are due to a mistake in method.

17. I regard Mark 12.32–4 as a secondary expansion. The evidence for this must be sought elsewhere.

With Jülicher, Klostermann, Bultmann, Michaelis, and Gollwitzer against Manson and Jeremias, I regard vv. 25–8 as a parallel to Mark 12.28–34.

The following grounds argue for the dependence of Luke 10.25–8:

1. As was already noticed by Tatian, Luke leaves out the question of the greatest commandment at the corresponding place in the Marcan order.

2. In view of the general observation that secondary development is to a considerable extent based on tradition, we are justified in making this assumption here too, in so far as the variations between the parallels can be explained through the effects of known tendencies in the history of tradition.

3. Among such tendencies are the change of scholastic dialogues into controversy dialogues. This may explain why the quotation is here put in the

mouth of the scribe. In a controversy dialogue a counter-question is part of the style (Bultmann, *HST*, pp. 42ff). Against Bultmann, however, one cannot, I believe, assume that this reshaping was carried out by Luke. The forms of controversy and scholastic dialogues are at home in Palestine. A Hellenist could hardly have mastered their stylistic laws to such an extent that this reshaping could be expected to come from him.

4. The fact that the question of eternal life is raised in the Lucan passage can be explained with Klostermann as an interpretation. Manson would infer a far-reaching difference in the units of tradition: in Mark an academic question is put, and in Luke a practical one. Against this it must be pointed out that *ekpeirazōn* is not well suited to a practical question. When Manson goes on to say later that the question "is the supreme religious question and so the supreme test of a religious teacher", he himself admits that it is not an existential question here, as it is in the pericope of the rich young man.

Not only is there a striking inconsistency between the question of the scribe and his intention. It must also be noticed that in v. 28 we have a double answer of Jesus. "You have answered right" is appropriate in the context of a scholarly question, but "Do this, and you will live", as the answer to an existential question. This juxtaposition is best explained by the intrusion of a later reinterpretation.

5. To say that the answer was put in the mouth of the scribe by the later Church as the only possible one is far more enlightening than the attempt of Manson to understand it from the historical situation. Certainly it must be granted that Jesus was not the only person for whom the linking of the command to love God and to love one's neighbour was possible. It is not this linking in itself that is the special feature in the answer of Jesus. It is that the question of the greatest commandment is answered by a unitary basic principle of the law of God, which was not in the least expected by the question nor part of the thought-forms of contemporary Judaism. But for just this reason, because it is not the utterance that is decisive but the attitude that is taken here towards the law, I cannot share Manson's view that Jesus constantly impressed on his listeners in conversation and preaching these two texts linked together as "great thoughts". Furthermore I cannot accept the view of the preaching of Jesus which lies behind it. Jesus was not a publicist who set out to propagate "great thoughts".

6. To assert the original unity of the pericope, Manson has to downgrade Luke 10.25–8 to an introduction: "It states what is common ground between Jesus and the lawyer." In this he overlooks the fact that this passage is not an historical report, but belongs to the stylized category of controversy dialogues, for which such a statement of agreement is unthinkable. Still more questionable is Manson's assumption that the scribe had begun the conversation from the outset with the intention of putting the question about the neighbour. In that case he would have had to foresee the course of the conversation right down to individual points, for Mark 10.19 shows that the answer to the question about eternal life could be put quite differently.

7. Controversy and scholastic dialogues normally show only a single exchange of dialogue. The only exceptions in the synoptic tradition are Mark 10.17–22, Mark 12.13–17, Mark 10.35–40, Mark 12.28–34. In the first two

cases this can be explained on obvious factual grounds; in the request of the Zebedees we have a secondary insertion, and in the question about the greatest commandment a secondary expansion (see above).

Manson's attempt to assert the originality of Luke 10.25–8 and the unity of 10.25–37 must therefore be regarded as untenable.

18. Cf. Billerbeck, I, pp. 901ff.
19. The only pre-Christian attempt preserved in tradition to "refer the whole of the individual demands of the Torah to a few great basic principles" comes from Hillel (20 B.C.) (see Billerbeck, I, p. 907). It must, however, be treated in its anecdotal context, and is not in my opinion intended to be a basic principle. (According to Billerbeck, I, p. 357, this saying in any case does not come from Hillel at all. For proof Billerbeck refers to his commentary, on Matt. 7.12; but I have not been able to find anything on this there.) In any case the tendency of Judaism at the time of Jesus went in the direction of the following saying: "An easy commandment should be as dear (precious) to you as a heavy (important) commandment (for God has commanded both of them)", Billerbeck, I, p. 903.
20. Cf. Bultmann, *HST*, pp. 41, 45 and 51f.
21. Cf. Klostermann, p. 119 and Bugge, p. 389.
22. See Manson, p. 261: "The reply of Jesus gives complete approval to this solution of the problem. He says in effect: 'That is my answer to the question'."
23. See Klostermann, p. 119.

2. THE PHARISEE AND THE TAX-COLLECTOR

1. Ebeling, *Unglaube und Glaube*, pp. 6f.
2. The interpretation of the beginning of v. 11 is disputed, and the textual tradition is divided. Is "with himself" to be connected with "stood" or with "prayed"? Does it mean that the Pharisee placed himself or stood "visibly" (Klostermann, Jeremias) or "on his own" (Zürich Bible) or does it mean that he prayed "with himself" (Jülicher, C. W. F. Smith)? Must praying "with himself" be understood in the sense of an inaudible prayer uttered in the heart, or is it equally possible to think of it as spoken in an undertone, not intelligible to the bystanders, as the Jewish rule was (cf. Berakoth V, 1; 31a)?
   According to Jeremias (p. 140) only the word order which connects "by himself" with "stood" corresponds to the Semitic idiom. "*Pros heauton* renders an Aramaic reflexive (*leh*) which lays a definite emphasis on the action".
3. Billerbeck, II, pp. 243f; Schlatter, p. 399; Jeremias, p. 140.
4. See Jeremias, p. 140.
5. Ibid., p. 140.
6. So Jeremias, p. 143; Jülicher, p. 603; Klostermann, p. 179; with some qualifications also Schlatter, p. 400.
7. Jeremias, p. 141.
8. Ibid., p. 143.

9. Ibid., p. 141.
10. Cf. C. W. F. Smith: "The judge in the matter is his own conscience, which is formed by the law as elucidated and applied by the scribes" (p. 121).
11. When our exposition here interprets the question, "Who is justified?" by another, "Who is just?", this is an attempt at translation in which original and rendering do not completely correspond. A completely appropriate translation seems to me impossible, since we cannot get behind the change of concept which has taken place—not least as a consequence of this parable.

So far as I can see, almost all expositors interpret v. 14a in the sense, "This one was forgiven and not the other". In so doing, they appear to have fallen under the spell of present-day linguistic usage. This matter of course equation of justification with forgiveness, "gracious acceptance", and the like was not possible for Jesus' listeners. Justification was for them the judicial recognition of the righteous, and Jesus' saying, which spoke of the justification of the sinner in place of the righteous, was for them an outrageous paradox, even from a linguistic point of view.

We find here the linguistic phenomenon for which I propose the name "interlocking". As it was understood until then, justification was the judicial recognition of the fact of righteousness. This justification, in which righteousness was ascribed to the man who was righteous, was, however, in no way understood as a simple establishment of facts. The emphasis which in this concept was laid on the act of judicial pronouncement was the linguistic prerequisite for the possibility of taking forgiveness, gracious acceptance, as equivalent to justification. Here was the axis around which the change in the meaning of the concept was effected. The linguistic paradox had to prove itself a genuine linguistic possibility, which ensured to the parable its effectiveness.

We must have already applied to the parable the dogmatic assumption that it is concerned with God's forgiveness to overlook the fact that forgiveness, "gracious acceptance", and the like, cannot possibly be the common heading under which the Pharisee and the tax-collector are brought. The Pharisee has not prayed for forgiveness—in the view of Jesus' listeners he did not need it at this moment anyway—so one can hardly say that it was refused him. Lines of thought such as Rom. 3.23 are certainly among the legitimate consequences of this parable, but were far from the minds of Jesus' audience, and in my opinion cannot be assumed for Jesus either.

It has far-reaching effects on the exposition of the parable if v. 14a is understood as saying that the tax-collector is forgiven and the Pharisee not, as is generally done, to the neglect of the situation portrayed in the parable. Verse 14a understood in the sense: "It is not the righteous who is justified but the wicked" gives a genuine paradox. The verdict of Jesus would, however, be meaningless if it had to mean, "The wicked is forgiven, but the righteous not". As soon as "justify" is replaced by "forgive", the Pharisee cannot be contrasted as the righteous one to the sinner in need of forgiveness, but must inevitably be characterized in a negative way.

So Jülicher describes the attitude of the Pharisee as "pride" and "arrogance", and contrasts it with the "humility" and "consciousness of sins" of the tax-collector. Klostermann speaks of the "proud Pharisee" and "the repentant tax-collector", and Jeremias describes the Pharisee as "self-righteous", though he avoids a term of virtue for the tax-collector ("despairing, hopeless sinner"). According to Michaelis (*Gleichnisse*) too, the Pharisee is "self-righteous". Such a characterization of types, however, is not only opposed to what has been established in respect of the historical situation, but also runs the risk of transferring the parable on to the level of moralizing.

The importance that this characterization has for the exposition is, however, very different in the individual expositors. In Jülicher it is dominant: "Even without the guidance given in 14a Jesus could expect from each listener who had been educated even for a little while in his school, in the sight of so clear . . . types of pride and consciousness of sin, the verdict: 'It is not the former whom God graciously receives, the latter will not be rejected by him'" (p. 607).

Jülicher overlooks (1) that the story is probably not spoken to the disciples; (2) that Jesus' listeners could hardly have regarded the attitude of the Pharisee as "pride" or "conceit". No more could the attitude of the tax-collector have appeared to them as "humility" or "consciousness of sin" in the sense of a virtue, a moral performance, or a religious attitude. And was Jesus really a teacher of virtue, who wanted to "teach that in all circumstances humility is more welcome to God than self-righteousness"? Then he would have won the full approval of his opponents, and they would hardly have crucified him! (See C. W. F. Smith, p. 122.)

Klostermann too seems to look for the motivation of v. 14a in the characterization of the two types ("Of the two that pray it is not the proud Pharisee who obtains . . . forgiveness but the repentant tax-collector.") The same is obviously true for Michaelis: it was because of the "perverted attitude" of the Pharisee, that he did not ask from God the gift of righteousness. "He believed that he had long been righteous in his own strength . . . but Jesus says: he was only self-righteous. But God does not recognize self-righteousness. . . . In fact a self-righteous man is separated from true righteousness for as long as he persists in his attitude" (*Gleichnisse*, p. 243). The strange thing is that in v. 14a not a word is said of the self-righteousness of the Pharisee!

In Schlatter the motivation of v. 14a by the characterization of the types becomes much less important. Correspondingly, however, Jesus' verdict, which in this interpretation has almost lost any basis in the narrative of the parable, takes on the character of a revelatory pronouncement: "The story would be worthless if God's verdict were not made clear. Hence it concludes with Jesus, as the one who knows the will of God and proclaims the judgement of God, making clear what each of the men who prayed obtained of God by their prayers" (p. 400). One can only accept direct revelatory pronouncements, however, from someone whose authority is patent and obvious. But this can hardly be the situation in which the "historical Jesus" was (see Matt. 11.6)! If Jesus had confronted his listeners with direct revelatory pronouncements, he would himself have been making it impossible for them to listen to him. Jesus, however, did want to be understood. This is proved by the fact that he spoke in parables.

Jeremias has corrected his position in his latest edition, and no longer puts it as, "God had forgiven him . . .", but as, "God had bestowed on him his favour, and not on the other" (p. 143—not yet altered in the English 2nd edition).

For Jeremias as for Schlatter the motivation of 14a by the character of the types portrayed recedes strongly in importance, and the verdict of Jesus appears for him too to be primarily an unmotivated revelatory pronouncement: "He simply says: That is God's decision" (p. 144). But then Jeremias tries nevertheless to find support for this verdict in the parable narrative. "The prayer of the publican is a quotation: he uses the opening words of Ps. 51. . . . But we find in the same psalm: 'The sacrifices of God are a broken spirit: a broken and a contrite heart, O God, thou will not despise.'" But Jeremias spoils this beginning because he does not connect what is said with the understanding of the listeners, but with the utterance of Jesus, and proceeds: "The character of God, says Jesus, is such as is described in Ps. 51."

12. Apart from its being found elsewhere in the tradition there are other arguments against the originality of 14b here:
   1. The verse does not fit the narrative:
      (a) One cannot say that the tax-collector has humbled himself (Jülicher, Bultmann).
      (b) The sentence gives the parable a "suggestion of popular morality which is wholly out of keeping with its wording" (Dibelius, *Formgeschichte*, p. 254 = *From Tradition to Gospel*, p. 253).
   2. "By the appeal to a generally valid sentence as the basis for the verdict passed in 14a the value of the story is . . . reduced" (Jülicher, II, p. 607).
   3. There is a tendency in the Gospels to add generalizing logia to parables as a conclusion (Jeremias, p. 107).

   In view of the number of the objections I cannot agree with Jeremias that it is not possible to decide with certainty whether 14b is original in this context (p. 144).

   Against Dibelius Jeremias refers to the possibility that the future tenses refer to God's action at the Last Judgement (p. 107), and expounds the verse in this future sense (p. 142). This overlooks the fact that the tax-collector is pronounced righteous *now*. If this interpretation of v. 14b were correct, it would be a further argument against the original connection of this verse with the narrative.

13. Verse 9 cannot be original; on this nearly all commentators are agreed. The only question is whether it was formed by Luke (Jülicher, II, p. 600; Bultmann, *HST*, p. 335 and—with less certainty—p. 193) or belongs to an earlier stage of the tradition (Jeremias, p. 93; some of the phrases of this verse are however in his view to be laid to the account of Luke; Bultmann, *HST*, p. 178).

3, THE SIMILITUDES OF THE LOST SHEEP AND THE LOST COIN

1. According to Bultmann (*HST*, p. 171) the shorter Matthean version is the original form of the parable. On this cf. above, pp. 64f, and notes 5 and 7 below.

2. Jeremias, p. 135.

3. See Jeremias, p. 135 and n. 11; Dalman, *The Words of Jesus*, pp. 209ff; Klostermann, p. 156. On the question of the originality of Luke 15.10 see above, p. 70, note h.

4. Jeremias, p. 134.

5. "The conclusion of the first parable (vs. 6, 7) is parallel to the conclusion of the Lost Coin (vs. 9, 10) and may have been assimilated from it. As a matter of fact the gathering of friends and neighbours to rejoice is proper and likely in the case of the woman, but rather unlikely in the case of the shepherd who presumably brings the recovered sheep to rejoin the others which are left 'in the wilderness'" (C. W. F. Smith, p. 105).

6. Bultmann (*HST*, pp. 194f) questions whether Luke 15.4–10 is an original double parable. 15.8–10 may possibly be a secondary variant. Schlatter (p. 346) and Jeremias (p. 91) regard the connection of 15.4–10 as original.

7. See Cadoux, p. 231: "Luke's closing verse 15.7 looks as though it was composed of the closing verse of the parable of the Lost Coin with the addition of a sentence that Matthew has in the body of the parable." Bultmann too (*HST*, p. 171) regards Luke 15.7 as a "secondary formulation, in which echoes are heard of the original ending (Matt. 18.13b)", since the Lucan version of the parable is secondary in other features also.

8. Jülicher urges against the originality of Matt. 18.14 that it does not give value to the chief features of the parable (II, p. 331). According to Bultmann it narrows the original sense of the parable to the point that "no member of the Christian community will be lost", and does not express "the joy over finding the lost, although this is obviously the essential feature of the similitude" (*HST*, p. 171). According to Jeremias too "the concluding sentence in Matthew has a ... different emphasis" (p. 39). "The emphasis does not lie, as in Luke, on the joy of the shepherd, but on the example of his persistent search" (p. 40). But on retranslation into Aramaic the concluding sentence in Matthew (18.14) strikes the same note, Jeremias claims, as the concluding sentence in Luke (15.7). Since the negative belongs in substance to the second half of the sentence, and the underlying Aramaic word which Matthew translates by *thelēma* (will) can as well have the meaning *eudokia* (good pleasure), the original meaning of Matt. 18.14, he says, is, "There is joy in the heart of God when even one of the very least escapes destruction." This "agrees exactly with Luke 15.7a" (p. 40). But *eudokia* (good pleasure), is in its nature something different from *chara* (joy), and the wording of Matt. 18.14 and Luke 15.7 is too divergent for it to be possible to derive both verses from a common Aramaic basis. Therefore no evidence for the genuineness of Matt. 18.14 can be drawn from this. (The discussion in Jeremias is not in connection with this question.)

9. Whether by the *mikroi*, "the little ones" in Matt. 18.10 and 14, weak and humble Christians, or Christians generally, are meant can be left open here. Even if G. Barth (*Tradition and Interpretation in Matthew*, pp. 84f and 121ff) is right that the *mikroi* in these verses means the Christians, I cannot agree with him that in Matt. 18 it becomes a "sustained designation of Christians". Apart from v. 14, which refers back to vv. 10f, Matthew uses the word only

F

in places where it has been given him by the tradition (this is true also of Matt.
10.42; cf. Bultmann, *HST*, p. 142).

10. See *TDNT*, II, pp. 57f, under *prosdechomai*.

11. Bornhäuser (p. 131) points out that *prosdechesthai* in the LXX is the "translation of nine Hebrew words". "Most are only rendered once or twice by
prosdechesthai", whereas we find it as the translation of *raṣah*—to have pleasure
in—thirteen times. So one can definitely say that it should as a rule be translated by "have pleasure in", "be pleased with". Since Luke, from whom the
introductory verses 15.1f come, is well known to have much in common with
the language of the LXX, one must allow for the possibility that he has used
prosdechesthai here in the sense of "have pleasure in".

12. Bornhäuser, ad loc.

13. So Dodd, p. 90: "The story . . . depicts vividly the concern which a person
feels about a loss which an outsider might consider comparatively trifling, and
his (or her) corresponding delight when the lost is found. The Lucan setting
is surely so far right, that the parables refer to the extravagant concern (as it
seemed to some) which Jesus displayed for the depressed classes of the Jewish
community." Cf. Jeremias, pp. 39f. Proof in the strict sense cannot of course
be given for this assignment of the parables to an historical situation. But if we
consider that the parables of Jesus were in general addressed to his opponents,
then we shall probably not leave the question undecided, as do Jülicher
(II, p. 331) and Bultmann (p. 199), whether Jesus "spoke the parables to con-
sole desperate sinners" or "aimed them in controversy against grumbling
Pharisees, to justify his own love of sinners".

14. See Billerbeck, II, p. 211: "The words of Sukka 5.4, 'Pious men and women
who busied themselves in good works, danced' (at the feast of the Drawing of
Water before all the people in the women's forecourt) were commented on in
Bar Sukka 53a: 'some of them said: 'Blessed be the time of our youth, for it
does not shame our old age' . . . (sc. these were the 'fully righteous'). Others
of them said: 'Blessed be our old age, for it has atoned for our youth' (these
were the 'penitent'). That the 'pious' did not scorn to share together with the
'penitent' to enhance the joy at the drawing of the water at the feast of
Tabernacles shows more than anything else that a lasting stain did not attach
in the minds of the public to the *ba'ale teshubah* [penitents] on account of their
earlier way of life."

    Bornhäuser too points out (p. 132) that the Pharisees did not refuse fellow-
ship to the penitent.

15. Schlatter seems to me to misjudge the historical situation when he says: "It
was not, however, impossible for a serious Pharisee to realize that for the
men whose fellowship with Jesus they were amazed at, it meant a complete
change of all their standards when they opened themselves to the word of
Jesus and sought his fellowship. . . . Jesus called it a fact visible to all, which
nothing ought to obscure, that what he was creating at his table was conversion" (*Lukas*, p. 348). Schlatter overlooks the opposition between the Pharisaic
understanding of penitence and what Jesus understood by conversion. Nor
does he notice that this understanding of conversion is indissolubly bound up
with the message of the nearness of the kingdom of God. If this nearness has
to be believed in, then neither can the conversion which this belief signifies

be "a fact visible to all, which nothing ought to obscure". "Undoubtedly *metanoia*" is the situation that "these men, living in sensuality without God, were so gripped by the word of Jesus that they sought his company", only for the Christian belief in Jesus as the Son of God (*Lukas*, p. 349). Schlatter's exposition is correct for the Christian interpretation of the parables in the applications, Luke 15.7 and 10, but not for the word of Jesus in the historical situation.

16. It has not, so far as I can see, been observed before by commentators that the description of the situation and the application of the parables are mutually exclusive.

17. The joy is connected in the parable with the event of finding, and only when a corresponding event can be pointed to in the situation to which the parable refers is the parable effective. The exposition must establish for the "reality part" too the anchoring of the joy in the event of finding .

Jülicher erroneously connects the joy with the object of the finding. He formulates the *tertium comparationis* of the parable in this way: "Joy over something lost and found again is greater than over many items of the same kind that have never been lost." He concludes from this that the Pharisees, since they are not penitents, "all of them together do not give God as much joy as *one* sinner won for God by Jesus" (II, p. 324). Jülicher wrongly takes the "greater value" of the penitent in the absolute, and so overlooks that the formula 1 = more than 99 is only "correct" at the moment of rediscovery (or of losing).

Jeremias too ignores the anchoring of the joy in the event of finding. He makes it a property of the *finder*: "Such is the character of God." "God's mercy is so infinite that his supreme joy is in forgiving" (p. 136). Jeremias ignores the structure of the event in the "reality part" too, in violently separating the moment of discovery of the lost and the time of the joy of God. This is because he understands the future in Luke 15.7 eschatologically. "At the final judgement God will rejoice when among the many righteous he finds a despised sinner upon whom he may pronounce absolution, nay more, it will give him even greater joy" (p. 136). Jülicher on the other hand rightly connects the time of the joy with the moment of finding. He rejects an eschatological and temporal understanding of the *estai*, and understands it as a future of necessary consequence, in the sense that there will be joy "in any case, even if only one sinner has repented" (II, p. 322).

18. This legend is taken from the book *In deinen Toren, Jerusalem*, Jewish legends retold by Else Schubert-Christaller, Heilbronn 1952. Only parts have been quoted literally, the rest retold with abbreviations. Compare on this Findlay, p. 74: "Indeed it is doubtful whether Pharisees of any period would have rejected even a publican if he expressed penitence, *and was willing to do what he could by way of reparation*. In *St Paul and Judaism* Montefiore argued with considerable force that Judaism has *never* taught salvation by works, but rather salvation by the mercy of God on the one side and the repentance of the sinner on the other. But is not repentance (along with the effort to make what reparation is possible) really a 'work'?"

19. Bornkamm, *Jesus*, pp. 83f.

20. See Fuchs, *Hermeneutik*, the chapter "Die Analogie", especially pp. 222f.

21. Against Schlatter the possibility cannot be allowed that Jesus speaks of the sinners as *his* property (p. 347: "Jesus speaks on the ground of his royal will. Those given up by the Pharisees are his property, for they belong to the community which is entrusted to him as its Lord"). Otherwise one introduces the faith of the Church in Jesus into the historical situation, instead of showing how the faith of the Church is grounded in Jesus' words and actions.

4. THE PARABLE OF THE PRODIGAL SON

1. According to Jeremias "the parable was addressed to men who were like the elder brother, men who were offended at the gospel" (p. 131). This gospel he describes some pages before (p. 124) in the words, "Jesus has come as a Saviour for *sinners*". In this he has hardly understood the historical situation correctly. To take offence at the *gospel*, his opponents would first have had to see in Jesus its authorized proclaimer. This can be excluded, however, because it cannot be harmonized with their open opposition to him.

   This criticism applies to Schlatter too, who also thinks that the protest of the Pharisees was directed against the fact that Jesus forgives sinners. Cf. p. 357: "When the Pharisee forbids Jesus to forgive, he shows that he himself cannot forgive."

2. See Madsen, p. 166: "It often happened among the Jews that a father already in his lifetime divided his property among his sons." As examples are quoted Gen. 24.36; 25.5f; B.M. 75b; B.B.8. In Jeremias, p. 129, n. 68, two further instances are given, "that legal settlement took place in the Talmudic period", Tos. B.B.2.5; b.B.B.47a.

   Cf. also Klostermann, p. 157: "It appears to follow indirectly from Ecclus. 33.19ff that this . . . demand . . . still implies no wrong."

   According to Schniewind (*Die Freude der Busse*, p. 56), "The demand of the younger son to be paid his portion . . . is to our own feelings, and still more to those of the time, disrespectful and a breach of love and fidelity." He omits, however, to produce any evidence for this.

   When Schlatter (p. 355) says, "The objection that the demand to administer his own property independently cannot be condemned as a sin . . . overlooks the fact that in the farming community, as Jesus knew it, there could be no independent administration of the inheritance by the son", he himself fails to notice that in every farming community there is a legal settlement upon the younger sons who are not entitled to the inheritance. If a son in this way "leaves the community", such conduct cannot in any way be equated with his "refusing obedience to his father".

   Instead of understanding the payment of the money to the younger son as a settlement, Bornkamm classes it as an inheritance, in order to draw from the idea of inheritance—which was not mentioned in the original text—the conclusion that the younger son "treats the father as if he were already dead" (*Jesus*, p. 126).

   The concern which lies behind the attempt to understand the request for payment and the departure from the father's house as itself a sin is made perfectly plain by the comment of *Christenlehre* on the passage: "The sin of the son does not consist just in his wasting the portion of his father's goods that falls to him. *That would be a moralistic understanding of the sin*. Rather, the sin is present and can be recognized at the moment when the son says to the father, 'Father, give me the share of the property that falls to me'" (Year 7 [1954] No. 3, Unterrichtshilfe, p. 39: my italics).

The danger which must here be avoided, however, is a result of the methodological mistake of interpreting the utterances of the parables as being directly theological, and leaving out of consideration the interplay of parable and historical situation.

3. So Bornhäuser, p. 103; Schmid, p. 252, with reference to Lev. 25.23ff. Jeremias (p.128) differs. According to him the younger son gets a third of the whole property.

4. See Jülicher, II, p. 338: "The vocative *pater* gives the imperative *dos moi*, like the *aphes* after *Kyrie* in 13.8, the character of a petition; *pater* sounds as affectionate as does *teknon* in v. 31."

5. Cf. Madsen, pp. 172ff, n. 191: "According to v. 29 it is only the younger son who has his portion put at his disposal; 'He divided the property *between them*' (v. 12) must accordingly mean that the elder son then merely acquired the reversion to his portion (cf. v. 31). This agrees precisely with b.Jeb.40a: 'How the firstborn gets nothing in the lifetime of his father . . . how the firstborn receives a double portion after the death of his father.'"

6. Jülicher, Bugge, Hauck, and Schmid would understand the emigration of the son to a far land from inferior motives of this sort (similarly too Schniewind and Schlatter, cf. n. 2). But the story only reports the fact, without commenting on the motive, and the inference of such an intention from the fact that the son goes to the bad, seems to me open to question. For the listeners to the story, moreover, it would hardly have been possible.

7. See Bornhäuser, pp. 109f; Jeremias, p. 129.

8. Bornhäuser, p. 111.

9. Baba Qamma 82b, quoted by Klostermann, p. 158.

10. See Jeremias, p. 129.

11. Jeremias (p. 129) translates v. 16—partly following Fridrichsen—" 'And he would have been only too glad to fill his belly with the carob-beans with which the swine were fed (sc. but he was too disgusted to do so), and no one gave him (sc. anything to eat).' Hence he must have stolen what food he got." Against this it can be argued: 1. It is improbable that the son when near to starvation should refuse in disgust a food that is admittedly not palatable, but quite edible, on which, e.g., Rabbi Hanina ben Dosa kept himself alive (Billerbeck, II, p. 214). 2. The assumption that the son takes on a job in which the only pay for the work consists in hunger (so Schniewind) is absurd. What could have decided him to take on this humiliating employment if not the prospect of keeping himself alive by it? He does get food, but never enough to satisfy his hunger, and the carob-beans with which he would have liked to fill his belly go not to him but to the animals. This is how Michaelis (*Gleichnisse*, p. 139) also understands the passage.

12. Quoted in Schniewind, *Die Freude der Busse*, p. 58.

13. Jeremias, p. 130.

14. Bornhäuser, p. 114.

15. Ibid., p. 113.
16. Jeremias, p. 130.
17. "Parables that are drawn from the natural compassion of a father to a son who has turned out badly are quite often met with in Rabbinic literature" (Billerbeck, II, p. 216).
18. When it is perceived that the conduct of the father is not a matter of course, the suggestion arises of a conformation here to the "reality part" (cf. Madsen, p. 174). But it is very important to determine correctly the connection between "picture" and "reality parts". According to Fuchs (*Hermeneutik*, p. 225) the three parables, Mark 4.3–9, Luke 15.11–32, and Matt. 20.1–15 show "the peculiarity that the application ('reality part') is in a hidden way identical with the 'picture part', because this obviously presupposes the event that is at issue. Nevertheless they are parabolic." The event, in this case, it seems to me, is the return of the lost, which Jesus celebrates with his table companions. It must be spoken of parabolically because this understanding of what is now happening in the presence of Jesus is not a matter of course, and the power of analogy must help the listener to come to agreement with Jesus. Cf. on this Fuchs again: "The truth brought to expression in them contains in fact one particular point. Everything in them is sustained by a hope that is anything but obvious, and therefore all the firmer" (ibid.).
    If, however, it is concluded from this anything but obvious behaviour of the father that the narrator has given the earthly father the features of the heavenly one, it is assumed that the narrator was at this point able to give up the use of the power of analogy. But does this fit the historical situation? Certainly God's fatherly goodness and his forgiving mercy were not something unknown to Jesus' listeners. But they had put in question the unconditional nature of God's forgiveness by the demands which they attached to repentance. This was in fact the reason why Jesus' table fellowship was bound to look to them like a gathering of sinners.
    The same is true if with Jeremias we understand the parable as a "description" of God's "abounding love" (p. 131). This again means one must assume that Jesus and his listeners were basically agreed on this point, for how otherwise could they have accepted this description from him? The decisive difference between Jesus and his listeners does not come to light here (cf. n. 1 and n. 26).
19. Jeremias, p. 130.
20. Occasionally commentators have discussed the question whether Luke 15. 25–32 is a secondary addition. Recently Eduard Schweizer has tried to produce proof of this (*TZ*, 4, 1948, pp. 469–71, "Zur Frage der Lukasquellen, Analyse von Lukas 15.11–32"; *TZ*, 5, 1949, pp. 231–3). It would take us too far to go into the many methodological objections that can be raised against Schweizer's argument. Jeremias must in any case be right in holding to the originality of Luke 15.25–32 against Schweizer (*TZ*, 5, 1949, pp. 228–31, cf. esp. pp. 230f). An important argument for the unity of the parable is put forward by C. W. F. Smith (p. 110): "The effort to divide the parable into two at v. 25 seems unnecessary and impossible. The place of the older son in the narrative is secured by references in vs. 11–13. There would be no point in this if the older son were to play no part in the story."

21. Against Bugge (p. 431), and Schniewind (*Die Freude der Busse*, p. 75). The word that is used in the Greek text admittedly means originally "to perform the duties of a slave". But in the LXX the word-group *doulos*, etc., is 'freed from the restriction to the service of slaves which marks its use in non-Biblical Greek. The reason for this is that it is almost always used for the root '*bd* and its denominatives" (Rengstorf, article "doulos", *TDNT*, II, p. 265). Jülicher (II, p. 355) and Klostermann (p. 160) understand *douleuō* as a word indicating respect.

22. This is how Jülicher (II, p. 357) understands the passage.

23. So Jeremias, p. 131.

24. The identification of the elder brother with the Pharisees is found in Schlatter, p. 354: "The elder brother represents what those people did who reproached Jesus for his fellowship with sinners"; in Schniewind, op. cit., p. 78: "As the eldest son behaves here against his father, so does the Pharisee against God"; in Jeremias, p. 131: "The Parable was addressed to men who were like the elder brother."

25. Cf. Fuchs, *Das urchristliche Sakramentsverständnis*, pp. 24 and 38.

26. When the basic decision that Jesus forces on his hearers by what he says is misunderstood, it changes unobtrusively into paraenesis, mere moral exhortation. |So in Jeremias, "To them Jesus says: 'Behold the greatness of God's love for his lost children, and contrast it with your own joyless, loveless, thankless and self-righteous lives. Cease then from your loveless ways, and be merciful . . . rejoice with him!'" (p. 131).

The opposition is seen as deeper in Schlatter's exposition: "God's will and his [the Pharisee's] will are completely at variance. God does not will the death of the sinner . . . but one who disowns and accuses his brother wills his death. He must incur death, so that God's right may be established and his superiority ensured" (p. 357). But although there is some truth in what Schlatter says as a judgement, it cannot be allowed to stand as it is as an exposition of the text. Schlatter has not grasped the situation correctly. One cannot say that "the Pharisee forbids Jesus to forgive".

Schniewind's exposition also loses sight of the conflict situation. It is summed up in the question: "Does the Pharisee . . . really understand that his joyless service is a sign of how he has *lost* his fellowship with the Father, although outwardly he remains in it, and strains himself with all his might to fulfil the Father's commandment? Does he notice that his anger over the goodness of the father is a sign of how far he himself is separated from the Father? . . . Does the Pharisee notice that he himself is thrown back on Jesus' mercy?" (op. cit., pp. 81f). Because Schniewind makes the methodological mistake of overinterpreting the parable narrative in order to edify, and identifies it with the historical situation, he misses the situation. The Pharisee is not angry at God's goodness! At the same time the way that parable and situation really work in together eludes him.

According to Jülicher the relation of the parable to the actual situation exists only in Luke's understanding of it (II, p. 359). The parable "is not so much a defence of Jesus the friend of sinners against the attacks of pious obscurantists as . . . a lofty revelation about a basic question of religion, namely, can the God of righteousness receive sinners graciously? This is a question Jesus had to answer at some time for himself and for his own followers, quite independently of any grumbling by the Pharisees" (II, p. 363). This view of the proclamation of Jesus, which makes of him a systematic theologian, can hardly be right.

For Jüngel (pp. 162f) in this parable "the kingdom of God acquires linguistic expression as love coming to pass". The point of the parable is: "You have been found by God's prevenient love as men who are called to joy over this love" (p. 164).

Jüngel does not consider how the hearers of the parable could deduce from the story of the love of the father towards both his sons, which Jesus of Nazareth tells them, that *they* have been found by the love of *God*, nor how the kingdom of God acquires linguistic expression for them through the parable. But one cannot give up the question of the situation in which the parable was told. In fact Jesus uses this parable to justify trust in the power of love. But this trust means, in concrete terms, table fellowship with tax-collectors and sinners.

5. THE PARABLE OF THE LABOURERS IN THE VINEYARD

1. Jeremias, p. 137.
2. Against Jeremias, p. 136: "The fact that between 4 and 5 p.m. the master of the house was still looking for more labour, shows that the work was unusually urgent."

   Michaelis also spoils the point in the same way. Cf. *Gleichnisse*, pp. 172f, esp. p. 173: "The owner must have been glad to have seen people who still had no work standing there when he came [at the eleventh hour]."
3. Against Billerbeck, IV, pp. 486f, cf. Jülicher, I, p. 461: "The text does not give the least indication of differences . . . in the trust placed in the owner."
4. For the same reason the translation suggested by Jeremias for v. 8b, "pay them all the (full day's) wages, including the last" (p. 36, cf. p. 137), seems to me inappropriate, although it is linguistically possible. The parable would be deprived of its effectiveness if the listener did not share the expectation of the first labourers that they would receive more.
5. Jeremias, p. 136.
6. Ibid., p. 137.
7. Jülicher, II, p. 462.
8. Ibid., p. 463; Jeremias, p. 137; cf. above, p. 10. The assumption that the owner (as is usual) is absent at the payment of wages inevitably involves supplying a scene in which the grumbling day-labourers press forward to the owner (see Jeremias, p. 137). It cannot, however, be methodologically justified to go behind the narrative of the parable in this way.
9. Jeremias, p. 137.
10. Bauer, *A Greek-English Lexicon of the New Testament*, p. 314.
11. These statements are based on the material given by Billerbeck, I, pp. 833ff.
12. While Schlatter and Billerbeck retain the connection with 19.30 and under-

stand the parable as a saying to the disciples, Jülicher, Klostermann, Dodd, Jeremias, and Fuchs assign the parable to the dispute which Jesus had to conduct with the Pharisees and scribes because of the attitude he took towards the tax-collectors and sinners.

The most probable solution is that this protest was kindled by Jesus' *behaviour*. In any case it could not be directed against the fact that Jesus "opens the gates of the kingdom of Heaven to tax-collectors and prostitutes" (Klostermann, in dependence on Jülicher). For this would presuppose the recognition by his opponents that Jesus has the power to do so. Nor is justice done to the historical situation if the protest is understood as a criticism of the gospel. Against the assumption that the parable is spoken to men "who criticized the good news" (Jeremias, p. 38), we are bound to ask in what *words* Jesus preached such a gospel for sinners, at which the critics could take offence. The parables cannot be adduced as evidence here, because they presuppose that this offence has already been taken. According to Percy (p. 26), there is "no certain proof that Jesus preached God's forgiveness as a message at all in the same way that he preached the nearness of the kingdom of God". If this assumption is correct, then Jeremias' verdict cannot be maintained: "the Gospel in the true sense of the word . . . says . . . Jesus has come as a saviour for *sinners*" (p. 124). Cf. on this Jeremias, p. 213, and my answer to his remarks, p. 178.

Cadoux sees the situation completely differently: with the expulsion of the money-changers from the forecourt of the gentiles in the temple, Jesus asserted that the temple had been given as a house of prayer "for all nations". "The Jewish objection would be: Why should they who have not borne 'the burden and heat of the day' now have equality in privilege?" (p. 102). Apart from the fact that Mark 11.17f is taken by Bultmann as an interpretative saying that has been added subsequently to Mark 11.15f (cf. *HST*, p. 36), the purification of the forecourt of the gentiles—which was in any case open to everyone—could not possibly make the Israelites think that by this action the gentiles were being assigned equal privileges.

13. Apart from the question whether the "evil eye" in v. 15b must be understood as envy, it is an error of method to draw conclusions directly from the parable to the historical situation. Usually there is an "interlocking" between parable and historical situation (cf. above, p. 27).

Jeremias seems to miss the basic character of the conflict when he assumes that Jesus wanted to show the Pharisees by the parable "how unjustified, hateful, loveless and unmerciful was their criticism" (p. 38).

14. Even if the introductory formula is not original—a possibility that must be allowed for—the assumption that Jesus is speaking here of *God's* goodness would remain materially correct, because in fact his attitude to tax-collectors and sinners, which is here at issue, has a connection with his proclamation of the arrival of the kingdom of God. Admittedly it is a difficult question how Jesus' *listeners* could see clearly that Jesus was alluding to God's action. Perhaps one may take into consideration the associations that the image of payment of wages must have suggested to them.

This must not, however, lead us to identify allegorically the payment of wages in the parable with the last judgement.

15. What answer does Jesus give his listeners to their criticism of his conduct by a parable that alludes to God's action? The answering of this question presents one of the leading problems for the exposition of this parable, which clearly none of the commentators has yet succeeded in solving properly.

The question stands in close connection with one's view of the historical situation in which Jesus told the parable. According to Jülicher the Pharisees regarded it as "a destruction of the righteousness of God" that Jesus "opened . . . the doors of the kingdom of Heaven to everyone". Jesus refutes them with a parable the point of which is that goodness can exist alongside justice. God deals "justly and unobjectionably when he holds open the one kingdom of Heaven for all who follow his summons, both sinners and righteous" (II, p. 466).

Could the objection of the Pharisees be that the conduct of Jesus destroyed the righteousness of God? One would in that case have to suppose that the unity between the conduct of Jesus and the action of God was an obvious and established idea to Jesus' opponents! It was *his own* conduct Jesus had to defend by the parable, not God's righteousness.

According to Dodd the parable is "a striking picture of the divine generosity which gives without regard to the measures of strict justice. But its 'setting in life' must surely be sought in the facts of the ministry of Jesus. The divine generosity was specifically exhibited in the calling of publicans and sinners who had no merit before God. The kingdom of God is like that. Such is Jesus' retort to the complaints of the legally minded who cavilled at Him as the friend of publicans and sinners" (p. 92).

Dodd, unlike Jülicher, has correctly seen that the attacks of the Pharisees were directed against *Jesus*. But would it have been an answer to these objections to set before them "a striking picture of the divine generosity"? It is certainly the faith of Jesus that God shows this generosity to tax-collectors and sinners. The only question is whether and how the parable could help Jesus' *listeners* to share this faith.

How does Dodd understand the sentence, "The kingdom of God is like that"? As instruction? This would suppose that Jesus' hearers acknowledged him as having authority to impart to them binding teaching about the kingdom of God! As an assertion? Jesus' choice of the parable form serves as proof that it was not enough for him to oppose his own view to that of his opponents about the situation, but that it was important for him to win their agreement.

According to Jeremias what Jesus says to his hearers by the parable is: "God acts like an employer who has compassion for the unemployed and their families. So he acts now. He gives to publicans and sinners a share, all undeserved, in his kingdom. So will he deal with them in the Last Day. That, says Jesus, is what he is like; and because he is like that, so am I; since I am acting under his orders and in his stead. Will you then murmur against God's goodness?" (p. 139).

The connection of Jesus' conduct with God's action is new compared with Dodd: *because* God is like that, so am I. This connection is correct as a fact, but it is wrong to regard it as being asserted by the parable. The parable makes no direct assertion about the connection between God's action and Jesus' conduct. Jesus' listeners could only discover such a link from the interplay of parable and situation.

Dodd and Jeremias, by making the parable an illustration of the goodness of God, miss the argumentative character of the parable, on which its effect depends.

According to Fuchs "coming from Jesus, the parable . . . declares: 'This is how things stand with regard to God's goodness—I know it and am showing it to you—it is like a great Lord, who once. . . .' And its unwritten introductory saying is: *Amēn, legō hymīn*, inasmuch as the parable effects and demands a decision" (*Studies*, p. 36). Fuchs, like Dodd and Jeremias, seems to understand the parable as an illustration of God's goodness. But in opposition to this a few lines later Fuchs declares: "The parable itself tells us that Jesus . . . solicits understanding by giving us to understand his conduct as God's conduct. *It is up to the person who understands the parable to give the verdict on the truth of Jesus' claim. It is the person who understands who has to decide*" (*Studies*, p. 37, cf. also p. 155). So here it is seen that the parable is not a communication of a revelation, but a saying that makes possible and demands a decision. But Fuchs does not go into the question *how* the parable can help Jesus' listeners to "understand his conduct as God's conduct".

For Schlatter the problem how the parable connects together God's action and Jesus' conduct does not arise, because he regards the connection of the parable with the logia Matt. 19.30 and 20.16 as original, and assumes that the parable was formed for the interpretation of 19.30 (cf. *Matt.*, p. 592). He renders its meaning as follows: "Now we know how the last can become first; it is through freely given grace. But we know also that when one who is first falls . . . Resistance to the goodness of God makes such people, who received more grace than others, become the last" (*Matt.*, p. 586).

Michaelis rightly points out: "So when the parable speaks in the first instance of the goodness of God . . . , there must have been a certain tension between this and the fact that Jesus wants to justify his own conduct towards tax-collectors and sinners by this parable" (*Gleichnisse*, p. 179). For him, however, this tension arouses "doubts about the connection of the parable with the Pharisees" (ibid.). Our view on the other hand is that this tension is necessarily given in Jesus' situation, because Jesus does in fact connect his own conduct with God's action.

The further objection which Michaelis raises against regarding the Pharisees as the intended audience of the parable only arises from a mistake in method, of giving meanings to individual features: "Had it really been the Pharisees who were aimed at, would it have been so obviously prescribed that the grumbling workers too were to receive their 'reward' as agreed on? Would it then not have been more strongly stressed—to avoid the Pharisaic idea of reward—that all reward is of grace, and that man has no claim before God to any reward . . . ?"

C. W. F. Smith fixes the point of the parable in the following way: "The sort of judgement expected . . . would certainly be that, though eccentric, the farmer had the right to be generous and to ignore calculation if he wished. On the spiritual plane it reminds us that God's dealings with man are independent of man's carefully calculated achievement" (p. 130). The exposition is based on a methodologically wrong emphasis on a subsidiary feature of the parable, the expectation of the whole-day labourers that they would get more (which can anyway hardly be described as "calculation"). Instead of the goodness of the householder, his sovereignty is made the point of the parable.

According to Cadoux, the parable deals with the objection of the Jews, "Why should the heathen, who have not borne the burden of the law, get the same rights?" (see n. 12). The answer it gives is "that this leaves out of count . . . the gentile's lack of opportunity, the goodness of God and the fact that religious truth is not an honorary privilege but a necessity of life" (p. 102). This exposition also rests essentially on subsidiary features of the parable, on the excuse of the last, "No man hath hired us", and the circumstance that in the end they do not receive just any large sum but the pay for the day, which is necessary for the support of life (cf. Cadoux, p. 103). This exposition is unable to catch the original meaning of the parable because it does not determine its situation correctly.

According to Bornkamm the parable is the "proclamation of the sovereign supremacy and freedom of God's goodness, in which fairness is quite certainly not excluded but included (v. 13), but which at the same time transcends all ideas of right and fairness. When this goodness appears it shames and condemns the heart of man. For the parable brings to light that behind the obstinate insistence of man on justice and order, the heart of man itself is ruled by injustice and disorder, possessed by envy and by the pressure of self-assertion" ("Der Lohngedanke im NT", p. 158, cf. p. 83). Bornkamm transforms the parable narrative into direct theological utterances. He fails to notice the interplay of parable and dialogue situation. Inevitably therefore he misses the *argumentative character* of the parable, which is dependent on the power of analogy. This becomes particularly clear in the following formulation: [The owner makes the last like the first], "an attitude which cuts through all the laws of civil order and justice. . . . This makes it abundantly clear, however, that this parable is meant to *proclaim* God's sovereignty, *in contrast to all human conceptions* of work and wages. . . ." (*Jesus*, p. 143, my italics. On the question of the unusual features, cf. above, pp. 28f). The parable "proclaims" something that is "in contrast to all human conceptions", in other words it imparts a revelation. "God's heart is here revealed. But also the heart of man . . ." (ibid., p. 143). But one can receive revelations only from a man who has identified himself already as one who can make revelations with authority. And the revelation discourse does not need the medium of the parable.

6. THE GREAT SUPPER

1. Billerbeck, II, pp. 202 and 204.
2. That the testing of the field and the proving of the performance of the yoke of oxen was a part of the purchase is shown by the passage quoted by Billerbeck, II, p. 208, on Luke 14.19: "AZ 15a (in no place may cattle be sold to the heathen, AZ 1, 6) Rammi b. Jeba (date unknown) said: 'This is a preventative measure . . ., in connection with the testing . . . ; for one could be selling

the beast before sunset on the eve of the Sabbath, and the purchaser could say to him (to the Israelite that was selling): Come, produce it for testing . . . and it could hear his voice and in consequence run, and because he is pleased that it runs, he would (if meanwhile the Sabbath had begun) be one that drives his cattle on the Sabbath; and whoever drives his cattle on the Sabbath is liable to a sacrifice for sin.'"

3. This seems to me to be shown at least for the purchase of a team from the passage quoted in n. 2. If it had not been usual to conduct a purchase and the testing connected with it in the evening, a prescription of that sort could hardly have arisen.

4. For further grounds that support this assumption see n. 8.

5. See Billerbeck, IV, 2, pp. 616f. I must thank Professor Jeremias for the reference to this passage.

6. It is widely assumed that vv. 22f are an allegorical expansion, which adds to the invitation to the tax-collectors and sinners in Israel, which was read out of v. 21, an invitation to the gentiles. But against this it can be argued:

    1. This conclusion is not justified by the fact that corresponding verses are not found in Matthew. The Lucan and Matthean versions of the parable are not parallels, but variant narratives, as is generally recognized. Variants, however, cannot be reduced to a common basic text by the help of the alternatives of abbreviation and expansion. Each variant has its independent narrative flow. In cases of divergence it must therefore always be asked whether they can be understood from their function in their own version of the story.

    2. The second of the subsequent invitations takes place on the grounds of information that there is still room, and with the intention that the house should be full. If this motif appeared only in v. 22 one could possibly see in it a narrative device by which to append the inserted verses to the preceding narrative. But the repetition shows that the motif has an independent significance.

    3. If vv. 22f were an allegorical expansion, not only the invitation of the people from the highways and hedges, but also its motivation, "the house must be filled", would have to be grounded in the reality part. This however is impossible:

    (a) The call of the gentiles could not be based theologically on the fact that not all the places in the kingdom of God could be filled by the repentant sinners in Israel;

    (b) Nor would a call of the gentiles with the *purpose* of excluding the pious in Israel from the kingdom of God be conceivable; but the command in v. 23 is explained by v. 24.

7. Jeremias, p. 177, following Hauck.

8. The firmly linked causal connection of vv. 21–4 makes the assumption inevitable, I believe, that the later invitation takes place with the express intention of excluding those originally invited. In v. 21 the invitation is motivated by the *wrath* of the master of the house. In vv. 22f it becomes clear that this measure, ordered in wrath, is to serve a specific *purpose*: the house must be filled.

    Considering the economy with which stories of this sort are fashioned, one must be prepared to allow that this trait, which is emphasized by repetition, has a particular function in the flow of the parable. As we have just seen, it cannot serve the purpose of inserting the second invitation of the substitute guests into the context of the story. On the other hand, to put it the other way round, the second invitation seems to have no other function than to add this motive, which could not be expressed in v. 21, since the wrath of the host had to be given here first of all as the motive for the later invitation. Cf. on this C. W. F. Smith, p. 177: "... the deliberateness of the redoubled effort to fill the places ... serves to heighten the drama and reinforce the point ... and ... establishes the climactic point, that the aim of the host is to fill every place ..."

Verse 24 declares the reason why the house must be filled right to the last place: none of those originally invited is to taste of the meal.

It is in this sense, I believe, that the future in v. 24 has to be understood. Since v. 24 is the key point which links together that "picture part" and the "reality part", it cannot here be a matter of a bare statement of fact, otherwise the parable would be without effect. Nor would a bare statement of fact be recounted, in view of the economy that prevails in parable narratives.

When we are told in vv. 21–4 that the master of the house takes specific measures to exclude the guests originally invited, the conduct of the host would be meaningless if the excuses of the guests had to be understood as refusals, as is generally assumed.

This problem of the parable has recently been set out by W. Salm: "It is not the guests, who simply do not want to come, but the host that is made to look ridiculous: this can at best be veiled by his vigorous concluding words" (p. 145). Salm therefore connects the parable with the story transmitted in J. Sanh, 6.23c, par. J. Hag. 2.77d of the tax-collector Bar Ma'jan, and sees in the host a tax-collector who tries in vain to get accepted by the highest circles.

This exposition faces the difficulty that it removes the correspondence between "picture part" and "reality part". In the "picture part" the host would be the one made to look foolish, his measures in vv. 21–3 an attempt to make a good show of it, and v. 24 a meaningless piece of rhetoric. In the "reality part" on the other hand it must be the other way round. In so far as the banquet is an allusion to the feast at the time of salvation, a point on which all the expositors agree, the host must here retain his superiority. For that anyone should seriously and voluntarily renounce a share in the kingdom of God is as unthinkable as is the idea that God's threat is empty talk. With such a contradiction between "picture part" and "reality part" the parable would not, as its task is, create the right attitude to the matter in question, but directly work against it.

This difficulty is shown up in Salm's exposition by the fact that the listeners have to be told in an explicit statement by Jesus what is meant by the parable: "... the epilogue sounds out short and harsh: 'In laughing at that poor fool, you are laughing, you specimens of cant and complacency, not at me but at God! What you have just laughed at and mocked at is—*mutatis mutandis*—the final picture which the earth experiences shortly before the coming of the end'" (Salm, p. 146).

But we are bound to ask how much of this "epilogue", so packed with a mass of thoughts, can really be deduced from v. 24.

One can hardly assert any dependence of the parable on the story handed down in J. Sanh. 6.23c, such as would make a consideration of it necessary for the exposition. There is no need of these parallels for the explanation of the unusual features, that "(1) the invited guests, one and all, as if by agreement 'all at once' decline the invitation, and (2) in their place the host deliberately invites the beggars and the homeless" (Jeremias, p. 178). One will have to look for the occasion of the unusual feature of the refusal by all in the "reality part", following Madsen's observation that it is just the unusual features of the parables that go back to the "reality part" (cf. above, pp. 28f). The invitation of the beggars and homeless is explained if what matters to the host is to get substitute guests "quickly" (v. 21). Guests that he could invite as stop-gaps from one minute to another would *have* to be sought among such people.

It cannot be right to connect the intention of the master of the house to exclude the original guests with the assumption that they might well change their minds. For a man to decline a banquet and yet afterwards to come is so unusual that no one surely takes measures against such an eventuality. The idea of such a change of mind is only conceivable in respect of men's attitude towards the kingdom of God. But the exposition has to start not from the "reality part" but from the "picture part" (against Jülicher, II, p. 432; C. W. F. Smith, p. 177; Madsen, p. 18).

The problem of the parable seems to me therefore to be insoluble—*unless* the excuses of the guests are to be thought of not as refusals, but as excuses for arriving later. We are then, however, compelled to take v. 20 as a secondary expansion. On this see n. 16.

Jeremias has considerably altered his exposition of the parable—probably under the influence of mine—in his latest edition. He gives the parable a completely new classification. It no longer comes under the heading "God's mercy for sinners", but under the newly created heading "It may be too late". It no longer asks "the critics of the Gospel": "Where do you get the right to pour scorn and derision on the wretched crowd who sit at my table?", but describes how "it may be too late" (p. 176).

Since, however, Jeremias does not accept my view that the excuses are for a late arrival, but continues to follow Salm in his exposition, we have a mixture of the new and the old, which seems to me to be unsuccessful. Jeremias says: "This parable, too, is not fully understood until attention is paid to the note of joy which rings through the summons: 'Everything is ready' (v. 17). 'Behold, now is the acceptable time; behold, now is the day of salvation' (2 Cor. 6.2). God fulfils his promises and comes forward out of his hiddenness" (p. 180). But how are the listeners to the parable to hear this note of joy, if v. 17 gives them the idea that a social upstart is trying to get in with the right people? Is it conceivable that they "must have been shocked" when Jesus, the master of the house [sic], sharply declares, "The house is full, the number is complete, the last place is occupied; close the doors, none henceforth may be admitted" (pp. 179f)? Even the postulated sharp cry of Jesus can hardly lead the listeners to think that the story of the host who has been exposed to ridicule, over which they have just burst into "audible laughter", is meant to convey to them that they are at this moment risking their right to a place at the table of God. As Jeremias interprets the parable, both now and previously, one listens in vain to hear how "it may be too late".

Jeremias (p. 178, n. 23) objects to my exposition on the ground that in the Gospel of Thomas, in Matthew's version, and in the story given in J. Sanh. 6.23c the replies are understood as definite refusals. This overlooks the fact that the differences of these texts within themselves and against Luke 14.16–24 are so considerable that the possibility of a difference on this point too must be admitted.

(a) J. Sanh. 6.23c lacks not only any sort of excuse or refusal by the guests, but also any equivalent whatever of Luke 14.22–4. But it is precisely these verses which compel us to the assumption that the excuses refer to a later arrival. The finality of the absence of the guests results in the Rabbinic narrative from the situation. But in Jesus' parable there is no support whatever for the idea that the host is to be thought of as a tax-collector. If Jesus had meant this, why should he not have said it? Could he expect that this Rabbinic narrative was the common property of his hearers? Could his listeners know that he had this story in mind, only because his story had in common with it three themes (invitation, unanimous refusal, substitute invitation [of the poor])? It is only the learned scholar, not the simple listener, who is used to identifying stories on the basis of themes found in common.

(b) On the divergences of the Matthean version, see above, pp. 93f. This version too has no equivalent to Luke 14.22–4, and the lack of any sort of excuse of the guests excludes in advance any idea of a later arrival.

(c) There is no equivalent to Luke 14.22–3 in the Gospel of Thomas either. The reasons for the excuses of the guests are also quite different from those in Luke and exclude in advance any idea of their later arrival (see below, n. 15).

Eichholz fails entirely to recognize the problem set by the parable—probably because (in contrast to his own principles) he falls into vigorous allegorization. The point of the parable eludes him because of this. Though he has certainly seen that this point lies in the situation indicated by v. 15, he is not able to hold firmly to this. For this reason the meaning of the parable is for him reduced to several scarcely connected theological statements: "What the parable impresses upon us and proclaims is the miracle of the *grace of invitation*. One can also say that it is about the sovereignty of the mercy of God. God's mercy can be forfeited . . . and God's table does not remain empty" (*Einführung in die Gleichnisse*, pp. 64f).

9. The close connection of v. 24 with v. 23 (the "for" shows v. 24 to be the grounds for v. 23 or vv. 21–3, and the words "my banquet" in v. 24 correspond to "my house" in v. 23) shows that this verse is still part of the parable narrative (see Jeremias, pp. 177f). The solemn manner of speaking is no objection to this, as is shown by the formal parallels Matt. 18.13; Luke 11.8; 18.14. These verses are definitely part of the parable narrative but are specially emphasized by the narrator, because they form the turning point that links the "picture part" with the "reality part." The difference in Luke 14.24 is that this utterance, belonging to the picture part, but referring ahead to the reality part, is not spoken by the narrator but in this strongly dialogue narrative

is put in the mouth of the leading character. It is only the plural in the address in v. 24 that creates difficulties; it cannot be directed to the one servant. But in my opinion it can be understood to mean that here the master of the house turns as it were to the general public, and explains to them the meaning and intention of the measures he has taken—a feature that is common in popular drama.

10. It seems to me conceivable that v. 15 belongs originally together with the parable. We have a formal parallel for the connection of a blessing with a polemical retort in Luke 11.27f. Furthermore we know from the controversy dialogues the custom of giving a polemical answer in the form of a parable.

If v. 15 does belong originally with the parable of the great supper, it must have undergone a slight alteration when it was inserted into its context in Luke. The beginning of the verse must previously have been something like: "A Pharisee said to him", which in the context of the Pharisee's banquet (Luke 14.1–14) could easily become "one of those invited".

Bultmann (*HST*, pp. 125, 129, 193), whom Klostermann follows, regards v. 15 as a redactional transition which the Evangelist has formed, making use of the blessing in v. 15b, which he has taken from the tradition. Against this can be raised the following objections:

1. The redactional activity of Luke in the introductory and transitional verses is in general considerably more modest than would allow us to attribute to him so complicated a process of linking.

2. The assumption that Luke has put into the mouth of some unnamed table companion of Jesus a piece of tradition, i.e. a logion, that was passed down to him as a saying of Jesus, seems to me untenable.

3. The blessing is besides much too general (and in fact just as possible for a Pharisee as for Jesus), to make it probable that it was passed down as a saying of Jesus. One only needs to contrast with it the beatitudes in the Sermon on the Mount to see this.

Our fixing of the historical setting of the parable is in any case independent of the genuineness of this verse.

11. See Schlatter, *Lukas* p. 336: "The Pharisee would expect Jesus to agree unconditionally with what he had said. Did not his beatitude too say, 'Yours is the kingdom of God'?"

What is here said of course becomes untrue as soon as it is understood as a psychological statement about the thoughts and feelings of an individual. We are dealing with *typical* features of the historical situation, which are expressed in an "idealized" scene.

12. Fuchs, *Das urchristliche Sakramentsverständnis*, p. 24. Cf. Bornkamm, *Jesus*, p. 81. Cf. also Dodd, p. 91: ". . . the words of invitation . . . : 'Come, for all is ready', correspond to the call of Jesus, 'Repent, for the kingdom of God has come.'"

13. Against Bultmann, *Jesus and the Word*, pp. 31f.

14. Cf. Otto, *Kingdom*, pp. 150–4.

15. The parallel in the Gospel of Thomas also belongs to the history of the exposition of the parable. It runs: "(64) Jesus said: A man had guest-friends, and when he had prepared the dinner, he sent his servant to invite the guest-

friends. He went to the first, he said to him: 'My master invites thee.' He said: 'I have some claims against some merchants; they will come to see me in the evening; I will go and give them my orders. I pray to be excused from the dinner.' He went to another, he said to him: 'My master has invited thee.' He said to him: 'I have bought a house and they request me for a day. I will have no time.' He came to another, he said to him: 'My master invites thee.' He said to him: 'My friend is to be married and I am to arrange a dinner; I shall not be able to come. I pray to be excused from the dinner.' He went to another, he said to him: 'My master invites thee.' He said to him: 'I have bought a farm, I go to collect the rent. I shall not be able to come. I pray to be excused.' The servant came, he said to his master: 'Those whom thou hast invited to the dinner have excused themselves.' The master said to his servant: 'Go out to the roads, bring those whom thou shalt find, so that they may dine. Tradesmen and merchants [shall] not [enter] the places of my Father.'" (*The Gospel according to Thomas*, ed. Guillaumont and others, pp. 35, 37. The Greek words in brackets have been left out.)

16. Although there are no absolutely compelling grounds for the assumption that v. 20 is secondary, a large number of points argue against the originality of this verse:

    1. In v. 20 the request to be excused, which occurs in the same form both in v. 18 and in v. 19, is lacking.

    2. Verse 20 has no equivalent in Matthew.

    3. The corresponding passage in the Gospel of Thomas (see n. 15) gives no direct parallel. Admittedly a wedding is there spoken of; it is not, however, the wedding of a guest which has just taken place, but a wedding feast which the man invited has to organize for a friend of his.

    4. The parallel in the Gospel of Thomas shows, I believe, that there was a tendency to multiply the number of excuses.

    5. The motive for a later supplementation of the verse is not hard to find. As soon as the parable was employed parenetically, and seen as a picture of the attitude men take towards God's invitation, the one-sidedness of the examples chosen must have been noticed. It is certainly not only possessions that hold men captive in this manner.

    6. In the context of the parable narrative, v. 20 offers material difficulties. From v. 16 one must suppose that those invited had originally accepted the invitation. While a favourable opportunity for a purchase may arise unforseeably and so provide a possible excuse for a sudden refusal, this cannot conceivably be said of a man's own wedding! With the wedding there could be a motive for the total rejection of an invitation ("Only men were invited to a banquet, and the newly married man does not wish to leave his young wife alone", Jeremias, p. 177), but not for a sudden subsequent refusal.

17. While only Lohmeyer among more recent exegetes has regarded Matt. 22.1–14 as a unitary element of tradition, Rengstorf has recently sought (in "Die Stadt der Mörder", *Judentum, Urchristentum, Kirche*, pp. 106–29) "to raise again the question of the original unity of the parable Matt. 22.1–14". He does this on the strength of the observation that vv. 6f contain "a theme that comes from the ancient East and was preserved into post-Biblical Palestinian Judaism" (p. 125). He gives as the "basic elements of the schema",

"King; assertion or expansion of lordship; struggle, above all for cities, and their destruction, with all consequences of this for the population" (p. 110).

There is no doubt that this observation is correct, but it settles nothing for the question of the unity of this pericope:

Vv. 6f cannot form "the centre of the parable in a decisive manner" (pp. 126f). If this theme were "the core of the whole" and if in this parable we had correspondingly "to deal with the representation of royal sovereignty and its enforcement" (p. 126), the parable would have had to end with v. 7. Vv. 8f cannot be understood from this motive. To see in the "free choice of guests" the expression of "royal sovereignty" (p. 126) is absurd. This freedom is open to every private citizen. In any case the point of comparison of the parable cannot lie in vv. 6f, because by the principles of structure it is to be sought at the end.

Vv. 6f clearly disturb the flow of the narrative. The verdict of the king in vv. 8f not only has an "insipid" effect (Schmid, *Matthäus*, p. 310) if it is to refer to the murderers mentioned in vv. 6f, but it also appears of no significance in its consequences (the invitation of substitute guests) if the destruction of the murderers (v. 7) has already been told. Similar difficulties are caused by the obscure juxtaposition of vv. 5 and 6: a climax is not achieved. The connection *hoi de loipoi* [but the rest] is blurred. Verse 5 is not worth telling alongside v. 6. Besides, it does not belong to the theme. The saying of the king in v. 8: "The marriage is ready" is only possible in immediate connection with v. 5.

Vaccari regards the insertion of the punishment in immediate connection with the murder of the servants of the king as a stylistic anticipation. But he overlooks the fact that a parable has no subsidiary course of events, but has a unitary flow of narrative.

Accordingly the theme of vv. 6f can only be a secondary insertion into the parable.

The need for such an expansion could arise only at a time when the parable was interpreted allegorically, and trait after trait of the narrative identified with the "reality". Vv. 6f can then be connected only with the destruction of Jerusalem. Their subordinate position in the context of the narrative excludes the possibility of understanding them as a prophetic threat. Consequently there only remains the assumption that these verses are already looking back to the fall of Jerusalem—as the majority of commentators assume.

The observation that vv. 6f contain a regular theme is no objection to this assumption. On the contrary it refutes objections that have been raised against it:

1. If the fall of Jerusalem has been added to the picture with the help of a traditional theme, it is irrelevant to point out that the verses "are kept much too general for the destruction of Jerusalem to have provided them with their model" (Michaelis, *Einleitung in das Neue Testament*, ed. 2, Berne, 1954, p. 41).

2. Then it is precisely the objection that for the mind of Judaism the catastrophe consisted less in the burning of the dwelling areas than in the destruction of the Temple (Rengstorf, p. 125) that cannot be made. One

cannot expect a general theme and the particular case to correspond exactly; yet the particular case can be appealed to by means of the theme.

To sum up, we can establish that the observation that vv. 6f contain a regular theme does not in the least lead to the assumption of the unity of Matt. 22.1–14, but only confirms the objections that have been raised against the authenticity of vv. 6f.

18. The reason the parable speaks of a wedding feast for the son does not have to be sought in an allegorical interest. The beginning of the parable Matt. 22.10c–13 is perhaps to be found in Matt. 22.2 (see Jeremias, p. 68; cf. Matt. 22.10, *ho nymphōn* [the wedding chamber]).

19. The double invitation in Matthew is not an allegorical expansion, as is widely supposed, but only a variant narrative of what is reported in Luke 14.16f: the king sends "his slaves (vv. 3 and 4) twice, once to invite, the second time to announce the hour of the banquet" (Schniewind). *Hoi keklēmenoi* in v. 3 are not those (already) invited, but those who are to be invited. There is a Semitism here: the perfect has a gerundive significance (Jeremias, p. 68, n. 74).

20. The numerous divergences of the passage in Matthew from the parallels in Luke, which can be understood neither as allegorical additions nor as redactional alterations, show that the allegory in Matt. 22.2–14 is not based on the Lucan version of the parable but on an independent variant of the narrative. It is also generally assumed that the two versions Luke 14 and Matt. 22 do not go back to the same prototype. (According to Hasler the Matthean version goes back to Q, while the Lucan version is from his special material.) But the differences in construction of the narrative flow of the two variants have as far as I am aware not been examined before. The two variants belong in any case to different types of parables, which Bugge has distinguished as illustrative and argumentative parables. The illustrative parable of Matt. 22 could easily pass over into allegory, for illustrative parables border on allegory (cf. Bugge, p. 60).

Trilling assumes that the allegorization of the pericope in Matthew has taken place in two stages. The earlier of the two, the accretion of vv. 10–14, will have been shaped by typical parenetic concerns, while the later stage, vv. 6 and 7, will have had a polemical aim, and have caused its connection with the polemical parables 21.28–32 and 21.33–46.

The prerequisite of this hypothesis is the view that the parable pursues two aims, "one polemical, which is directed at the failure of Israel in the history of salvation, and one parenetic". Its consequence is the thesis "that we have to allow for a fairly lengthy period of transmission . . . which lies . . . between Mark and Q and the final redaction". One cannot place the "whole redaction" "on one literary level".

Against this it must be pointed out that the insertion of verses 6 and 7 would never have made an effective polemic out of the postulated parenetic allegory of 22.1–5, 8–14. For this reason I cannot agree with the assumption that this insertion was made with polemical intent, nor with the view that the parable had a polemical as well as its parenetic aim. I can only here mention, without establishing it in detail, that the arguments brought forward for the assumption of different levels of redaction in Matthew's Gospel seem to me insufficient.

Hasler's attempt to demonstrate in Matt. 22.1–14 three redactional layers in Matthew's reworking of the traditional material found in Q does not seem to me to be successful. Hasler in fact confines himself to showing the biases which he thinks have been at work in the individual layers and to pointing them out in individual features of the parable. He does not undertake any literary-critical division of the individual layers, which would be needed to prove his case here—but seems to be impossible to carry out on the basis of his comments.

21. Verse 13b is for Matthew a "characteristic (Matthew 6 times, Luke once) closing formula" (Jeremias, p. 104). The "furthermost darkness" is also "characteristic of him" (cf. Matt. 25.30 with Luke 19.24, 25, Matt. 8.12 with Luke 13.28). Probably there originally stood in Matt. 22.13a as in Luke 13.28 a simple *exō*.

The reading of D in v. 13a in spite of its weak attestation makes the more authentic impression, because it does not bear the traces of the allegorical understanding of the parable. This is also the view of A. Merx (*Das Evangelium des Matthäus*, Berlin, 1902, p. 299), J. Wellhausen (*Das Evangelium Matthäi*, Berlin, 1904, p. 111), and Klostermann (*Matt.*, p. 177). The binding of the damned is a regular feature in representations of the last judgement (cf. Mark 6.17; Shabbath 152b; Plato Rep. X.615e; quoted in Klostermann, *Matt.*, p. 177). There is one parallel for throwing out by seizing hands and feet (Yalkuth I, 867, quoted by Klostermann, p. 177).

If the variant of the Western text is authentic, as is supported by the parataxis, it must go back to a subsidiary tradition. Since the parable was already understood allegorically by the Evangelist, the reading of the great majority of the manuscripts no doubt goes back to him.

G. Barth ("Matthew's Understanding of the Law", in *Tradition and Interpretation in Matthew*, p. 59, n. 9) regards Matt. 22.11–13 as a formation by Matthew. The mistake he makes of referring to Jeremias for support could only have been made because he has overlooked the main discussion on pp. 187ff, and only refers to pp. 30 and 65f.

Barth tries to demonstrate Matthean authorship by proof of Matthean peculiarities of language. His evidence, however, does not seem to me compelling. *Theasasthai*, used by Matthew once more than by Luke, settles nothing. The threefold occurrence of *hetaire* in Matthew (not otherwise in the New Testament) proves nothing: in Matt. 20.13 it stands in a piece of tradition; why not here too? Instead of *dēsantes ekballete* some manuscripts offer a reading without this Matthean characteristic. Verse 13 need not have been formed by Matthew, but can just as well have been expanded by him: cf. Luke 13.28 with Matt. 8.12. He could have used *endyma* to replace a less familiar expression in his source—this happens frequently in the course of tradition. The remaining points, the introductory participial construction in v. 11 and the *tote* (v. 13) which is characteristic of Matthew, are hardly sufficient to prove Matthean authorship.

The strongest argument against it lies in the fact that Matthew has read the whole pericope as an allegory, but vv. 11–13 contain a series of concrete features which could not have arisen if these verses were only intended to supply a missing thought in picture form. (It is instructive to compare it from this point of view with vv. 6f.)

22. Jeremias, p. 187.
23. Schniewind, p. 215. According to Jeremias the parable of the "Guest without a wedding garment" is a crisis-parable, with the meaning, "The summons may come at any moment. Woe to the unprepared!" But Jeremias only achieves this sense by going behind the parable to a Rabbinic parallel, and gathering from it that the guest "was invited, but he was a fool; the summons to the wedding-feast came earlier than he had expected" (p. 188). But such a procedure cannot be methodologically justified. Though the parable agrees in some features with the Rabbinic parable, there are considerable differences between the two in construction and in individual features; and it has already been learnt from the comparison of Matt. 22.1–9 with Luke 14.16–24 how little one is justified in introducing into a parable features from a variant. If the parable of the guest without a wedding garment were concerned with the thought that the call to the banquet catches the man while he is still unprepared, this would somehow have to be expressed, perhaps as an answer to the king's question.

Jeremias would understand the wedding garment as a "symbol of the righteousness awarded by God"; "God offers you the clean garment of forgiveness and imputed righteousness. Put it on, one day before the Flood arrives, one day before the inspection of the wedding guests—to-day!" (p. 189). But "the garment is on the contrary *not* given, and the question at issue is not that of 'calling', but of worthiness" (Trilling, p. 259). In the passages quoted by Jeremias in favour of his view the "garment of salvation" is never connected with the forgiveness of sins. On the contrary in Rev. 19.8 it is connected with "the righteous deeds of the saints" (cf. also Isa. 61.10 with 61.8). To quote Luke 15.22 here is a mistake of method. The conferment of the garment of honour is certainly a sign of the father's forgiveness, but it is not thought of in a generalized way as a metaphor for forgiveness.

The meaning of the parable which results from this is not characteristic for Jesus. We must therefore allow for the possibility that it first came into existence in the early Church, perhaps under the influence of the Rabbinic parallel.

24. Jeremias, p. 106.

7. THE UNIQUE OPPORTUNITY

1. Jeremias, who previously regarded the two passages as a double parable, now takes the view that "they are closely connected, but will have been spoken on different occasions" (p. 198). Bultmann (*HST*, p. 173) considers the possibility that the second parable is a later addition, since 13.45 is sharply separated from 13.44 by the new introduction.
2. It is generally assumed that the finder of the treasure is a day-labourer. But it is only in C. W. F. Smith, p. 94, that I have been able to find reasons given for this.

3. It seems to me open to question whether one can, with Jeremias (p. 198), draw from the only occurring parallel J. Hor. 3.48a the definite conclusion for Matt. 13.44 that "his ox sinks into a hole while ploughing". Was this the only possible picture that the narrator could connect with what he says, or that this would create for his listeners? It must also be remembered that the Rabbinic story is fashioned by a motif that is lacking here, that misfortune (the cow breaks a leg) turns out through God's dispensation to be a piece of good fortune.

4. See Derrett. The other motif suggested by Jeremias of burying as a security against theft does not seem to me to be present here. In the exposition of a parable one must in my opinion keep to the motifs that govern the parable *narrative* and not to complexes of motifs that could possibly be at work in the situation described by the parable. This also needs saying with reference to Cadoux's exposition. According to him the reburial of the treasure is to serve to keep the secret: "Let the secret get out, and not all he had would make the field and its treasure his" (p. 143). The thought is certainly correct, but has no part to play in the parable narrative. Cadoux leaves the flow of the narrative completely out of consideration and rests his exposition on an insignificant (in fact not once mentioned!) subsidiary point, when he asserts: "No explanation of the parable that does not do justice to this, its outstanding feature, has any right to be considered." The parable has according to him "special aptitude to what we have seen to be Jesus' ideal for his people—that they should lead the world into God's kingdom by teaching it to know the true God; for we saw that this hope, if it was ever to be realized, must for a time be hidden" (p. 143). This is not the place to go into the questions which need to be raised about this view of Jesus' preaching.

5. Jeremias, p. 199. To answer this question, one would have to know whether the finder, after he had discovered the treasure, had the right to leave it where it was until he could remove it as his own undoubted property (cf. Derrett on this).

6. Jeremias, p. 199.

7. Klostermann, *Matt.*, p. 125.

8. In the Gospel of Thomas a variant to the parable is found, which sees the event a little differently: "(76) Jesus said: The kingdom of the Father is like a man, a merchant, who possessed merchandise (and) found a pearl. That merchant was prudent. He sold the merchandise, he bought the one pearl for himself." (*Gospel of Thomas*, ed. Guillaumont and others, pp. 41–3. The Greek words in brackets have been left out.)

"The situation is obviously represented as being that the merchant is on a purchasing mission. He has already bought all sorts of goods when the pearl comes to his notice. Then he does not stop for thought—he disposes of all the rest of his goods to be able to buy this one pearl, which will be his greatest deal. This is how a good merchant does business" (Hunzinger, p. 220). By contrast, according to Hunzinger, "the version in Matt. 13.46 is less enlightening. To sell all his possessions goes completely beyond what a prudent business man does. The feature is exaggerated in its effect and precisely for that reason unconvincing." Hunzinger conjectures that the version of the parable in Matthew goes back to a secondary assimilation to the parable of the Treasure in the Field.

9. So C. W. F. Smith: "The assumption is that the dealer is not himself a collector but knows a collector who will pay so much for this pearl that the investment of all the dealer's wealth . . . will be more than repaid by a handsome profit" (pp. 96f).

Similarly Jülicher, II, pp. 584f.

Lohmeyer on the other hand assumes that the pearl merchant buys the pearl "for his own possession, only to give up his trading at the same time and to live, though desperately poor, with his treasure" (p. 227). He understands the conduct of the day-labourer similarly: "he gives up . . . all his possessions . . . in order to crouch over a chest containing precious stones and precious metals" (p. 226). Lohmeyer is, however, only able to assume such pointless conduct on the part of the finder because he interprets the parables allegorically, and therefore the "picture part" taken on its own does not need to be meaningful. Having connected the parables with the story of the rich young man, he concludes that they provide "a vivid example of what a disciple has to do" (p. 226). He derives meanings from the parables accordingly. The meaning which the parables had in the mouth of Jesus cannot, however, be ascertained by these methods.

None of Jesus' hearers could have understood the position of the lucky finder as an acceptance of voluntary poverty in order to possess an object of value. The formalized widespread picture of finding a treasure was firmly bound up with the idea of becoming rich, that is, to have opportunities that were out of the question for the poor man, not with the idea of living a life of misery while having a valuable possession.

The direction in which the ideas of Jesus' listeners must have gone is shown not only by the stories quoted in Billerbeck, I, p. 674, but also by the parallel section in the Gospel of Thomas: "(109) Jesus said: The kingdom is like a man who had a treasure [hidden] in his field, without knowing it. And [after] he died, he left it to his [son. The] son did not know (about it), he accepted that field, he sold [it]. And he who bought it, he went, while he was ploughing [he found] the treasure. He began to lend money to whomever he wished" (*Gospel of Thomas*, ed. Guillaumont and others, p. 55).

10. This counts against Klostermann and Schniewind, for whom the parables describe the value of the kingdom of God. In Jülicher and Schlatter also the thought of value is predominant; cf. against this Michaelis, *Gleichnisse*, p. 65.

11. Bultmann, Klostermann, Schniewind, and Schlatter speak of sacrifice. Jeremias, following Gulin, wants to exclude the thought of sacrifice from the exposition of these parables. The double parable has in reality been "completely misunderstood if it is interpreted as an imperious call to heroic action. . . . The decisive thing in the twin parable is not that the two men sacrifice, but the reason for their sacrifice; the overwhelming experience of the splendour of their discovery" (pp. 200f).

Instead of excluding the idea of sacrifice from the exposition from the start, Jeremias tries to play off against one another "sacrifice" and "reason for sacrifice". This is not possible, for both are variations of the same phenomenon. They can only be played off against one another in the question what the point of the parable is. But this is not the overpowering joy, but the risking of all ((cf. p. 101 and notes 13 and 14). Against Jeremias cf. also Michaelis, *Gleichnisse*, pp. 65f.

12. Schniewind, Klostermann, and Schlatter represent the need to sacrifice everything as a consequence of the greatness of the treasure.

13. Cf. Madsen, p. 141: "In the 'picture part' the (more unusual) feature, the discovery of the treasure, has been chosen with an eye on the first feature of the 'reality part'. Its being hidden in a field, the reburial, and the joy were by contrast all phenomena which were bound up in various ways with the discovery. . . . It was different with the sale of all one's possessions. This feature can be explained only as an analogous construction from the reality."

An interpretation which ignores the fact that what matters to the narrator is the risking of all misses the point of the passage. One cannot object, as Jüngel does (p. 145), that the conduct of the lucky finder is governed by the greater value of the thing found. Both belong together, and the difficulty of the exposition lies in relating them correctly.

Pp. 102 and 105 of my book certainly do not say that "both parables lead to an association of thoughts which emphasizes the need 'to turn about, to repent'". Jüngel's assumption (p. 145, n. 3) that my interpretation still results in the thought of sacrifice would seem to rest on a misunderstanding.

The overpowering joy cannot be the point of comparison of the parables any more than the value of the discovery. That the joy is unfolded in the direction of "giving everything up" is not founded in the event but in the stage-management of the narrator. Joy could be expressed quite as well in other ways (cf. Matt 18.13; Luke 15.9). But for the narrator it is risking all that matters. This (against Jeremias) is left as the point of comparison of the parables.

14. To show that the motif of the lucky discovery must also be based on the "reality part", cf. the passage from Madsen quoted in the previous note. In the exposition accordingly weight must be given to the time factor which is contained in the phenomenon of the "unique opportunity". This time factor is the real problem of interpretation which the parables face. Only Dodd, so far as I can see, has considered it explicitly: "You agree that the kingdom of God is the highest good: it is within your power to possess it here and now . . ." (p. 86).

Jülicher derives from the parable the teaching, which is formulated as a principle (and so is timeless), that "as a price for the kingdom of God absolutely nothing . . . can be too dear" (II, p. 585). He reintroduces the time factor in the hypothetical statement; "*Where* [my italics] the acquisition of the kingdom of God is endangered through holding on to former possessions, one should gladly let them go."

Klostermann (*Matt.*, p. 124) and Bultmann (*Theology of the New Testament*, I, p. 11) remove the time factor by drawing from the parable a statement of principle, "One must sacrifice all for the kingdom of God." For Bultmann, however, the time factor comes back again in his notion of "historicity". "For the positive thing that corresponds to this renunciation, the thing, that is, which constitutes readiness for God's reign, is the fulfilment of God's will, as Jesus makes that will evident in combating Jewish legalism."

Schlatter too does not give value to the time factor. In his *Erläuterungen zum neuen Testament* he strangely makes the event of the finding dependent on the conduct of the finder. "Jesus says that we only find God's gift when we put everything else second to it" (p. 163). Here there can of course be no idea of a "unique opportunity". In his *Der Evangelist Matthäus* he says: "The profit is certain: the treasure is extremely rich, and the pearl has unique value" (p. 447). Value is a timeless motif: the "now" of the favourable opportunity is suppressed.

Schniewind and the *Interpreter's Bible* also exclude the time factor by basing their exposition on the motif of timeless value.

In Lohmeyer's formulation of the aim: "When you find the kingdom of God, go and do likewise" (p. 226), the time factor is admittedly retained, but displaced into the hypothetical, which can hardly do justice to Jesus' parable.

In Jeremias' exposition the time factor does not come into consideration: "Thus it is with the kingdom of God. The effect of the joyful news is overpowering; it fills the heart with gladness; it makes life's whole aim the consummation of the divine community and produces most whole-hearted self-sacrifice" (p. 201). The parables appear as a timelessly valid description of what happens when the "joyful news" meets a man. Is such a description conceivable as a saying of Jesus to his listeners? And is it permissible to identify the kingdom of God in this way with the "joyful news"?

It is impossible to give value to the time factor by connecting the moment of finding with encounter with Jesus, as Michaelis does: "The discovery . . . means encounter with Jesus. Jesus is the one who brings the joyful news of the coming kingdom, as he is also the one who one day will make this kingdom a reality" (*Gleichnisse*, p. 66). What does this "encounter with Jesus" mean? What significance could Jesus himself assign to the "encounter"? And how were his listeners to know that the parables are talking of encounter with him? Here dogmatic theology outstrips exegesis! This is even more true when Michaelis asserts: "There can be no suggestion that just as the two men . . . really come into full possession of the treasure and the pearl, in exactly this way the kingdom of God can here and now become the possession of man. Participation in the kingdom is only in the future." Little is achieved by such assertions. What the case is with the kingdom of God is in fact the question that must be answered by the *text*, not by one's dogmatic theology.

The time factor in the parables will have to be understood as a time announcement, as the announcement of the arrival of the kingdom of God, which Jesus' preaching consistently speaks of.

15. Against the *Interpreter's Bible*: "The kingdom of God is so desirable that . . . a man will sell all his worldly possessions to have it . . ."

16. According to Dodd, Jesus uses the double parable to summon people to follow him: "We have to conjecture a situation in which the idea of great sacrifices for a worthy end is prominent. There is no difficulty in finding such a situation. In Mark 10.17–30, and other kindred passages, Jesus is represented as calling for volunteers to join a cause. It may mean leaving home and friends, property and business; it may mean a vagrant life of hardship, with an ignominious death at the end. . . . The parables before us fit such a situa-

tion. They are . . . intended . . . to enforce an appeal which Jesus was making for a specific course of action then and there. . . . We may state the argument thus: 'You agree that the kingdom of God is the highest good: it is within your power to possess it here and now, if, like the treasure-finder and the pearl merchant, you will throw caution to the winds: follow me!'" (pp. 85f).

This interpretation presupposes "that Jesus saw in his own ministry the coming of the kingdom of God" (ibid.). The open question is whether and how Jesus' *listeners* could come to see a connection between following Jesus and obtaining the kingdom of God. Is in fact "the kingdom of God in some way identified with the cause of Jesus" in their eyes too?

According to C. W. F. Smith the parables are directed against Israel, which fears to lose the *status quo* which it has, thanks to the forbearance of Rome, in "complete commitment" (p. 95). Against this rendering of the situation it must be remembered that Jesus was neither a Pharisee who increased the possibilities of conflict with Rome by intensifying the legal duties that set Israel apart, nor a Zealot who demanded revolt against the Roman authorities.

According to Cadoux the parable of the precious pearl gives "the one likely and tolerable explanation . . . to one of the most important, striking and puzzling features of Jesus' work that, with sympathies and aim wide as the world, he confined his work and the immediate work of his disciples to Israel. . . . It was concentration in the interest of extension. He must at all cost to his wider sympathies limit himself to Israel, for otherwise as we have seen, he could not hope to win Israel; but having gained Israel, he could through Israel gain the world" (p. 147).

Cadoux treats the parable as an allegorical representation of the work of Jesus. For him it is the answer to a question which can hardly have been of concern to Jesus' contemporaries. It arises only for those who, like Cadoux, when discussing the mission to the gentiles do not distinguish between the attitude of Jesus and that of the early Church, and because of this have to try to put original sayings of Jesus and secondary formulations of the Church under a common heading.

I cannot here go into Fuchs' comments on this parable (*Studies*, pp. 123–30, cf. pp. 94f), for that would demand too far-reaching a discussion of questions of methods.

8. THE PARABLE OF THE UNMERCIFUL SERVANT

1. The assumption that the parable is concerned with forgiveness is no doubt right. There is a Rabbinic parallel too which uses remission of tax debts as an image of God's forgiveness (Billerbeck, I, p. 799, on Matt. 18.27). As Professor Jeremias has informed me orally, Aramaic has only the word *ḥōba* for sin, which also means a money debt. For forgiveness it uses *šᵉbaq*, which also has the meaning "forgo a debt".

2. Jeremias further points out that the "'*dia touto*' (Matt. 18.23) indicating the

link between Matt. 18.21f and the parable of the Unmerciful Servant, is a linguistic peculiarity of Matthew" (p. 97).

3. See Bultmann, *HST*, p. 141. Possibly the piece of tradition which corresponds to Luke 17.3 already lay before the Evangelist in the expanded version of Matt. 18.15–17 (or –18) (without 16b) (Bultmann, *HST*, ibid.; G. Barth, *Tradition and Interpretation in Matthew*, p. 84). But then it will have to be assumed that *at the same time* he had before him the unit of tradition Luke 17.3f. Otherwise it cannot be explained why Matthew a few verses later gives an equivalent to Luke 17.4. A piece of tradition in which an equivalent of Luke 17.4 followed Matt. 18.17 (or 18) immediately is inconceivable.

4. Billerbeck, I, p. 795, produced the proof that the passage Tos. Yoma 5.13, "Three times one forgives, a fourth time one does not forgive", is to be referred to the forgiveness of God. In spite of this Schlatter, even in the later editions of his *Der Evangelist Matthäus*, still maintains that Peter's question is to be understood in the light of a casuistic limitation of the forgiveness of sins in the Synagogue. He does not recognize the literary motives that led to the formation of Peter's question.

   Lohmeyer too still understands Peter's question along the lines of the tradition in Chrysostom that Peter "thinks he is saying something great" (because he offers sevenfold instead of threefold forgiveness). He does admit that the practice of only threefold forgiveness cannot be securely attested, but does not recognize that the assumption of such a usage and the need to produce evidence for it only arise from misunderstanding the literary background of Peter's question. Even Käsemann, though he himself refers to the literary position, swings over to the line of this tradition when he says that "Jesus here destroys all casuistry".

5. In the discussion of the priority of Luke 17.4 as against Matt 18.22 it is usually adduced that Luke 17.4 presupposes an apology, but Matt. 18.22 does not. Harnack for this reason regards the Lucan version as secondary, and Klostermann agrees with him; Jülicher asserts the opposite. It must, however, be noticed that the difference arises from the fact that in Matthew the connection between the two verses has been destroyed, but in Luke it still exists. When v. 3 talks of the brother being rebuked for his sin, naturally the *declaration* of forgiveness cannot follow unless the man addressed admits his fault. If a dialogue like this is not presupposed, forgiveness can nevertheless follow without there being a request for it. The Rabbis certainly held it was a man's duty to make his peace with anyone he had offended by asking for forgiveness, but they still demanded that the man injured should pray for mercy for the offender, even if he has not asked for forgiveness.

6. Although Käsemann realizes the literary origin of Matt. 18.21f, he treats the parable from the outset as one addressed to the disciples. This is probably because he wants to connect the mercy of the king with the divine forgiveness which happens in Christ and is proclaimed by him. But of course only the disciples of Jesus can be addressed about this. For a technical argument against this exposition see below.

7. Linguistic usage suggests that this verse comes from Matthew. Only Matthew makes Jesus speak to others of *his* father in heaven, in order to express that he stands closer to God than all other men, that he is the Son who in a special way

can call God his Father. We can recognize his interest in this from the way he has occasionally strikingly altered the Marcan tradition that he had before him on this point (cf. Mark 3.35 with Matt. 12.50; Mark 10.40 with Matt. 20.23; Mark 14.25 with Matt. 26.29. The evidence is given in Schrenk, *TWNT*, V, pp. 987ff).

8. The view is occasionally found that in the parable of the unmerciful servant "the metaphor of king for God has been only subsequently inserted" but "not fully carried through". It is, however, a necessary conclusion from the parable narrative that the "Lord" is thought of as a king.

Verse 25 would be meaningless if it meant just any kind of master, and accordingly not a high official (cf. n. 9) but a slave, in the case of the "servant". The attempt of Michaelis (*Hochzeitliches Kleid*, p. 155) to refute this is questionable. (In his "*Gleichnisse*" he passes over the problem in silence, although here too he regards the servant as a "bondman", p. 192.)

Verse 30 also would then be unintelligible. Michaelis reasons back improperly from the parable to the reality when he says (*Gleichnisse*, pp. 192f): the servant is "a bondman certainly . . . but . . . a well-to-do and influential man, who according to 18.30 could even put a fellow-servant in prison without having to ask his master".

For a king being addressed as *kyrie* cf. Matt. 25.37,44. The reason that in the parable *kyrios* is used and not *basileus* could be that *kyrios* is the counterpart of *doulos*. To set the thoughts of the listeners on the right lines, it was sufficient to mention the *basileus* in v. 23.

It is only the word *daneion* in v. 27 that gives rise to difficulties. If we think of the "Lord" as a king we shall accordingly understand the debt as taxes not paid over, which is also suggested by the size of the total sum (so Jeremias). *Daneion*, however, is rendered as "loan" by the dictionaries. Whether this meaning, which is certainly the most frequent, is also the only possible one, I am not in a position to judge. The basic meaning of *dainymi*, "to divide up", or "to assign", would also allow another possibility. The verb *apodidōmi* does not demand that we should understand *daneion* as a loan. It means not only "to pay back" (something received) but has the wider sense of "to give or do something which one should in fulfilment of an obligation or expectation" (Büchsel, *TDNT*, II, p. 167). Jeremias (p. 211) points out that the Syriac translations render *daneion* with a word that means "debt", and supposes that this word in Aramaic underlies our text, while the translation by *daneion* is an unjustified narrowing of the sense.

9. *Douloi* is attested as a description for the subordinates of a king (see Rengstorf, *TDNT*, II, pp. 261–79). "The king is always the absolute ruler of his subjects, and they are under him like slaves at the whim of their masters. The word group [*douleuein*] is well adapted to denote this, because it always stands in opposition to the thought of freedom. It thus expresses with singular force both the extreme of power demanded and exercised on the one side and the extreme of objective subjection and subjective bondage present and experienced on the other" (pp. 266–7).

10. I owe to an oral communication from Professor Jeremias the information that hearsay familiarity with the conditions of non-Israelite States and legal systems can be presumed.

11. Against Jeremias I cannot assume that the Governor is brought out of prison. The words *prosagō* and *prospherō* can mean producing someone by force, but are not confined to this meaning. *Prosagō*, for example, is also used for bringing someone forward for an audience with the king, *prospherō* is found in the usage "to bring the sick to Jesus", see Bauer, *A Greek-English Lexicon of the New Testament*, pp. 718, 726f. Professor Jeremias has pointed out to me orally that the *passive* of the verb could have undergone such a narrowing in meaning. At present, however, there is no known instance of this. The context of the parable does not suggest the picture of the debtor being brought in from prison. According to v. 23 the reckoning is to be made with *all* the servants. Verse 24 suggests that his inability to pay only comes to light during the reckoning (so also Michaelis, *Gleichnisse*, p. 261, n. 125). Verse 27, "he released him", means that the debtor will not be sold into slavery.

12. Jeremias, p. 210. It is therefore not necessary to explain the enormous sum as an intrusion from the "reality part", as most commentators do. Once this line is taken one has to struggle, as Schlatter does, with the difficulty that alongside the huge debt to God the sin against the neighbour appears insignificant, the debt to the neighbour can no longer be included in that to God, and transgression against God must now be restricted to "deficit in the service of God". So far as the proportion of the totals does not contribute to the effectiveness of the parable narrative it is in my opinion to be understood by analogy with Matt. 7.1ff: a log in one's own eye, a mote in one's brother's eye.

13. Jeremias, p. 211.

14. Since, against Jeremias, it cannot be assumed that he was already in prison for debt, *apelysen auton* cannot be understood to mean that the king releases him from imprisonment for debt. Only the simple *lyō* is used in the LXX for releasing people in prison, while *apolyō* in the LXX and in the NT occurs primarily in the sense of "dismiss, release, liberate" (see Procksch, *TWNT*, IV, p. 329).

15. M. Doerne, *Er kommt auch noch heute*, ed. 4, Berlin, 1955, p. 149.

16. According to Fuchs (*Studies*, p. 153) the conclusion of the parable, verses 32-4, oversteps "the limit of the image, for something new appears which is seldom the case in daily life: the pitiless man, who had himself experienced mercy, is severely punished and the previous act of mercy annulled. This means that God does not stand for the misuse of his kindness (cf. Gal. 6.7a). In fact, it is obvious that the one who has a right to kindness will not allow this right to be abused or derided through unintended consequences of the kindness (cf. also Rom. 12.19). But this thought contains a reflection which hardly does justice to the dignity of the kindness itself—would it not watch over its honour in silence?—and which contradicts rather than confirms Matt. 5.45."

One cannot in my opinion say that the parable "oversteps the limit of the image". Certainly its development does not remain within the framework of everyday life, but it remains within the bounds of possibility. The parable remains "in the picture", and does not talk directly of God and man.

The thought in v. 33 has the listener in mind. It does not "lament" over the "misuse of goodness" (that would be a monologue!) but it does give us to understand that goodness must claim consequences, as the listener could well be aware, but knows only too well how to conceal.

If v. 35 is ignored, as it is by Fuchs also (p. 153), the parable has to my mind no "threatening tone". It is meant not only to proclaim "that God calls a person to account when he abuses his compassionate gift" (*Studies*, p. 110), but refers the listener (as does Luke 12.57-9 in Fuchs' exposition) to his own possibility of living under the ordinance of mercy which makes claims on him. I can see no reason for refusing to attribute the parable to Jesus.

17. The point of comparison of the parable, according to Jülicher, lies "in the refusal of mercy to one who himself refuses it to others who asked him for mercy". But his fixing of the point of comparison does not correspond to the flow of the parable narrative. At its end comes not the request for mercy and the refusal of this request (we are not entitled to combine the two scenes before the king!) but the verdict (supported by the story) that the mercy received "is a basis for demands" (Käsemann).

Jülicher does establish that the attitude of the wicked servant "could only evoke the intended impression between the two acts", that is between the mercy of the king and the later condemnation of the wicked servant (II, p. 312). He fails to see, however, that the priority of the mercy of the king is not only a technical necessity for the story, but has a significance in the reality on which the technical necessity depends.

Accordingly, Jülicher draws no consequences for the interpretation of the parable from this important realization. His statement of the point of it is obviously centred on the (secondary) application of the parable (v. 35). It runs, in short: God will not forgive us if we have refused forgiveness to our debtors.

But the parable is more than a warning or a threat. For this reason we cannot agree with Klostermann and Bultmann that its meaning "is correctly expressed by the application" (though they leave open the question of its originality). Behind the exposition of Jülicher, Klostermann and Bultmann one can see a particular understanding of the nature of parables. It is assumed that a parable is for imparting instruction, which can be naturally summarized in such a statement. It is not realized how a parable is linked with a concrete situation and affects it, or that it does not impart instruction but sets in motion a process of understanding.

Schlatter takes the mercifulness of the king as a description (!) of the grace of God. He sees accordingly in the parable a picture from which the relation between God and man can be read off, a sort of map which spreads out the relative positions of God and man before the hearer or reader, so that he can read off from it at what point he is. Correspondingly all the individual points are transferred (this is not to be confused with allegorizing): the unearned mercy of the king to the debtor "describes the justification of sinners as the act of pure grace", and the great debt of the wicked servant describes man's debt in the sight of God. The precedence of mercy means that acquittal has been won for the disciples through their adherence to Jesus. The final punishment of the wicked servant means "that the grace received is taken away from the disciples if it does not govern their behaviour" (*Matt.*, pp. 560f).

Käsemann follows Schlatter very closely. ("Jesus here too proclaims that God with royal generosity gives and forgives, with its reverse side that grace is a ground for demands and makes judgement possible. . . . It is from forgiveness that the rules for dealing with one's brother are to be obtained, by which forgiveness becomes a demand in one's dealings. . . . Grace is understood as the power that demands and makes possible obedience.") Käsemann, like Schlatter, ignores the character of the parable, in that direct theological statements are read off from the parable. A further point of importance is that Schlatter and Käsemann presuppose that the parable is connected with a forgiveness imparted or declared to the disciples by Jesus. (Schlatter: "All the debt that has arisen in relation to God is . . . for the disciples . . . blotted out. With their adherence to Jesus, justification became the property of the disciple." Käsemann: "With his gift God sets up his dominion.") Against this it can be argued:

1. It is only the context in Matthew that makes the parable one addressed to the disciples.

2. The idea of the bestowal of forgiveness on the disciples by Jesus is a belief of the early Church, but cannot be assumed for Jesus. It could not be grounded on a "Messianic consciousness", for Judaism had no belief in a forgiveness of sins by the Messiah. (On the other hand we do find forgiveness of sins as an element in the eschatological salvation, Jer. 31). "There is no sure evidence that Jesus proclaimed the forgiveness of sins at all in the same way as he proclaimed the nearness of the kingdom of God." (Percy, p. 23; cf. Fuchs, *Studies*, p. 147: "Jesus did not forgive sins, but he called sinners.") The only evidence for a proclamation of forgiveness of sins by Jesus (which would include a claim to authority) are Mark 2.1–12 and Luke 7.36–50. But the interpretation of these passages is still an open question.

The point that needs to be proved is whether there are parables which can be claimed as a pronouncement of the forgiveness of sins by Jesus. The general remark "that Jesus . . . prefers to express himself, not in the language of theology, but by similes, parables, parabolic actions, in short, in the established language of symbols" (Jeremias, p. 213) cannot take the place of a demonstration *which* parables Jesus employed to pronounce to his listeners the forgiveness of sins. It would still be necessary to prove that Jesus understood his intimacy with tax-collectors and sinners as a pronouncement of forgiveness. (Jeremias limits himself on p. 227 to understanding it as the announcement of the *age* of forgiveness.)

In short, it remains to be proved whether there is a "misconception" in our assumption that it is only the early Church that knows a bestowal of forgiveness of sins by Jesus.

The assumption that the parable in Matt. 18.23–35 proclaimed God's forgiveness is possible only if one fails to recognize how parables function. If this parable was to be at all effective, it had to presuppose a knowledge of mercy received. Because Jesus' listeners were Jews, there were no difficulties in this. They were aware of living under the mercy of God. Cf. the passage quoted by Billerbeck on Matt. 18.33: "If ever you take your neighbour's garment in pledge, you shall restore it to him before the sun goes down (Ex. 22.26 [22.25 in the Hebrew]). God says, 'How much you owe me! You sin before me, and I have patience with you . . . and your soul ascends daily evening by evening to me (when you sleep), to hold conversation and to answer (for the deeds of the man in the course of the previous day), and even if it has done wrong I give you your soul (every morning) back again, which you are indebted for to me. So you too, although he is indebted to you, should give it him back before sunset, if you have taken it as a pledge'" (I, p. 800).

If the parable "works" for us too this means that we also know what it is to receive mercy, even when we do not connect it with God. Mercy belongs to the structure of our existence inasmuch as man always counts on goodness— directed towards himself—because he has to count on it. In this or that area of life he may be able to satisfy abstract standards, but never in the whole area of his existence. As soon as he is unable to balance it out, his need becomes obvious. From this everyone can realize that his neighbour stands in need of goodness, and that he must therefore love him "like himself", by turning from abstract standards (which demand judgement and condemnation) towards the person of the neighbour in goodness.

According to Jeremias the parable of the wicked servant is a parable of the Last Judgement. However, the text offers no support for this—unless the fact that the "picture part" speaks of reckoning and judgement can be taken as evidence for this. This is, however, methodologically inadmissible.

In Jeremias' view the parable fulfils a double purpose. On the one hand it is warning and exhortation, on the other hand it offers instruction and makes a contribution to a theological discussion.

As exhortation and warning it is supposed to say all of the following: "God has extended to you in the gospel, through the offer of forgiveness, a merciful gift beyond conceiving, but God will revoke the forgiveness of sin if you do not wholeheartedly share the forgiveness you have experienced, but harden your heart against your brother. Everything is here at stake. Woe unto you if you try to stand on your rights; God will then stand on his and see that his sentence is executed rigorously" (p. 213).

On top of this, the parable as instruction is supposed not only to represent over against Jewish apocalyptic the view that God will let the measure of mercy prevail in the last judgement too, but also to answer the question that only then follows, when God will use the measure of mercy, and when that of judgement. This it does in the following way: "'Where God's forgiveness produces a readiness to forgive, there God's mercy grants forgiveness of debts again at the Last Judgement; but he who abuses God's gift, faces the full severity of Judgement, as if he had never received forgiveness (Matt. 6.14f)" (p. 214).

It seems to me that an interpretation of this sort ascribes more to the capacity of a parable and to the comprehension of its hearers than they can bear. And surely too much is left to the reader of the interpretation also, if the decision is left to him whether he is to see in the audience of the parable disciples of Jesus, as on p. 213, or apocalyptic theologians, as on p. 214.

But Jeremias is right to point out that Ex.R. 45 (101a) cannot be quoted against his interpretation, as was done in the first German edition of this book.

9. THE PARABLE OF
THE SOWER AND ITS INTERPRETATION

1. Basing this on Jeremias, p. 14, note 11, and taking account of Bultmann, *HST*, p. 325 and n. 1, I should like to suggest the following stages for the earlier history of Mark 4:

    1. Oral tradition put together the parable of the sower (4.3–9), of the seed growing by itself (4.26–9), and of the Mustard Seed (4.30–2).

    2. The three parables were united by the framework of vv. 2 and 33 as a parable discourse of Jesus, and the parable of the sower was extended by means of the interpretation, vv. 13–20. This interpretation was probably introduced by the stylistically appropriate question of the disciples: *Kai ērōtōn auton hoi peri auton tēn parabolēn* ("and those who were about him asked him about the parable"). Against Jeremias I take the view that the description of the change of situation, which (*a*) goes further than the question of the disciples, (*b*) contradicts the framework verse v. 33 which belongs to this layer of tradition, and (*c*) is obviously connected with Mark's theory of parables (cf. v. 34), is the work of Mark.

    3. Mark expanded this collection of parables with those of the Lamp under the Bushel (4.21–3) and the Measure (vv. 24f), himself wrote vv. 1 and 34, inserted vv. 11f, and reworked v. 2 and v. 10. Possibly v. 13 too is either in whole or in part the work of the Evangelist.

2. Against Jeremias, Fuchs, and others I take the view that the sower does not stand at the centre of the parable. Apart from the introductory verse, Mark 4.3 par., there is no mention of the sower in the whole parable. It is also to be noticed how the real action begins at Mark 4.4 with *kai egeneto en*, which is omitted in Matthew and Luke. It seems to me completely unjustified to read out of the parable even the frame of mind and personal qualities of the sower ("resolute", "persistent", etc).

    The German title of the parable, "the field with four different kinds of soil", is misleading, and only justified by reference to the interpretation. But since all these titles seem to suffer from the start from a misunderstanding of method I have not attempted to find a new one for this parable.

3. I have tried to harmonize the sometimes contradictory statements of Dalman in "Viererlei Acker", *PJ*, 22, pp. 120–32, and in *Arbeit und Sitte in Palästina*, II, pp. 180ff, 194f, as best I could. In his article on the parable, Dalman, who is an expert in the conditions of the country, obviously assumes that there is no ploughing at all before the sowing, but in *Arbeit und Sitte* he allows that between harvest and sowing, ploughing can take place several times, although it is not always done. If I have understood him aright the ploughing, when it is done only once or twice, takes place soon after the harvest. Immediately before sowing, however, the land is never ploughed unless it has been left fallow.

4. Dalman, *PJ*, 22, p. 122.

5. In his article, *PJ*, 22, Dalman leaves it in the end obscure whether one is to assume that the way is ploughed up and afterwards trodden out again or whether it is left by the plough. Jeremias assumes the first. But can one then

explain why the seed on the way is eaten by the birds, but that on the field is not?

6. Schniewind, *Matt.*, p. 165.
7. Sprenger, p. 81; Hauck, *Markus*, p. 52.
8. Klostermann, *Markus*, p. 40.
9. Jülicher, II, pp. 517f.
10. Dalman, *PJ*, 22, p. 125.
11. Ibid., p. 128.
12. Ibid., p. 128.
13. Against Jeremias, p. 150, cf. Dalman, *PJ*, 22, p. 130, and Lohmeyer, *Matt.*, pp. 196f. The yield of the field is calculated from the *whole* of the seed. Otherwise it would have to say: "The field bore thirty-, sixty-, a hundred-fold." This is how the passage runs in the Gospel of Thomas: "And others fell on the good earth; and it brought forth good fruit; it bore sixty per measure and one hundred and twenty per measure" (*Gospel of Thomas*, ed. Guillaumont and others, No. 9, p. 7, with the omission of a Greek word in brackets). Regarded as the yield of individual ears the figures remain entirely within the bounds of possibility and can hardly be interpreted as signs of eschatological plenty, particularly when one compares the fantastic figures given in the Rabbinic parallels.
14. Dalman, *PJ*, 22, p. 128, Sprenger, p. 84. One could also think of it as being the case that the individual wheat plant has offshoots and produces several stalks. But it is improbable that the narrator had this in view.
15. Cf. Bultmann, *HST*, pp. 199f: "*The original meaning of many parables has become irrecoverable in the course* of the tradition . . . And as for the parable of the Sower in Mark 4.3–9!—is it a consolation for every man when his labour does not all bear fruit? Is it in this sense a monologue by Jesus, half of resignation, half of thankfulness? Is it an exhortation to the hearers of the divine Word? Or of Jesus' preaching? Or of the message of the Church? Or was there in the original parable no reflection at all on the Word, and have we to understand it roughly in the sense of 2 Esdras 8.41?"

I cannot but regard the efforts made, nevertheless, by the various commentators to recover the original meaning of the parable as having failed. They do not do justice either to the historical situation or to the parable, or even to both:

1. According to Dodd the parable answers an objection against Jesus' proclamation that now the time of the end, the time of the harvest, has come. The objection runs: Even John the Baptist has not brought about the "restoration of all things . . . which is generally expected as the immediate prelude to the Day of the Lord", for much of his work had been a failure. Whereupon Jesus, according to Dodd, answers with the parable: "True; but no farmer yet delayed to reap the harvest because there were bare patches in the field. In spite of all the harvest is plentiful" (pp. 136f).

The argument itself would certainly be possible. No farmer puts off the harvest because certain places show stunted growth. But it has no connection with the parable, in which the question of the *time* of the harvest is not touched on.

Again, Dodd's determination of the historical situation is hardly correct.

The objection against Jesus which Dodd conjectures: "Even the work of
John the Baptist has not brought about the complete 'restoration of all
things' (Mark 9.12) . . . Much of his work has been a failure", is artificial and
improbable. No contemporary of Jesus could confuse the preaching of
repentance by the Baptist, and the "restoration of all things" in this way, as
Dodd does. We are dealing with two entirely different complexes of thought.

The "restoration of all things" was expected to come with the return of
Elijah, who would appear immediately (one or three days) before the
Messiah, and was to bring the good news to Israel. When it was said of Elijah
that he would convert Israel, the idea could only be of a miraculous act, not of
a prophetic preaching of repentance. There was no room in this picture of the
return of Elijah for a preacher of repentance.

A preacher of repentance could have a rôle in the coming of the kingdom
of God only in so far as it was expected that as soon as *all* Israel repented,
the Messiah must come.

The connection between the Baptist, the preacher of repentance, and the
complex of ideas associated with the return of Elijah must have been first
made by primitive Christianity, which made John the forerunner of Jesus, and
thus identified him with the forerunner of the Messiah who brings in the
time of the end (cf. Bultmann, *HST*, p. 124, on Mark 9.12). But even if it
were conceded to Dodd that *Jesus* saw in the Baptist the eschatological forerunner (cf. Dodd, pp. 38f), one cannot expect to find this interpretation,
which considerably reinterprets received ideas, with Jesus' contemporaries at
all. Anyone who saw in John the forerunner must also have agreed with Jesus'
determination of the eschatological time. But anyone who denied Jesus'
announcement of the time (*a*) could point out that Israel had not yet repented
(but would he have appealed to the failure of the Baptist for this?); (*b*) could
argue that there were still no signs of the events of the end, which were
expected with the arrival of the messianic age. He would have to say that
Elijah had not yet returned, not that the Baptist had not brought the restoration of all things.

The thought that in spite of everything the harvest is plentiful, which comes
nearer to the "picture part" of the parable, is added on in Dodd's exposition
without any connection. It does not belong to the argument of the picture.
With a bad harvest the farmer would just as much go straight on without
delay to get it in! Nor does it make sense in the "reality part". If the harvest
is taken as a metaphor for the time of salvation which is breaking in, it would
make no sense to talk of "more" or "less" in connection with it.

2. According to Dahl, the parable answers the question whether Jesus
could be "the coming one", although his work was without success in many
respects. The answer runs: "Look at the sower: even if much of the seed was
uselessly scattered, yet he could get a harvest of immense richness. And even
though the ministry of Jesus in Israel often did not lead to anything, yet it was
the condition for and the beginning realization of the coming of kingdom of
God" (*The Parables of Growth*, p. 154).

The point of the "picture part" is credibly formulated, but the formulation of the "reality part" is not covered by the parable. The parable could
certainly say that the work of Jesus, in spite of its failure, is bringing in the

kingdom of God, as sowing brings in the harvest. But it cannot at the same time bear the burden of proof that Jesus' work and the coming of the kingdom are related as are the sowing and harvest, as cause and effect. Apart from this it must be asked on a point of fact whether Jesus did connect his work with the kingdom of God in such a way.

(a) This appears to be ruled out by the concept of the kingdom of God. It means the eschatological *revelation* of the now still hidden reign of God. But one can hardly say that the preaching of Jesus is the necessary condition of this revelation of God.

(b) No sayings of Jesus can be found, in my opinion, which suggest that he understood his work in this way as the beginning of the kingdom of God, or that it formed a necessary presupposition for it, as the sowing is for the harvest. Jesus' preaching does not bring in the coming of the kingdom of God but challenges us to believe in it.

(c) Nor did the early Church, as far as I can tell, understand the preaching of Jesus as the beginning of the kingdom of God.

(d) Dahl's thesis, that Jesus expected the events of the end to take a particular course, and gave his ministry a place among them—which forms the starting-point for his widely accepted exposition of the parables of growth—is not established by the passages he quotes (Mark 9.11f; Matt. 18.7; Mark 8.31; Luke 12.50; Mark 10.38; 14.36; 13.9–13; 13.1f; 12.1–12; 13.10). These passages are for the most part secondary, and in those whose authenticity is at least open to discussion the eschatological connection of the *dei* is in my opinion not obvious. The methodological conclusion that the *number* of passages pointing in this direction justifies the assumption that Jesus shared these thoughts seems to me open to question as a matter of method. Against Dahl cf. also Bultmann, *HST*, p. 418.

3. What has been said against Dahl is for the most part equally applicable to Jeremias, who likewise connects the "failure" of the sower with the failure of Jesus, and understands the activity of Jesus as the "hopeless beginnings" from which God "brings forth the triumphant end which he had promised" (p. 150).

Jeremias determines the situation too in the same way as Dahl: The parable answers doubts about Jesus' mission, which have been occasioned "by apparently ineffectual preaching . . . the bitter hostility . . . and the increasing desertions" (p. 151). But against this it must be pointed out that in the situation of the "historical Jesus" the conditions were not yet present in which alone the failure of the preaching and the falling away acquire theological relevance and become a genuine problem for believers. Not till after Easter was that possible, when the preaching was understood as an event of salvation, and the eschatological community was gathered. Only then could one really speak of falling away. If missionary success is seen as an event effected by God, then its failure inevitably becomes a problem. If the Church understands itself as the community of the elect, it can hardly understand any member withdrawing from this community.

The objection against Jesus of those outside could not, however, be derived from the failures of his work, because this work itself did not in any case run along the lines of the Messianic expectations by which they must have measured him (cf. Schlatter, *Matt.*, p. 425).

4. C. W. F. Smith follows the order of Mark's Gospel to find the setting of the parable, and places it at the beginning of Jesus' activity outside the synagogues after these had been closed to him as places of activity. "In spite of the inevitable loss of some of the seed", the parable will have told the listeners, "the rewards are so great that the sower finds it worth while . . . to sow his seed year after year, persistently, knowing that the harvest far outweighs the loss" (p. 63). "Just as the sower expects to lose a proportion of his seed, and is not thereby discouraged nor deterred from sowing, but expects a plentiful crop, so in the spiritual realm God also is persistent . . . in setting forward his kingdom in the certainty . . . that it will come to fruition" (p. 64). So in the parable one must see "Jesus' proclamation of his purpose to pursue his task in the face of all opposition and failure" (p. 65).

On this it must be said that the parable is no more concerned with the persistence of the sower than it is with his frame of mind. This would show itself in repeated sowing, which the parable does not mention, and in the presence of stronger opposition than the (on Smith's own view) relatively small loss of seed. Jesus' listeners could therefore not take the conduct of the sower as persistence which is not discouraged in spite of all opposition, and will hardly have understood the parable as a proclamation by Jesus that in spite of all opposition he would press on with his work. Besides this the connection in Smith's exposition of the activity of Jesus with the coming of the kingdom of God is of course also open to question.

5. Lohmeyer's exposition in his commentary on Matthew is undoubtedly a very fine sermon on the passage, but it can hardly be correct as exegesis. The predestinarian idea, "each land is how it is, a man is what is given him, and from this givenness he receives life or death", can I believe be found neither with Jesus nor with the early Church.

6. According to Schlatter, the connection of the parable with the situation resulted "from the fact that Jesus gave the people and the disciples nothing but the word. This is, however, often spoken in vain . . . yet Jesus said of his word that the kingdom of God comes through it. From this the question of how the kingdom of God was related to what Jesus was doing resulted forcibly . . . Does Jesus act like a King? He answers 'Yes'. For the word has creative power in itself . . . as certainly as the harvest resulted from the seed, God's kingdom comes through the word" (*Matt.*, p. 426).

(*a*) I can find no saying of Jesus which declares that the kingdom of God comes about through his word.

(*b*) That Jesus' word has creative power in itself could at best be deduced from the interpretation of the parable, Mark 4.14ff. This, however, is secondary, and in any case does not have the "creative power of the word" in view at all.

(*c*) There is no mention of the kingdom of God anywhere in the parable, apart from the secondary formulation *logos tēs basileias* in Matt. 13.19. Still less is it said that the kingdom of God comes through the word. The word is mentioned only in the interpretation, and there it is not the kingdom of God that comes out of it "as the harvest from the seed", but the fruit of the heart.

16. The interpretation covering the individual points in Mark 4.14–20, must have been preceded—not temporally but materially—by a new total understanding of the parable. The total understanding that underlies the exposition of individual points was not yet possible in the lifetime of Jesus. The parable has therefore been reinterpreted. Since, however, we do not know its original meaning, we cannot grasp the nature of the reinterpretation. We cannot therefore begin with the passage, but must try to start from the situation of the early Church to which the application of the parable refers us.

It would in my view also be conceivable that the parable does not go back to Jesus, but was first created in the early Church, in the situation mentioned above. The question cannot, however, be decided, since there are no criteria for it.

The interpretation of the parable cannot possibly come from Jesus, as is proved by considerations of language and content (see Jeremias, pp. 77ff).

10. THE UNJUST JUDGE

1. Jülicher: "'Unjust' is probably too weak a word . . . *adikos* and *adikia* include what is evil or sinful in the widest possible sense of the words . . . , it is not meant just to assert a violation of the duties of his judicial office, but to describe the man as through and through 'bad'" (II, p. 278). Bultmann speaks of the "godless judge" (p. 175). Bugge says: "The judge was what we would call a man without a conscience." According to Jeremias, on the other hand, the description "seems intended to characterize the judge as corrupt" (p. 153). This can hardly be correct: linguistically it is improbable and in the story so far as I can see there is no support for it.
2. Schlatter, *Kennen wir Jesus?*, p. 359.
3. Jeremias, p. 153.
4. Bornhäuser, p. 162; Jülicher, II, p. 279.
5. Bornhäuser, p. 162.
6. *Ercheto* is an iterative imperfect, so Jülicher (II, p. 279), Bugge (p. 468), Jeremias (p. 153, n. 4).
7. "In a soliloquy . . . the judge repeats the characterization of his personality given by Jesus in v. 2—one would regard it as irony, if the words were not necessary for the narrative, to provide a motive for his change of behaviour" (Klostermann, pp. 177f).
8. Jülicher, Bugge, Klostermann, Madsen, Michaelis, and Bauer understand *hypōpiazein* in the sense of acts of violence. Only Jeremias among the more recent expositors gives the word its traditional meaning here. It is linguistically possible (see Jülicher, II, p. 282, and Bauer, p. 856). A further argument in favour of it is that only persistence and not possible acts of violence can be the point of comparison of the parable. Although the commentators regard the acts of violence as the "necessary climax" to the persistent coming, they contradict themselves by leaving it out of consideration completely as the point of comparison.

As an explanation of the trouble feared the final clause would not be at all a "worthless repetition" (Jülicher, II, p. 282), but a necessary emphasis on the main point of the parable, which has not yet been brought out clearly enough just by the iterative imperfect in v. 3.

9. Jeremias, p. 154.

10. "So drastic a phrase was hardly chosen just for want of a better": In this Jülicher (II, p. 282) is no doubt right. This is, however, no argument against the assumption that it is used here in a transferred sense. The shining through of the original meaning gives the phrase a sufficient emphasis to motivate the judge's change of mind.

11. See Jülicher, II, p. 282; Jeremias, first ed., p. 115. It may be correct that *eis telos* in itself has no iterative meaning (Delling, p. 12, n. 45). This still results, however, from the connection with *erchomenē*: "coming for ever" can mean repeated coming.

12. Klostermann, *Lukas*, p. 178.

13. Verse 7 is an old *crux interpretum*. How can the second half of the verse be so understood that it does not seriously disturb either the meaning or the construction of the sentence?

If *makrothymein* is translated as "be long suffering", "have patience", and 7b taken as an independent indicative sentence in the sense, "'and he lets his forbearance govern his elect', in that only out of compassion for their weakness does he still put off the last judgement" (Klostermann), this contradicts v. 8, where it is precisely a rapid *ekdikēsis* that is promised. Furthermore there would be no point of contact in the parable for this idea in the application. If on the other hand *ep' autois* were connected with the opponents, and the sentence understood "as a continuation of the question, with the meaning: 'and should he perhaps exercise patience *against the enemies*?'" (Klostermann), we face the difficulty "that the second question does not expect the answer 'certainly' but 'no', i.e. it would be necessary to supply to *makrothymei* just the interrogative *mē* (with loss of the *ou*)" (Klostermann), and to postulate a grammatical mistake. A further argument against this view is the change from the subjunctive (*poiēsē*) to the indicative (*makrothymei*), because "this change of mood makes v. 7b an independent sentence" (Jeremias).

According to Jeremias (p. 154), who is here following Sahlin, we have here an Aramaizing construction. "(a) The principal sentence *kai makrothymei ep' autois* represents a relative clause: 'and to which he listens patiently'; (b) the participial construction (*tōn boōntōn*, etc.) stands for an adverbial clause: 'when they cry to him'. Accordingly, we should render the verse: 'Will not God hasten to the rescue of his elect, he who listens patiently to them when they cry to him day and night?'"

But there are three objections to be made to this:

1. The persistent crying of the elect, the point of comparison with the parable, recedes completely into the background on this understanding of the construction.

2. The thought of God's patience in hearing prayers, which comes to the fore in place of this, has no point of contact in the parable.

3. Furthermore its contents are open to question. The man who prays does not expect God to endure his prayer patiently. He expects it to be granted. Jülicher must still be right here in his criticism of the thesis

already proposed by Weiss and Blass, that patience "is not the most meaningful description for the effectiveness of prayer" (p. 287).

Ljungvik suggests the following translation for Luke 18.7: "'Will not God
vindicate his elect, who cry day and night to him, but has patience with
them?'"

This yields no sense, however, and it must be assumed that the author has
been the victim of linguistic difficulties.

With Jülicher, Bugge, and Bauer, we shall accordingly understand
makrothymein as "put off for long", "delay", for which linguistic support is
not lacking, and follow the translation of Weizsäcker: "and does he delay
long with them?" The change in mood can in my opinion be explained
from the fact that v. 7b is not part of the first affirmative question, but is an
independent interrogative sentence. This is already probable from its contents: the answer to this question was by no means an obvious one to the
listeners to the parable, but is the decisive utterance of the pericope. With
this there disappears also the difficulty which seemed to arise from the connection of an affirmative question with a negative one.

14. The question of the authenticity of the parable is indissolubly connected with
the question whether verses 6–8a are original. This is denied by Jülicher and
Bultmann. Klostermann leaves the question open. Bugge, Schlatter, Madsen,
and Michaelis take its authenticity for granted without going into the problem seriously. Only in Kümmel and Jeremias is a positive verdict supported
by arguments.

Against authenticity it can be adduced that:

1. The applications of parables are frequently secondary.

2. Nowhere else is the application so sharply separated from the parable.
Even Luke 16.8 can hardly be adduced for comparison, because direct speech
is not found there.

3. The concept of the *eklektoi* is not found in any genuine saying of Jesus,
but is on the other hand very frequent in primitive Christianity. Apart from
this who can be meant by the "elect"? The Jewish people, who are here
promised release from their oppressors in the near future? There is no trace
at all in Jesus' preaching of any such nationalistic future expectation. The
disciples of Jesus? There are weighty objections to be raised against the
assumption that Jesus gathered "elect" men as the eschatological community.

Could Jesus have been addressing a Jewish group which regarded itself as
elect (Delling, p. 22)? Who could be intended? To whom could *Jesus* award
the title of "elect"? (The attempts of Delling to demonstrate a reserve in
Jesus' language [p. 24] are unconvincing.) And what Jewish group could be
specified, which at the time of Jesus (*a*) was expecting the Parousia in the near
future, (*b*) was suffering from severe persecution (cf. Jeremias, p. 156,
n. 18)?

On these grounds the assumption of the authenticity of 6–8a seems to me
to be untenable.

Jeremias adduces a linguistic criterion for authenticity: "The Aramaizing
construction is evidence of the antiquity of the tradition" (p. 155). Apart
from objections on grounds of content to his interpretation of v. 7, which
put in question the presence of an Aramaism, it must be pointed out that the

H

antiquity and Palestinian origin of a unit of tradition are not enough to prove that it is original.

Kümmel argues for authenticity that "the interpretation 18.6–8a is in no way a re-interpretation, since the parable, as a metaphor, can bear a particular as well as a general application and can scarcely do without one altogether" (*PF*, p. 59). On the other hand "the decision of the judge 'to vindicate' the woman is probably a metaphorical feature which is intended to suggest an application to the vindication by God of the elect". In this he is no doubt right. The need to have an interpretation of this parable can also be shown by the argument that the application here must follow *a minore ad maius* or *e contrario* and cannot therefore be read off directly from the "picture part". (Delling, pp. 3f, takes a similar view.) But in view of the strong objections to the authenticity of the application this evidence that the parable and interpretation belong together argues against the originality of the whole pericope. So Fuchs: "If one accepts Kümmel's defence of Luke 18.1–8a as a unity, then the passage must have first appeared in the early Church, despite the fact that Kümmel ascribes it to Jesus" (*Aufsätze*, II, p. 70).

There are no formal criteria that argue against the originality of the parable, vv. 2–5, but there are still objections from the content.

In the mouth of Jesus the parable would mean one of two things. Either it would be a general exhortation to persistence in prayer when it is not granted. But is it characteristic of Jesus to give general religious exhortations?

Or it is an exhortation to persistent prayer for the coming of the kingdom of God. But this exhortation is more likely for the contemporaries of Jesus than for him. Certainly he shares their prayer for the kingdom (compare the second petition of the Our Father with the Jewish Qaddish prayer). But at the same time he proclaims that the kingdom of God is already arriving. He does not exhort them to bring it in by persistent prayer, but demands that they should take its arrival seriously.

Finally, the parable could also be a declaration to those who were praying so persistently, that their prayers were fulfilled. But how could Jesus, who called his contemporaries to repentance in view of the coming of the kingdom of God, have regarded the arrival of the kingdom as the consequence of their persistent piety? In view of these difficulties it would seem more probable that the parable (together with the interpretation) first arose in the early Church in the situation described above.

15. Schlatter, *Kennen wir Jesus?*, pp. 359f.
16. Bornhäuser, Sahlin, and Jeremias understand *en tachei* in the sense of "suddenly", "unforeseen". This translation is, however, not made likely by the basic meaning of the word, nor can it be taken as proved by the passages of the Bible quoted for it. Deut. 11.17 has in the original *mᵉhērah*. Derived from *māhar* (Pi.), it means "speedily", "quickly". The same word is used in Josh. 8.19. Again, *kim'at*, which the LXX in Ps. 2.12 renders by *en tachei*, does not mean "suddenly" but "soon", "in a little". Furthermore the sense does not allow us to translate *en tachei* by "suddenly" in any of the passages quoted. This is also true for Ezek. 29.5 and Ecclus. 27.3. In connection with the threat *en tachei* must mean that the punishment is already hanging over their heads, and not that at some time in the future it will come suddenly.

Although Delling, in contrast to the authors mentioned, translates *en tachei* by "swiftly" (p. 19, cf. n. 83), he wishes to establish that no information is thereby given about the interval until the Parousia. He gives for this the strange reason that for the oppressed the time now appears long, but after the coming of the Parousia in retrospect it will seem short. The parable does not, however, say that "shortly" is to be understood *sub specie aeternitatis*.

17. Jülicher, Bultmann, Klostermann, and Kümmel regard 8b as secondary. They say that it is noteworthy that it is no longer God who appears as the judge, but the Son of Man. The change of subject cannot be played down by the postulated transition, "God fulfils the prayer for his judgement by sending the Son of Man" (Delling). Since it could not be of concern to the author of the parable to give more precise information about the divine judgement, the introduction of the Son of Man, of whom there is no mention in 7a, remains unmotivated. If this transition in thought were present, 8b would probably then have been put: "Yet when he sends the Son of Man. . . ." Also a certain inconsistency with v. 7 cannot be missed: do those who "cry every day and night to God" need this question to warn them? But the strongest argument against v. 8b having originally belonged to the parable is that an adversative continuation of the parable does not suit an application. Although Jeremias may be correct in his assumption that the verse is pre-Lucan (p. 155, in contrast to the earlier edition, where in agreement with Jülicher he assumed a Lucan usage in v. 8b), this does not prove that the connection of 8b with Luke 18. 2–8a is original.

18. So Jülicher, II, p. 289, Bultmann, p. 335, Delling, p. 5, Jeremias, p. 156 (v. 1 exhibits "Lucan peculiarities").

19. Bugge, p. 467, Schlatter, *Kennen wir Jesus?*, p. 360. Since it can hardly be a question here of incessant prayer, Billerbeck cannot be right in his view that "this exhortation did not conform to the Jewish outlook and custom" (II, p. 237). Cf. II, p. 238: "If a man realizes that he is praying without his prayer being granted, let him pray again and again."

20. Sabbe (p. 368) sees in the parable "a stimulus to eschatological prayer for the Son of Man to come soon". In this he may have hit upon the Evangelist's interpretation, but not the original meaning of the passage. The application of the parable is formulated as a promise that God will shortly vindicate his elect, not as a call to pray for that vindication.

11. THE PARABLE OF THE WISE AND FOOLISH VIRGINS

1. The defectiveness of our material for late Jewish wedding customs is alluded to by Jeremias (pp. 172f). Burkitt (*JTS*, 30 (1929), pp. 267–70) would understand the situation as being that the bridegroom has gone to meet the bride, to escort her to his parents' house, and the girls from the neighbourhood go to meet him on his return. He bases his case on the weakly attested reading (in D Θ al latt sy), which inserts "and the bride" in v. 1 after "the

bridegroom". But the mention of the bride cannot be original, since she is not mentioned in vv. 5 and 6, although the bride is the leading character in a wedding procession. For that reason it is also not possible to understand the omission of any mention of her in the great mass of manuscripts from a striving "to strengthen the allegorical features" (Schniewind, p. 243; cf. against this Meinertz, "Die Tragweite", p. 95). The insertion of the bride may go back to the fact that the procession of honour at a wedding was usually the bride's procession.

2. In the frequently discussed problem of whether all the features of the parable "can be included in the picture of an ordinary wedding", it is constantly overlooked that a parable does not have to give a regular instance, but usually describes an abnormal individual case. The occurrence of unusual features does not of itself make it an allegory (cf. above, pp. 28f). The question whether Matt. 25.1–12 is an allegory or a parable cannot therefore be decided by whether parallels can be found for the source of events assumed in the text or not.

3. Billerbeck, I, p. 969.

4. Jeremias, p. 175.

5. Klostermann, *Matt.*, p. 201.

6. The heightened tone does not turn verse 12 into an allegorical feature. The fact of the exclusion is motivated by the flow of the story and is not made intelligible only by the reality. On the other hand a realization of the function of the verse prevents us from seeking the point of "the severity of the refusal" in the dependent status of the girls (as against Jeremias, p. 175).

7. The views of the commentators on the parable of the Ten Virgins are very varied. Dodd, Jeremias, Jülicher, Kümmel, Meinertz, Michaelis, Schlatter, Schmid, Schniewind, and C. W. F. Smith regard it as an authentic parable of Jesus, though their understanding of it varies enormously. Bornkamm, Bultmann, Fuchs, Grässer, Klostermann, Madsen, and Strobel see Matt. 25.1–12 as a secondary Church formation, though Klostermann and Bultmann leave open the possibility that underlying it there may be an original version that goes back to Jesus.

The numerous attempts to treat the parable as a genuine saying of Jesus, for all their variations of interpretation, have one thing in common: they do not correspond to the point of comparison of the parable as it results from the flow of the story.

According to Dodd "all the vivid dramatic detail is intended only to emphasize the folly of unpreparedness and the wisdom of preparedness—preparedness, as I take it, for the developments actually in process in the ministry of Jesus" (p. 128). Dodd fails to see that the individual features of the parable have a function in its development, and does not notice that the unpreparedness of the virgins is due to their failure to allow for the delay of the bridegroom. A narrator who only wanted to denounce the folly of inadequate preparation would have used some more obvious examples. Further, the choice of pictorial matter is not quite as unimportant as Dodd would have us believe. A narrator who wants to speak of a "judgement" that brings with it such "catastrophes" as his own persecution, the persecution of his disciples, the destruction of the Temple and of the Jewish nation (Dodd, p. 126) would hardly hit upon the image of a wedding! (Cf. on this Kümmel, *PF*, p. 130.)

Jeremias too understands the parable as a crisis parable, though he understands the crisis in the strict sense of the word as eschatological. He stresses more strongly than Dodd the theme of suddenness: "The sudden coming of the bridegroom (v. 6) has its parallels in the sudden downpour of the flood, in the unexpected entry of the thief, or in the unlooked-for return of the master of the house from the feast or the journey. The common element of suddenness is a figure of the unexpected incidence of catastrophe. The crisis is at the door. It will come as unexpectedly as the midnight cry in the parable, 'Behold the bridegroom cometh!'. . . Woe to those whom that hour finds unprepared!" (p. 53). But the cry that announces the coming of the bridegroom to the virgins does not "surprise" them—they had been waiting for it all the time! (so too Michaelis, p. 93). And he only comes "suddenly" inasmuch as "anyone who is not punctual comes 'suddenly' at any later moment" (Grässer, p. 125, n. 5). It is not the sudden coming but the long delay of the bridegroom that embarrasses the "foolish" virgins. It is the *delay* that makes readiness a problem.

For Jülicher Jesus wants to illustrate by the parable "the fatal folly of a half preparation": "either you are ready whenever God's kingdom comes, or you put off the preparation for one reason or another, counting on your luck instead of on sure facts, and then you miss your aim grievously" (II, p. 457). But the virgins have not "put off" their preparation. They have not wantonly trusted their luck. Their only mistake was that they did not reckon on a long time of waiting. It is from this that the point of comparison of the parable must be determined.

For Kümmel "it follows from all these exhortations to be on the alert and to be prepared"—among which he includes the parable of the Ten Virgins—"that Jesus describes the coming of the Son of Man and therewith the entry of the kingdom of God as possibly very imminent, and in any case pressingly near, although its actual date was completely unknown" (*PF*, p. 59). To reach this result he has to assert that "the trait 'while the bridegroom tarries' belongs only to the vivid embellishment of the 'picture part'" (p. 58). This is, however, untenable. "This trait belongs so firmly to the substance of the parable that the treatment of individual points can only be understood from it" (Bornkamm, "Verzögerung", p. 120). "In fact it is from this trait alone that it is determined why the one group are called foolish, the other wise" (ibid.). This means, however, that the parable can be understood only from the problem of the delay of the Parousia, and is not evidence for Jesus' own "near expectation".

For Michaelis ("Kennen die Synoptiker eine Verzögerung der Parousia?", pp. 119f) the parable does not mean "to describe by the examples of the ten virgins how one should behave when one has to prepare oneself for a long wait. Rather it is meant to describe how one must behave if one does not want to be found surprised and unprepared, if it should take longer, so as to come too late to the really decisive event." But Michaelis' contrast is unreal. What is preparation for the possibility that it will "take longer," other than "to prepare oneself for a long wait"! "Either way the delay is presupposed as a fact" (Grässer, p. 127). Nor can the reference to the delay of the Parousia be removed from the parable by the observation that in the parable the problem found in 2 Pet. 3.4 has left no deposit. The mockery of opponents is not the only, nor by any means the first problem that the delay of the Parousia brought with it (cf. Grässer, p. 126).

Schlatter holds that Jesus wants to warn the disciples by the parable against seeing a guarantee of salvation in membership of the Church. "Membership of the church is no substitute for the personal conduct of the individual, who must himself find in his hope strength to prepare for the day of Christ" (*Matt.*, p. 720). Schlatter builds his interpretation on a subsidiary feature of the parable. It is not vv. 8f but v. 5 that is decisive for the flow of the narrative. It cannot be read out of the parable that the foolish virgins thought no preparation was needed or that each one simply relied upon the others. There is no reflection on the thoughts and motives of the characters.

For Schmid "the folly or guilt of the foolish virgins lies in the fact that they were not sufficiently prepared for their task" (p. 344). A correct demonstration that v. 5 "is indispensable to the flow of the action" leads him to the conclusion that the trait is "not important . . . for the interpretation of the parable" (cf. pp. 343 and 345), and that the parable accordingly has no connection with the delay of the Parousia. But although v. 5 does not demand an "allegorical interpretation", that does not mean that this trait of the picture has no connection with the reality.

Schniewind's verdict is: "Our parable exhorts us to true wisdom, perhaps most pressingly of all the similar sayings of Jesus" (p. 243). He does indeed ask himself "whether v. 5 is to be given the meaning that all Christians without exception become weary of the non-arrival of the Parousia?" (ibid.), but draws no conclusions from this connection with the delay of the Parousia. Probably this is because he has put the question in the wrong terms. Verse 5 is not to be "given a meaning" allegorically, still less the sleep of the virgins, which in the parable is a completely unstressed, subsidiary feature. The point of comparison of the parable does not lie in what is common to all the virgins, but simply and solely in what divides the wise ones from the foolish.

According to C. W. F. Smith the parable imparts the lesson: "'When the call comes, be wholly committed to do what is demanded.' Only instant response finds the door open. The emphasis is here on the two types and two responses, rather than upon the delay, for the delay was not entirely unexpected (the wise took extra oil) and, 'now while the bridegroom tarried', is quite casually introduced to provide the explanation of their going to sleep (vs. 4f)" (p. 169). But the folly of the virgins does not consist in their delay at the decisive moment. Nor does the parable reproach them for not being fully committed to the cause in hand from the very beginning, unlike the wise ones (so Smith, cf. p. 168). The virgins do not leave their jars of oil at home because they are thinking of something else, but because they do not think they will need them. But the reserve of oil is only needed because the bridegroom "tarries". It turns things upside down if the delay of the bridegroom has to explain the sleep of the virgins. Their sleeping is not necessary for the flow of the parable, but the delay is.

8. Those scholars who observe the connection of the parable with the problem of the delay of the Parousia regard it as an allegory, or as a "formation of the Church, permeated with allegorical features".

This verdict is based above all on the fact that the connection between picture and reality, which is certainly present in v. 5, is understood as one of allegorical identity. It is overlooked that a parable too is evolved with an eye to the reality, and that the narrator does not limit himself at all to natural situations but carries out his stage production independently, being concerned only to keep the story, which he shapes in accordance with his intentions, within the bounds of possibility, so that his listeners follow him (cf. above, pp. 28f).

But it is also argued against its being a parable that "a mass of individual features of the parable" cannot be explained from the procedure of an ordinary wedding. But one must distinguish between what is not the rule, and what crosses the bounds of possibility. As far as individual points are concerned:

1. Escorting the bridegroom is not the rule. But that is not to say that it could not occur, perhaps if the wedding were held in the house of the bride, which did occasionally happen (cf. Billerbeck, I, p. 511; Midr. Esther I, 4; Tobit 8.18). While it is the *bridegroom* in 25.12 who sends away the foolish, we cannot conclude from this that it must be *his* house. The narrator did not need to make this presupposition to win acceptance for his stage management, which made the bridegroom, corresponding to but not identified with Jesus the Judge of the world, speak the verdict in v. 12.

2. The coming of the bridegroom at midnight is unusual. However, the parable does not represent it as the rule, but as a possibility for which one must allow. And such a delay is always possible, particularly when the bridegroom is coming from elsewhere. The trait is still within the bounds of possibility. Furthermore it has a function in the development of the narrative. The coming of the bridegroom is expected at night, as the virgins' lamps show. It needs to be a fairly long delay—how can this be better expressed than by the mention of this plainly proverbial hour? (Cf. in our language the phrase, "in the middle of the night".)

Bornkamm ("Verzögerung", p. 125) and Grässer (p. 122) try to explain this feature from "the early Christian expectation that the Messiah and the end of the world would come by night". But there is no evidence for such an expectation. It is impossible to quote Rom. 13.11 or Eph. 5.14 for this. The motif used in 1 Thess. 5.1ff, and Rev. 3.3, "coming as a thief in the night", is obviously linked by the context with the theme of surprise, not with coming at an hour in the night. Nor can Rev. 16.15 be quoted, for "watching" is there meant in a transferred sense. For this and the remaining passages Mark 13.33ff; Luke 12.35ff; Matt. 24.42ff. Meinertz's verdict is correct, that the examples quoted "stand in connection with an exhortation to wakefulness, just as in our parable. But one can only say 'stay awake' at a time when sleeping is normal, so at night. . . . When therefore an exhortation to wakefulness is given in an image, the night time inevitably serves as the background. But this is obviously only an image and does not in the least permit the conclusion that the Parousia will come by night" ("Die Tragweite", p. 104).

3. The escorting of the bridegroom is claimed to go back to a constitutional usage which has entered into the early Christian expectation of the Parousia, and left its mark in 1 Thess. 4.17. As the population of a city escorts a dignitary in with festivity, so the Christians come to escort their returning Lord (E. Peterson, *ZsT*, 7 (1930), pp. 682–702; Bornkamm, "Verzögerung", p. 123; Grässer, p. 123). Whether this exegesis is correct for 1 Thess. 4.17 is a question which may be passed over here. For Matt. 25.1ff it certainly cannot be upheld. It presupposes a confusion of ideas which is quite unthinkable. The place of the Messianic banquet is not on earth, but is where "Abraham and Isaac and Jacob" sit at table (Matt. 8.11; cf. Mark 14.25), the "Garden of Eden" (see Billerbeck, IV, pp. 840, 1146, 1154ff, and often). But if Peterson is right the escorting of the *Kyrios* takes place on earth. The pictures of escorting the Lord and of the Messianic meal do not fit in together. The latter can, however, be assumed for the parable with far greater right than the former, and consequently rules it out.

4. Bornkamm considers the possibility, and Grässer takes it as an actual fact, that the *kraugē* in v. 6 "is more than a mere loud cry", is in fact the eschatological cry which precedes the end of the world and announces it. The passages quoted show certainly that *kraugē* and *krazein* do occur in eschatological contexts, and that they *can* have the sense of inspired speech (the citation of Acts 7.57 and 23.9, however, must be a mistake). But there is ample evidence that the words are not limited to this usage. The cry in v. 6 has a genuine function in the narrative. The advance announcement of the bridegroom's coming secures a span of time in which the foolish virgins realize that they have not got enough oil, and set off to walk to the shop. Furthermore, after the sleep of the virgins had been narrated, it had to be mentioned that they were woken up as well.

5. The view is found that Matt. 25.1–12 is based on the allegory "bridegroom = Messiah" and "bride = Church", in the formation of which "the myth, widely spread in Gnosticism, of the *sōtēr* [Saviour] as *nymphios* [bridegroom] has played a part" (Grässer, p. 121). The occurrence of this allegory in early Christianity is not to be disputed. (Cf. 2 Cor. 11.2f; Eph. 5.23ff; Rev. 19.7, 9; 21.2, 9. John 3.9 may not be quoted for this. The verse is "a genuine figurative saying" [Bultmann, *Das Evangelium des Johannes*, p. 126, n. 12]. The same is true of Mark 2.19a. In 19b, 20 this figurative saying is admittedly turned into a metaphor and the bridegroom identified with Jesus, but all reference to the bride is lacking. The place of the Church is taken by the "wedding guests".) For Matt. 25.1–12, however, this allegory cannot be assumed to be present. The bride is not mentioned here. If "the aim of the story makes her dispensable", this is precisely to say that the narrator did not have this allegory in mind at all in constructing the parable. It is turning an assertion into a presupposition to say that the place of the bride (= Church) is here taken by the virgins, who symbolize the Church. In this way one can certainly decide that "'the representation of the bride and bridesmaids has been confused' and the whole picture 'distorted' (Wellhausen)"

(Klostermann, pp. 200f). But it is not the parable that is "distorted" but the exegesis.

Bornkamm's statement that "in the . . . picture of a wedding the pictorial use of 'virgins' was already implicit" (op. cit., p. 122), puts us on to the right track. One only needs to disagree with Bornkamm when he says that this wedding image was "first shaped in the early Christian hope of the Parousia", by which he means to say that it goes back to this allegory. But the image of the wedding does not originate in the allegory. The representation of the Messianic age as a wedding time is admittedly not very well attested (cf. Billerbeck, I, p. 517, and Jeremias, *Jesus als Weltvollender*, Gütersloh 1930, pp. 21ff). The representation of the time of fulfilment as a banquet was, however, widespread. But a wedding was one of *the* occasions for being invited to a banquet. For that reason the picture of participation in a wedding could easily be connected with the thought of the banquet at the end of time. (Cf. Pesiq. R. 41 [174b], "Why 'will Jacob rejoice', Ps. 14.7? If a man has a son to circumcise or takes a wife, who rejoices? The man who has been invited to the banquet. And just so has Jacob been invited to the banquet of the Holy One, blessed be he, which he will at some time prepare for the righteous in the future.")

6. Apart from this C. W. F. Smith is right in saying that "an allegorical treatment raises more difficulties than it solves" (p. 165). These difficulties cannot be met by a warning against "going too far in allegorizing". It is a methodological mistake to say: "There is no reason to give a meaning to the number of the virgins, and the equal number of wise and foolish, nor may one allegorize the lamps, oil, shopkeeper, etc." (Bornkamm, p. 124). We should not have to ask what we "may allegorize" and what not, but must ask whether the text has been developed from the reality, i.e. allegorically, or whether in spite of its connection with the reality it is an independent narrative. Then it turns out that the traits already mentioned have not developed out of the reality. It is, however, inconceivable that the narrator in his development of the story should jump about, partly arranging the narrative so that it is for him identical with the "reality", partly letting the story go its own way independently. It involves quite different thought-processes when a parable is being developed and when an allegory is being created. When links between picture and reality occur in a parable apart from the point of comparison, they are of a different nature from allegorical identification.

7. If allegorical and non-allegorical elements in the parable cannot be distinguished and the allegorical elements excluded as secondary, then the assumption that beneath the parable lies a different original form that goes back to Jesus has no basis whatever in the text.

For Strobel the parable is a "symbolically arranged parable" which owes its origin to the passover expectation of the Quartodecimans. He makes great efforts to derive all the themes of the parable from the "theology of the passover". This attempt seems, however, to me to be unsuccessful:

(a) It is true that the connection of the passover meal with the eschatological banquet is attested occasionally in the tradition. But one may not by any means assume on the strength of this that wherever any allusion to the eschatological banquet is found, a connection with the passover meal is implied.

(b) An expectation that the Messiah would come at the passover meal can certainly be attested. But this tradition is not according to the evidence so widespread that every allusion to the coming of the Messiah must have a connection with the passover meal.

(c) The filling of the lights belongs to every feast at night-time, and for that reason also to the night of the passover, not the other way round.

(d) The mention of midnight, which the parable shares with the passover haggadah, results naturally from the development of the parable (see above) and need not go back to the haggadah.

(e) The cry which wakes the virgins has its own function in the narrative. Since it is not a cry of lamentation but a cry of joy it can have nothing to do with Ex. 12.30 and Wisd. 18.10.

(f) The assumption that the theme of the *closed* door is a development of the theme of the *open* door of the passover and belongs within the "framework of the Passover theology", shows clearly the exaggerated efforts of the writer to derive every single point from the "theology of the passover" which he postulates.

The themes adduced do indeed occur in the passover haggadah or the passover feast also, but none of them is so characteristic of these that it could only be explained as coming from them. Some of them form part of the content of every feast at night, some belong to the eschatological expectation, which was only connected secondarily, and then not in every case, with a "theology of the passover". The characteristic themes of the passover haggadah, the blood, the lamb, and the unleavened bread, are completely missing.

9. *Tote* is "one of Matthew's favourite and characteristic transition particles" (Jeremias, p. 52; cf. p. 82, n. 52).

10. See Bultmann, *HST*, pp. 176f, Klostermann, p. 200, Fuchs, *Studies*, p. 122.

11. On v. 13 cf. Jeremias p. 52: "The exhortation to watchfulness in v. 13 is one of those hortatory additions which people were so inclined to add to the parables; it repeats Matt. 24.42 and belonged originally to the parable of the doorkeeper (Mark 13.35)." No argument against the authenticity of v. 13 can be produced, however, from the contrast between sleeping (v. 5) and waking (v. 13) (against Jeremias, ibid.). The decisive ground for the assumption that v. 13 is not the original application of the parable can lie only in the fact that this verse does not continue the basic thought of the parable, which insists that only those can be ready who make allowance for a lengthy period of waiting.

Bibliography

Abbreviations

Indexes

Bibliography

(Abbreviations of Journals and Series are listed below. Where there is no danger
of misunderstanding, books are quoted only by the name of the author.)

Baldermann, I., *Biblische Didaktik*, Hamburg, 1963.
Bartsch, H. W., *Probleme der theologischen Wissenchaft seit Kreigsausgang*
(Evangelischer Schriftendienst, 13/14), Schwäbisch Gmünd, 1947.
— "Zum Problem der Parusieverzögerung bei den Synoptikern", *EvTh*, 19
(1959), pp. 116–31.
Bauer, W., "Jesus der Galiläer", *Festgabe für A. Jülicher*, Tübingen, 1927,
pp. 16–34.
— *A Greek-English Lexicon of the New Testament and other Early Christian
Literature* (ET and adapted by Arndt, W. F., and Gingrich, F. W.),
Cambridge, 1957.
Biehl, P., "Zur Frage nach dem historischen Jesus", *TR, NF*, 24 (1956/57),
pp. 54–76.
Billerbeck: see under Strack, H. and Billerbeck, P.
Binder, H., "Das Gleichnis vom barmherzigen Samariter", *TZ*, 15 (1959),
pp. 176–94.
Black, M., "The Kingdom has come", *Expository Times*, 63 (1952), pp. 289–
96; 64 (1953), pp. 89–91.
— *An Aramaic Approach to the Gospels and Acts*, ed. 2, Oxford, 1954.
Blair, E. P., "Recent Studies of the Sources of Matthew", *TZ*, 15 (1959),
pp. 206–10.
Blass, F., and Debrunner, A., *A Greek Grammar of the New Testament*, Cam-
bridge, 1961.
Bornhäuser, K., *Studien zum Sondergut des Lukas*, Gütersloh, 1934.
Bornkamm, G., "Der Lohngedanke im Neuen Testament", *Studien zu Antike
und Urchristentum*, ed. 2, Munich, 1962, pp. 69–92.
— "Die Verzögerung der Parusie", *In Memoriam Ernst Lohmeyer*, Stuttgart,
1951, pp. 116–26 (quoted as Bornkamm, "Verzögerung").
— "Das Doppelgebot der Liebe", *Neutestamentliche Studien für Rudolf Bultmann*
(BZNW, 21, 1954), pp. 85–93.
— *Jesus of Nazareth*, London, 1960 (quoted as: Bornkamm, *Jesus*).
Bornkamm, G., Barth, G., Held, H. J., *Tradition and Interpretation in Matthew*,
London, 1963.

Braun, H., *Spätjüdisch-häretischer und frühchristlicher Radikalismus*, Tübingen, 1957 (Beiträge zur historischen Theologie, 24).

— *Gesammelte Studien zum Neuen Testament und seiner Umwelt*, Tübingen, 1962.

Brown, R. E., "Parable and Allegory Reconsidered", *NovTest*, 5 (1962), pp. 36–45.

Bugge, C. A., *Die Hauptparabeln Jesu*, I, Giessen, 1903.

Bultmann, R., "Das Problem einer theologischen Exegese des Neuen Testaments", *Zwischen den Zeiten*, 3 (1925), pp. 334–57.

— "Reich Gottes und Menschensohn", *TR*, NF, 9 (1937), pp. 1–35.

— "The Study of the Synoptic Gospels", *Form Criticism: A New Method of New Testament Research*, ed. and tr. F. C. Grant, Chicago, 1934, pp. 11–75.

— "Zur eschatologischen Verkündigung Jesu", *TLZ*, 72 (1947), cols. 271–4.

— *Theology of the New Testament*, London, vol. I, 1952; vol. II, 1955.

— *Glauben und Verstehen*, vol. I, ed. 4, Tübingen, 1961; vol. 2, ed. 3, Tübingen, 1961; vol. 3, ed. 2, Tübingen, 1962; ET of vol. 2, *Essays Philosophical and Theological*, London, 1955.

— *Primitive Christianity in its Contemporary Setting*, London, 1956.

— *Jesus and the Word*, Glasgow, 1958.

— *Das Verhältnis der urchristlichen Christusbotschaft zum historischen Jesus*, ed. 2, Heidelberg, 1961 (Sitzungsberichte der Heidelberger Akademie der Wissenschaften, 1960/3).

— *Das Evangelium des Johannes*, ed. 17, Göttingen, 1962 (*MeyerK* II).

— *History of the Synoptic Tradition*, Oxford, 1963 (quoted as Bultmann, *HST*).

Buri, F., "Replik", *TZ*, 3 (1947), pp. 422–8 (reply to Cullmann, ibid., pp. 177–91).

Burkitt, F. C., "The Parable of the Ten Virgins", *JTS*, 30 (1929), pp. 267–70.

Cadoux, A. T., *The Parables of Jesus. Their Art and Use*, New York, 1931.

Cander, G., "Le procédé de l'économe infidèle décrit Lucas 16.5–7, est-il répréhensible ou louable?", *Verbum Caro*, 7 (1953), pp. 128–41.

Die Christenlehre, Year 3 (1950), part 2; Unterrichtshilfe, pp. 21–8 (Lukas 10.25–37).

— Year 7 (1954), part 3; Unterrichtshilfe, pp. 37–44 (Lukas 15.11–32).

Conzelmann, H., "R. Morgenthaler, Kommendes Reich," *TZ*, 9 (1953), pp. 306f.

— "Gegenwart und Zukunft in der Synoptischen Tradition", *ZTK*, 54 (1957), pp. 277–96.

— *Zur Methode der Leben-Jesu-Forschung*, BZTK, 56 (1959), pp. 2–13.

— *The Theology of Saint Luke*, London, 1960 (quoted as Conzelmann, *TSL*).

— "Jesus Christus", *RGG*, ed. 3, vol. 3, cols. 619–53.

— "Eschatologie im Urchristentum", *RGG*, ed. 3, vol. 2, cols. 665–72.

— "Randbemerkungen zur Lage im 'Neuen Testament'", *EvTh*, 22 (1962), pp. 225–33.

Cullmann, O., "Das wahre durch die ausgebliebene Parusie gestellte neutestamentliche Problem", *TZ*, 3 (1947), pp. 177–91.

Cullmann, O., "Duplik", *TZ*, 3 (1947), pp. 428–32.
— "Parusieverzögerung und Urchristentum", *TLZ*, 83 (1958), cols. 1–12.
Curtis, W. A., "The Parable of the Labourers" (Matt. 20.1–16), *Festgabe für A. Jülicher*, Tübingen, 1927, pp. 61–9.
Dahl, N. A., "The Parables of Growth", *Studia Theologica*, 5 (1951), pp. 132–65.
— "Der historische Jesus als geschichtswissenschaftliches und theologisches Problem", *Kerygma und Dogma*, 1 (1955), pp. 104–32; ET in *Kerygma and History*, ed. Braaten, C. E. and Harrisville, R. A., New York, 1962, pp. 138–71.
Dalman, G. H., "Viererlei Acker", *PJ*, 22 (1926), pp. 120–32.
— *Die Worte Jesu*, ed. 2, Leipzig, 1930; ET of ed. 1, *The Words of Jesus*, Edinburgh, 1902.
— *Arbeit und Sitte in Palästina*, vol. II, Gütersloh, 1932.
Deissmann, A., *Light from the Ancient East*, rev. ed., London, 1927.
Delling, G., "Das Gleichnis vom gottlosen Richter", *ZNW*, 53 (1962), pp. 1–25.
Derrett, J. D. M., "Law in the New Testament: The treasure in the field (Matt. XIII,44)", *ZNW*, 54 (1963), pp. 31–42.
Dibelius, M., "Zur Formgeschichte der Evangelien", *TR*, NF, 1 (1929).
— *Gospel Criticism and Christology*, London, 1935.
— *Formgeschichte des Evangeliums*, ed. 4, Tübingen, 1961; *From Tradition to Gospel*, ET of ed. 2, London, 1934.
— *Jesus*, London, 1963.
Diem, H., *Der irdische Jesus und der Christus des Glaubens*, Tübingen, 1957 (SgV, 215); ET, "The earthly Jesus and the Christ of Faith", in *Kerygma and History*, ed. Braaten, C. E., and Harrisville, R. A., New York, 1962, pp. 197–211.
Dinkler, E., "Bibelautorität und Bibelkritik", *ZTK*, 47 (1950), pp. 70–93.
Dodd, C. H., *The Parables of the Kingdom*, rev. ed., Glasgow, 1961.
Ebeling, G., *Die Geschichtlichkeit der Kirche und ihrer Verkündigung als theologisches Problem*, Tübingen, 1954 (SgV 207/208).
— "Unglaube und Glaube. Predigt über Lukas 18.9–14", *Predigten für Jedermann*, Year 4 (1957), No. 10, Bad Cannstatt, 1957.
— *Was heisst Glauben?*, Tübingen, 1958 (SgV 216).
— "Hermeneutik", *RGG*, ed. 3, vol. 3, cols. 242–62.
— *The Nature of Faith*, London, 1961.
— "Der Grund christlicher Theologie", *ZTK*, 58 (1961), pp. 227–44.
— *Theologie und Verkündigung*, Tübingen, ed. 2, 1963 (HUT, 1).
— *Word and Faith*, London, 1963.
Ebeling, H. J., *Das Messiasgeheimnis und die Botschaft des Markus-Evangelisten* (BZNW, 19), Berlin, 1939.
Eichholz, G., "Das Gleichnis als Spiel", *Ev Th*, 21 (1961), pp. 309–26.

Eichholz, G., *Jesus Christus und der Nächste*, Neukirchen, n.d. (BSt, 9).

— *Einführung in die Gleichnisse*, Neukirchen, 1963 (BSt, 37).

Eissfeldt, O, *Der Maschal im Alten Testament*, Beihefte zur Zeitschrift für die alttestamentliche Wissenschaft, 24 (1913).

Fascher, E., *Vom Verstehen des Neuen Testamentes*, Giessen, 1930.

Fiebig, P., *Die Gleichnisreden Jesu im Lichte der rabbinischen Gleichnisse des neutestamentlichen Zeitalters*, Tübingen, 1912.

— *Der Erzählungsstil der Evangelien* (Untersuchungen zum Neuen Testament 11), Leipzig, 1925.

Findlay, J. A., *Jesus and His Parables*, London, 1950.

Förster, W., "Das Gleichnis von der anvertrauten Pfunden", *Verbum Dei manet in aeternum* (Festschrift für O. Schmitz), Witten, 1953, pp. 37–56.

Frör, K., *Biblische Hermeneutik*, Munich, 1961.

Fuchs, E., "Jesu Freude als des Christen Trost und Mut. Predigt über Lukas 15.11–32", *Predigten für Jedermann*, ed. Müllerschön, O., Year 3 (1956), No. 9, Bad Cannstatt, 1956.

— *Das urchristliche Sakramentsverständnis* (Schriftenreihe der Kirchlich-Theologische Sozietät in Württemberg, 8), Bad Cannstatt, [1958].

— "The Parable of the Unmerciful Servant (Matt. 18.23–35)", *Studia Evangelica*, ed. Aland, K., and others, Berlin, 1959 (TU 73), pp. 487–94.

— *Zum hermeneutischen Problem in der Theologie*, Tübingen, 1959 (Aufsätze I).

— *Zur Frage nach dem historischen Jesus*, Tübingen, 1960 (Aufsätze II) (quoted as Fuchs, *Aufsätze* II).

— *Das Programm der Entmythologisierung*, ed. 2, Bad Cannstatt, 1960 (Schriftenreihe der Kirchlich-Theologische Sozietät in Württemberg, 3).

— "2. sonntag nach Trinitatis. Lukas 14.15–24", *Göttinger Predigtmeditationen* (1961), pp. 190–2.

— "Das neue Testament und das hermenutische Problem", in Aufsätze III, pp. 136–73; ET in *The New Hermeneutic*, 1964, pp. 111–45.

— "Über die Aufgabe einer christlichen Theologie", *ZTK*, 58 (1961), pp. 245–67.

— *Hermeneutik*, ed. 3, Bad Cannstatt, 1963.

— *Studies of the Historical Jesus*, London, 1964 (ET of part of Aufsätze II) (quoted as Fuchs, *Studies*).

— *Glaube und Erfahrung*, Tübingen, 1965 (Aufsätze III).

Gerhardsson, B., *The Good Samaritan—The Good Shepherd?*, Lund and Copenhagen, 1958 (Coniectanea Neotestamentica, XVI).

"Gleichnis und Parabel", *RGG*, ed. 2 (Winternitz, Gunkel, Bultmann).

"Gleichnis und Parabel", *RGG*, ed. 3 (Edsman, Fohrer, Dietrich, Dahl, Frör).

Gloege, G., "Entmythologisierung", *VF*, 1956/57 (1957/59), pp. 62–101.

Glombitza, O., "Der Perlenkaufmann", *NTS*, 7 (1960/61), pp. 153–61.

— "Das grosse Abendmahl. Lukas 14.12–24", *NovTest*, 5 (1962), pp. 10–16.

Gogarten, F., *Die Verkündigung Jesu Christi*, Heidelberg, 1948.

Gogarten, F., "Theologie und Geschichte", *ZTK*, 50 (1953), pp. 339–94.
— *Was ist Christentum?*, Göttingen, 1956.
— *Die Wirklichkeit des Glaubens*, Stuttgart, 1957.
— *Verhängnis und Hoffnung der Neuzeit*, ed. 2, Stuttgart, 1958.
— *Der Mensch zwischen Gott und Welt*, ed. 3, Stuttgart, 1962.
Gollwitzer, H., *Das Gleichnis vom barmherzigen Samariter*, Neukirchen, 1962 (BSt, 34).
Goudge, H. L., "The parable of the Ten Virgins", *JTS*, 30 (1929), pp. 399–401.
Grässer, E., *Das Problem der Parusieverzögerung in den synoptischen Evangelien und in der Apostelgeschichte* (BZNW, 22), ed. 2, Berlin, 1960.
Greeven, H., "Wer unter euch . . .?", *Wort und Dienst*, NF, 3 (1952), pp. 86–101.
Gressmann, H., *Vom reichen Mann und armen Lazarus*, Abhandlungen der Preussischen Akademie der Wissenschaften, 1918, philosophisch-historische Klasse, No. 7.
Grobel, K., "Amerikanische Literatur zum Neuen Testament seit 1938", *TR*, NF, 17 (1948/49), pp. 142–56.
Guillaumont, A., Puech, H.-C., Quispel, G., Till, W., and †Yassah ʿAbd al Masīḥ, *The Gospel according to Thomas, Coptic Text established and translated*, Leiden and London, 1959.
Gutbrod, W., "Aus der neueren englischen Literatur zum Neuen Testament", *TR*, NF, 11 (1939), pp. 263–77; 12 (1940), pp. 1–23; 73–84.
Guttmann, T., *Das Maschal-Gleichnis in tannaitischer Zeit*, Frankfurt [1929] (doctoral thesis).
Haenchen, E., *Die Botschaft des Thomas-Evangeliums*, Berlin, 1961.
Hasler, V., "Die Königliche Hochzeit. Matt. 22.1–14", *TZ*, 18 (1962), pp. 25–35.
Hauck, F. *Das Evangelium des Markus*, Leipzig, 1931 (THK, 2) (quoted as *Markus*).
— *Das Evangelium des Lukas*, Leipzig, 1934 (THK, 3).
Heidegger, M., *Unterwegs zur Sprache*, ed. 2, Pfullingen, 1960.
— *Being and Time*, London, 1962.
Heitzsch, E., "Die Aporie des historischen Jesus als Problem theologischer Hermeneutik", *ZTK*, 53 (1956), pp. 192–209.
Hick, L., "Zum Verständnis des neutestamentlichen Parabelbegriffes", *Bibel und Kirche*, 1 (1954), pp. 4–17.
Higgins, A. J. B., "Non-Gnostic Sayings in the Gospel of Thomas", *NovTest*, 4 (1960), pp. 292–306.
Hoskyns, E. C. and Davey, F. N., *The Riddle of the New Testament*, ed. 3, London, 1947.
Hunter, A. M., *Interpreting the Parables*, London, 1960.

Hunzinger, C. H., "Unbekannte Gleichnisse Jesu aus dem Thomasevangelium", *Judentum, Urchristentum, Kirche* (Essays presented to Prof. Jeremias on his 60th Birthday), Berlin, 1960, pp. 209–20.

Iber, G., "Zur Formgeschichte der Evangelien", *TR*, NF, 24 (1957/58), pp. 283–338.

The Interpreter's Bible, vol. 7, New York, 1951.

Jepsen, A., "Eschatologie im Alten Testament", *RGG*, ed. 3, vol. 2, cols. 655–62.

Jeremias, J., "Eine neue Schau der Zukunftsaussagen Jesu", *ThBl*, 20 (1941), pp. 216–22.

— "Zum Gleichnis vom verlorenen Sohn", *TZ*, 5 (1949), pp. 228–31.

— *Jerusalem zur Zeit Jesu*, ed. 3, Göttingen, 1962.

— *The Parables of Jesus*, rev. ed., London, 1963 (quoted as Jeremias).

— *The Problem of the Historical Jesus*, Philadelphia, 1964.

Jolles, A., *Einfache Formen*, ed. 2, Tübingen, 1958.

Jülicher, A., *Die Gleichnisreden Jesu*, 2 vols., ed. 2, Tübingen, 1910.

Jüngel, E., *Paulus und Jesus*, Tübingen, ed. 2, 1964 (HUT, 2).

Kähler, M., *The so-called Historical Jesus and the Historic, Biblical Christ*, Philadelphia, 1964.

Käsemann, E., "Aus der neutestamentlichen Arbeit der letzten Jahre", *VF*, 47/48 (1949/50), pp. 195–225.

— "Probleme neutestamentlicher Arbeit in Deutschland", *Die Freiheit des Evangeliums und die Ordnung der Gesellschaft*, Beiträge zur *EvTh*, 15 (1952), pp. 133–52.

— *Das Evangelium des Matthäus*, II, Vorlesung Sommersemester 1953, Göttingen.

— *Exegetische Versuche und Besinnungen*, vol. 2, Göttingen, 1964.

— *Essays on New Testament Themes*, London, 1964.

Kenyon, F. G., *The Text of the Greek Bible*, London, 1937.

Kittel, G., and Friedrich, G., ed., *Theologisches Wörterbuch zum neuen Testament*, Stuttgart, 1932ff (quoted as *TWNT*); ET, *Theological Dictionary of the New Testament*, Grand Rapids, Michigan, vols. 1 and 2, 1964 (quoted as *TDNT*).

Klein, E. F., *Gestalten aus Jesu Umwelt*, Berlin, 1956.

Klostermann, E., *Das Matthäusevangelium*, ed. 2, Tübingen, 1927 (HNT, 4) (quoted as Klostermann, *Matt.*).

— *Das Lukasevangelium*, ed. 2, Tübingen, 1929 (HNT, 5).

— *Das Markusevangelium*, ed. 4, Tübingen, 1950 (HNT, 3) (quoted as Klostermann, *Markus*).

Kögel, J., *Zum Gleichnis vom ungerechten Haushalter*, Gütersloh, 1914.

Kreck, W., "Die Frage nach dem historischen Jesus als dogmatisches Problem", *EvTh*, 22 (1962), pp. 460–78.

Krengel, J., "Mashal", *The Jewish Universal Encyclopedia*, New York, 1939ff, vol. 7, pp. 394–6.

Kümmel, W. G., "Das Gleichnis von den bösen Weingärtnern (Markus 12.1–9)", *Aux sources de la tradition chrétienne* (Goguel memorial volume), Neuchâtel and Paris, 1950.

— *Promise and Fulfilment. The eschatological message of Jesus*, London, 1957 (quoted as Kümmel, *PF*).

— *Das Neue Testament. Geschichte der Erforschung seiner Probleme* (Orbis Academicus, III, 3), Freiburg and Munich, 1958.

— "Futurische und präsentische Eschatologie im ältesten Urchristentum", *NTS*, 5 (1958/9), pp. 113–26.

Leenhardt, F. J., "Das Gleichnis vom barmherzigen Samariter", Gollwitzer, H., *Das Gleichnis vom barmherzigen Samariter*, Neukirchen, 1962 (BSt, 34), pp. 97–106.

Leipoldt, J., "Ein neues Evangelium? Das koptische Thomasevangelium übersetzt und besprochen", *TLZ*, 83 (1958), cols. 481–96.

Lindeskog, G., "Nordische Literatur zum Neuen Testament 1939–49", *TR*, NF, 18 (1950), pp. 216–38; 288–306.

— "Christuskerygma und Jesustradition", *NovTest*, 5 (1962), pp. 144–56.

Linnemann, E., "Überlegungen zur Parabel vom grossen Abendmahl (Lukas 14.15–24/Matt. 22.2–14)", *ZNW*, 51, 1960, pp. 246–55.

Ljungvik, H., "Zur Erklärung einer Lukasstelle. Lukas XVIII, 7", *NTS*, 10 (1963/4), pp. 289–94.

Lohmeyer, E., *Urchristliche Mystik*, Darmstadt, 1955.

— *Das Evangelium des Markus*, ed. 15, Göttingen, 1959 (*MeyerK*, I, 2).

— *Das Evangelium des Matthäus* (ed. W. Schmauch), ed. 3, Göttingen, 1962 (*MeyerK*, Sonderband).

Lohse, E., "Die Gottesherrschaft in den Gleichnissen Jesu", *EvTh*, 18 (1958), pp. 145–57.

Madsen, I. K., *Die Parabeln der Evangelien und die heutige Psychologie*, Copenhagen and Leipzig, 1936.

Manson, T. W., *The Sayings of Jesus*, London, 1949.

Marxsen, W., "Redaktionsgeschichtliche Erklärung der sogenannten Parabeltheorie des Markus", *ZTK*, 52 (1955), pp. 255–71.

— *Der Evangelist Markus. Studien zur Redaktionsgeschichte des Evangeliums.* (Forschungen zur Religion und Literatur des Alten und Neuen Testamentes, NF, 49), Göttingen, 1956.

— *Exegese und Verkündigung*, Munich, 1957 (Theologische Existenz heute, NF, 59).

— *Anfangsprobleme der Christologie*, Gütersloh, 1960.

Meier, A., *Die Umwelt Jesu und seiner Apostel*, ed. 2, Basle, 1944.

Meinertz, M., *Die Gleichnisse Jesu*, ed. 4, Münster, 1948.

— "Die Tragweite des Gleichnisses von den zehn Jungfrauen", *Synoptische Studien* (presented to A. Wikenhauser), Munich, 1954, pp. 94–106 (quoted as Meinertz, "Die Tragweite").

— "Zum Verständis der Gleichnisse Jesu", *Das Heilige Land*, 86 (1954), pp. 41–7.

Meyer, R., "Eschatologie im Judentum", *RGG*, ed. 3, vol. II, cols. 662–5.

Mezger, M., "Die Anleitung zur Predigt", *ZTK*, 56 (1959), pp. 377–97.

Michaelis, W., *Das hochzeitliche Kleid*, Berlin 1939 (quoted as Michaelis, *Hochzeitliches Kleid*).

— "Kennen die Synoptiker eine Verzögerung der Parusie?", *Synoptische Studien* (presented to A. Wikenhauser), Munich, 1954, pp. 107–23.

— *Die Gleichnisse Jesu*, ed. 3, Hamburg 1956 (quoted as Michaelis, *Gleichnisse*).

Montefiore, H. W., "A Comparison of the Parables of the Gospel according to Thomas and of the Synoptic Gospels", *NTS*, 7 (1960/61), pp. 220–48.

Morgenthaler, R., "Formgeschichte und Gleichnisauslegung", *TZ*, 6 (1950), pp. 1–16.

— *Kommendes Reich*, Zürich, 1952.

Mussner, F., *Die Botschaft der Gleichnisse Jesu*, Munich, 1961.

— "Der historische Jesus under der Christus des Glaubens", *BZ*, NF, 1 (1957), pp. 224–52.

Nötscher, F. "Jüdische Mönchsgemeinde und Ursprung des Christentums nach den jüngst am Toten Meer aufgefundenen hebräischen Handschriften", *Bibel und Kirche*, 1952, pp. 21–38.

— *Zur theologischen Terminologie der Qumrantexte*, Bonn, 1956 (Bonner biblische Beiträge, 10), pp. 149ff.

— "Wahrheitssucher im Zeitalter Jesu nach den Handschriften von Qumran am Toten Meer", *Das Heilige Land*, 89 (1957), pp. 1–13.

Otto, R., *The Kingdom of God and the Son of Man*, London, ed. 2, 1943 (quoted as Otto, *Kingdom*).

Percy, E., *Die Botschaft Jesu. Eine traditionskritische und exegetische Untersuchung*, Lund, 1953 (Lunds universitets Årsskrift, NF, Avd. 1, vol. 49, no. 5).

Peterson, E., "Die Einholung des Kyrios", *ZsT*, 7 (1930), pp. 682–702.

Preisker, H., "Lukas 16, 1–7", *TLZ*, 74 (1949), pp. 85–92.

Rengstorf, K. H., "Die Stadt der Mörder (Matt. 22,7)", *Judentum, Urchristentum, Kirche* (Essays presented to Prof. Jeremias on his 60th Birthday), Berlin, 1960, pp. 106–29.

Ristow, H., and Matthiae, K. (ed.), *Der historische Jesus und der kerygmatische Christus*, Beiträge zum Christusverständnis in Forschung und Verkündigung, ed. 2, Berlin, 1961.

Robinson, J. M., "Jesus' Understanding of History", *JBR*, 23 (1955), pp. 17–24.

— "The Quest of the Historical Jesus Today", *Theology Today*, 15 (1958), pp. 183–97.

— "New Testament Faith Today", *JBR*, 27 (1959), pp. 233–42.

— *A New Quest of the Historical Jesus*, London, 1959; rev. ed. in German, *Kerygma und historischer Jesus*, Zürich, 1960.

Royen, J. van, *Jesus en Johannes de Doper*, Leiden, 1953.

Sabbe, M., "Het eschatologisch gebed in Lukas 18.1–8", *Collationes Brugenses et Gandavenses*, 1 (1955), pp. 361–69.

Sahlin, H., "Zwei Lukas-Stellen. Lukas 6.43–45; 18.7", *Symbolae Biblicae Upsalienses*, 4 (1945).

Salm, W., *Beiträge zur Gleichnisforschung*, Göttingen Dissertation, 1953.

Sattler, W., "Die Anawim im Zeitalter Jesu", *Festgabe für A. Jülicher*, Tübingen, 1927, pp. 1–15.

Schelke, K. H., "Zur neueren katholischen Exegese des Neuen Testaments", *TR*, NF, 14 (1942), pp. 173–99.

Schlatter, A., *Erläuterungen zum Neuen Testament*, vol. 1: *Die Evangelien und die Apostelgeschichte*, Calw and Stuttgart, 1908.

— *Kennen wir Jesus? Ein Gang durch ein Jahr im Gespräch mit Ihm*, Stuttgart, 1937, pp. 359f.

— *Der Evangelist Matthäus*, ed. 5, Stuttgart, 1959 (quoted as Schlatter, *Matt.*).

— *Das Evangelium des Lukas aus seinen Quellen erklärt*, ed. 2, Stuttgart, 1960 (quoted as Schlatter, *Lukas*).

Schmid, J., *Das Evangelium nach Matthäus*, ed. 4, Regensburg, 1959 (Regensburger NT, 1).

— *Das Evangelium nach Lukas*, ed. 4, Regensburg, 1960 (Regensburger NT, 3).

— *Das Evangelium nach Markus*, ed. 5, Regensburg, 1963 (Regensburger NT, 2).

Schneemelcher, H. (ed.): *Das Problem der Sprache in Theologie und Kirche*, Berlin, 1959.

Schniewind, J., "Zur Synoptiker-Exegese", *TR*, NF, 2 (1930), pp. 129–89.

— *Das Evangelium nach Matthäus*, ed. 9, Göttingen, 1960 (NTD, 2)

— *Das Evangelium nach Markus*, ed. 10, Göttingen, 1963 (NTD, 1).

— "Das Gleichnis vom verlorenen Sohn", *Die Freude der Busse*, Göttingen, 1956, pp. 34–87.

Schürmann, H., "Das Thomasevangelium und das lukanische Sondergut", *BZ*, NF, 7 (1963), pp. 236–60.

Schuster, H., "Die konsequente Eschatologie in der Interpretation des Neuen Testaments, kritisch betrachtet", *ZNW*, 47 (1956), pp. 1–25.

Schweitzer, A., *The Quest of the Historical Jesus*, London, ed. 3, 1954.

Schweizer, E., "Zur Frage der Lukasquellen, Analyse von Lukas 15.11–32", *TZ*, 4 (1948), pp. 469–71.

— "Antwort auf Jeremias", *TZ*, 5 (1949), pp. 231–3.

— "Der Menschensohn (Zur eschatologischen Verkündigung Jesu)", *ZNW*, 50 (1959), pp. 185–209, and *Neotestamentica*, Zürich and Stuttgart, 1963, pp. 56–84.

— "The Son of Man Again", *Neotestamentica*, pp. 85–92.

Smith, B. T. D., *The Parables of the Synoptic Gospels*, Cambridge, 1937.

Smith, C. W. F., *The Jesus of the Parables*, Philadelphia, 1948.

Snell, B., *The Discovery of the Mind*, Oxford, 1953 (chap. 9: From Myth to Logic: the Role of the Comparison, pp. 191–226).

Die Sprache, issued by the Bayerische Akademie der schönen Künste, Darmstadt, 1959.

Sprenger, G., "Jesu Säe- und Erntegleichnisse", *PJ*, 9 (1913), pp. 79–97.

Stählin, G., "Die Gleichnishandlungen Jesu", *Kosmos und Ekklesia, Festschrift für W. Stählin*, Kassel, 1953, pp. 9–22.

Stählin, W., *Vom Sinn des Leibes*, ed. 3, Stuttgart, 1952, pp. 90–100.

— *Symbolon. Vom gleichnishaften Denken*, Stuttgart, 1958.

Stallmann, M.: *Was ist Säkularisierung?*, Tübingen, 1960 (SgV, 227/8).

— *Die biblische Geschichte im Unterricht*, Göttingen, 1963.

Stauffer, E., *Christ and the Caesars*, London, 1955.

Stock, H., *Studien zur Auslegung der synoptischen Evangelien im Unterricht*, ed. 2, Gütersloh, 1961.

Strack, H., and Billerbeck, P., *Kommentar zum Neuen Testament aus Talmud und Midrasch*, vols. 1–4, ed. 2, Munich, 1956 (quoted as Billerbeck).

Strobel, F. A., "Zum Verständnis von Matt. 25.1–13", *NovTest*, 2 (1958), pp. 199–227.

Svanholm, C., "Hovedproblemene i fortolkningen av Jesus Lignelser is den nyere Teologi fra Jülicher av", *Tidskrift for Teologi og Kirke*, 24 (1953), pp. 164–76.

Thielicke, H., *The Waiting Father, Sermons on the Parables*, London, 1960.

Tödt, H. E., *The Son of Man in the Synoptic Tradition*, London, 1965.

Torm, F., *Hermeneutik des Neuen Testamentes*, Göttingen, 1930, pp. 109–27.

Trilling, W., "Zur Überlieferungsgeschichte des Gleichnisses vom Hochzeitsmahl Matt. 22.1–14", *BZ*, NF, 4 (1960), pp. 251–65.

Vaccari, A., "La Parabole du Festin des Noces (Matt. 22.1–14). Notes d'Exégèse", *Recherches de Science Religieuse*, 39 (1951), pp. 138–45.

Veit, M., *Die Auffassung der Person Jesu im Urchristentum nach den neuesten Forschungen*, Marburg, 1946.

Vielhauer, P., "Gottesreich und Menschensohn in der Verkündigung Jesu", *Festschrift für G. Dehn zum 75. Geburtstag*, Neukirchen, 1957, pp. 51–79 (quoted as Vielhauer, "Gottesreich").

— "Jesus und der Menschensohn. Zur Diskussion mit Heinz Eduard Tödt und Eduard Schweizer", *ZTK*, 60 (1963), pp. 133–77.

Vincent, J. J., "The Parables of Jesus as Self-Revelation", *Studia Evangelica*, Berlin, 1959 (TU 73), pp. 79–99.

Weinel, H., *Die Gleichnisse Jesu*, ed. 5, Leipzig and Berlin, 1929 (Aus Natur und Geisteswelt, 46).

Weiss, J., *Die Predigt Jesu vom Reiche Gottes*, ed. 2, Göttingen, 1900.

Wrede, W., *Das Messiasgeheimnis in den Evangelien*, ed. 2, Göttingen, 1913.

Abbreviations

TZ   *Theologische Zeitschrift*

TU   Texte und Untersuchungen zur Geschichte der altchristlichen Literatur

VF   *Verkündigung und Forschung*

ZNW *Zeitschrift für die neutestamentliche Wissenschaft und die Kunde der älteren Kirche*

ZsT *Zeitschrift für systematische Theologie*

ZTK *Zeitschrift für Theologie und Kirche*

Index of Subjects

(This index is selective, and is intended primarily to help the reader to find his way back to the key concepts of the book.)

Index of References to the Synoptic Gospels

(Figures in bold type refer to the detailed treatments of each parable. An asterisk indicates that the reference is to a parable or part of a parable.)

Index of Authors